THE PAGAN ROAD TO SALVATION

ROMEL RIVERA

Coracii Publishing

Coracii Publishing LLC
coracii.org

© 2025 by Romel Rivera. All rights reserved.

ISBN 979-8-30853-689-5 (Paperback)
ISBN 979-8-89704-416-0 (eBook)

Library of Congress Cataloging in Publication Data
Name: Rivera, Romel, author
Title: The Pagan Road to Salvation
Includes bibliographical references and index
Library of Congress Control Number: 2025901560

Cover Design by Romel Rivera
Cover Image, public domain
Author's photograph by Sofía Skuza Rivera

First Edition, March 5, 2025

CONTENTS

Preface 9
Introduction 13
Chapter Summaries 19
PART I, Beliefs and Secularity 23
1. A Roll of the Dice 25
2. The Secular Avalanche 35
   2.1. NDEs 37
      Anita Moorjani 38
      Mary Neal 46
      Other NDE Cases 46
      Omni Vision for the Blind 49
      Summary of NDE Findings 56
      Prospective NDE Research 58
      Criticism of NDE Research 59
   2.2. Spontaneous Recollection of Past Lives 61
      James 3 63
      Other Past Life Cases 65
   2.3. Subconscious Recollection of Past Lives 68
      Santorini 1863 B.C 68
      Sadness Clouds the Eyes 69
      Evidence Based? 70

2.4. Conscious Access to Nonlocal Existences 71

2.5. Non-Physical Individual Differentiation 75

2.6. A Foundation for Secularity 76

3. Beliefs 81

   3.1. Beliefs 81

      Adoption and Internalization 85

      Capitulation 86

      The Flip 89

      A Belief in Superiority 90

      Belief Sublimation 91

      Faith and Trust 92

   3.2. Blanket Beliefs 94

   3.3. Selective Beliefs 96

   3.4. Inspirational Motivation 97

      Demeaning the Starting Point 101

   3.5. Collective Internalization 102

   3.6. Beliefs and Exclusivity 103

4. Beliefs and Surrogacy 105

   4.1. Religion, the Mother of Blanket Beliefs 106

   4.2. Scientific Beliefs 119

      Hyper Extending into Pseudo-Science 120

      Provable by Real Science 127

   4.3. Philosophical Joe 130

The Bouncy Floor of Self-Evidence 132
The Closing of the American Mind 136
The Context in the 1950's 141
4.4. Doodling and the Rabbit Hole 143
Pinker's Rationality 148
Gatekeepers of the Self 157
4.5. Democracy and Self-Combustion 164
Equality 168
Inequality 169
Politics of the Herd 173
4.6. A Paper-Thin Unidimensionality 175
PART II, Dismantling Beliefs 177
5. Deconstructing Beliefs 179
5.1. My Beliefs, My Gods 179
Gods Without a Cause 180
Fusion of Essentials 186
You Got Nothing, You Are Nothing 191
You Never Left 193
Truths Worth Lying for 197
5.2. The Dance Around Fear 198
5.3. All Roads Lead to Rome 202
5.4. Nothing to Learn 205
5.5. Enormity by Invisibility 209
6. Reality and Duplicity 215
Putrid Disregard 215
Masters of Reality 217

The Colossal Juxtaposition... 217
PART III, Baby Steps..223
7. Truth..225
   7.1. Truth Formation...228
   7.2. Crying, the Perpetuation of Conviction 231
   7.3. Truth, Self-Centric...233
   7.4. Truth and Credit 234
   7.5. Truth Ephemeral..240
   7.6. Truth Exposed..243
      The Cocoon that Broke the Other Way.......................244
      Fear of Freedom..245
      The Unbearable Weight of a Late Invitation..............246
      The Suspensive Stupefaction of the Naïve.................248
   7.7. Truth Recognized..250
   7.8. Truth and the Homeless Civilization.........................253
   7.9. The Language of Truth Formation 255
      Poetry...256
   7.10. The Emotional Horizon..257
   7.11. Truth and Lope de Vega 259
8. Life, the Personification of Truth.....................................261
   8.1. Descent and Surrender...263
      State of Decoy..264

An Inadvertent Winding Descent 264
The Open Wound 268
Dungeons of Insanity 273
Loose Emotional Intensity 279
8.2. The Strength of Our Individuality 279
8.3. Love is Everything and Nothing 280
8.4. Love in the Days of the Jaguar 282
8.5. The Purpose of Being 285
8.6. A Tale of Three Purposes 286
9. Present Time 289
9.1. The Echo of the Past 289
9.2. Elusive Togetherness 295
9.3. Intuition and the Blink of an Eye 297
9.4. Arrival to Present Time 301
9.5. Blossoms that Cling to the Vine 308
10. While Today is Still Forever 311
PART IV, Addendum 317
A.1. Unsubstantiated NDE Cases 319
A.2. James 3, a Past Life Remembered 323
A.3. Joe and the Closing of the American Mind 337
Education, Know Thyself 340
Instamatic Philosophy 344
Plowing with a Rake 347
The Backflow 349
Acknowledgments 351

Author Quotes 353
Bibliography 361
Index 373

Preface

This book presents the inaugural claim to our emotional autonomy, igniting a profound, self-centric paradigm shift that challenges civilization's 5000-year addiction to beliefs. The survival of humanity is at stake. By breaking free from our addiction to beliefs, myths, blind subservience and surrender to anything that moves, we shed the social clothes that keep us hidden, rendering us unrecognizable as we walk on the face of the earth. In doing so, we are compelled to confront our emotional core, where deep inside lies the individual autonomy and independence our civilization has never seen.

This book highlights our compulsion to internalize and become addicted to beliefs, such as religion, mythology, political and intellectual ideologies, and social disciplines. However, its purpose is not to engage with or debate these beliefs but to examine the mechanisms through which they are internalized. By understanding these processes, this book seeks to reveal how they undermine the emotional constitution and autonomy of individuals. Therefore, this book is not about religion, nor does it engage in religious rhetoric, or make claims about the divine nature of religious proclamations. However, when necessary, I will not divert from exposing the implausibility of certain man-made promulgations of faith. This is done solely to clear the path and guide conversation to the deeper, more essential issues at hand.

This book is not about religion, myths, beliefs, or intellectualized social disciplines, which I consider peripheral and of zero value to the human condition. It is about what matters: reclaiming our emotional self and rescuing our intuition from 5000 years of suppression and condemnation. It is a book about 5000 years of emotional occlusion—though forgive me for not having been there throughout its entirety.

This book, above all, is about our continuing state of emotional orphanhood. It explores how our addiction to beliefs and mythology serves as proof of this haunting state of emotional homelessness. Beliefs and myths are merely a fragile decoy, exposing the persistent absence of our emotional foundation over the past 5000 years. Just as mathematical logicians use scenarios to ground their arguments in provable contexts, I use our dependency on beliefs and mythology as a framework to validate my thesis. Without examining the damaging effect of these constructs, discussions about our emotional state risk being dismissed as mere conjecture. But if you skip this commentary, you may misunderstand the purpose. Beliefs are not the focus of this book; they are simply a means to illuminate the far-reaching effects of civilization on individual emotionality. By the time you're halfway through reading, it will become clear that this book has never been about beliefs—and you'll begin to realize we are not in Kansas anymore.

The central theme in this book is the inexistence of an individual emotional foundation throughout the entire human civilization. While history is filled with displays of emotional intensity—some genuine, but many choreographed dramatizations marked by plenty of screaming, crying, and dying—what remains missing in either case is the emotional foundation needed to provide perspective, grounding, stability, and a deeper connection to reality. An emotion can be extremely intense and lead to wars and death, but if it does not reflect a deep, enduring, sober reality, what is it? In 5000 years, this foundation has never existed, does not exist, and has never been acknowledged by society as something that needs to exist.

Beliefs are used as a framework to illustrate and expose the concept of the vacuous emotional self, bringing to light the monumental damage this void has inflicted on civilization and bringing it to public trial.

This is not an intellectual book. However, I have to invade the intellectual sanctuary erected by disciplines such as philosophy and psychology to reclaim all the notions long misappropriated by them. I am a soldier of fortune making incursions on foreign soil, parachuting to set foot into the enemy territory of intellectuality with just enough time to rescue the hijacked treasures that belong to us, then flee. I am not an intellectual. As a chapter in the book, I introduce *"Philosophical Joe,"* my alter ego, who knows how to scrap with anything intellectual without stepping into the lofty sanctuary of pompous intellectual reasoning.

This book is not about providing self-improvement recipes, tickling you on the belly, or standing on a pulpit to preach, inspire, and motivate thy kingdom come. If I were to make a list of all the things I would like to be, a preacher would be number 1001, right after dying young for failing to follow my intuition.

This book is personal. There is a je ne sais quoi, anecdotal personal tone engraved in the book. After all, everything in the universe is personal—the impersonal being the most personal. After all, if we walk the earth one foot in front of the other, we are leaving a trace, and that makes us storytellers, so how can we not be? We can divide the world in two halves in any which way we want—young and old, northern and southern, friendly and unfriendly. We can also divide it into self-improvement recipe givers and storytellers, and I am not a recipe giver.

At its core, this book is about drawing the battlelines between intellect and emotion: the biggest confrontation in human civilization.

Introduction

The claim to our emotional autonomy requires a profound self-centric paradigm shift to break civilization's 5000-year addiction to beliefs that have distorted reality and alienated our sense of identity, shielding access to our deeper, often uncomfortable emotions and the fluid nature of our true selves.

This book is about the emotional process of freeing ourselves from our dependence on deeply ingrained beliefs—particularly the socialized notions we internalize that shape and often dominate our sense of identity. Beliefs provide structure, certainty but also a misunderstanding of who we are in an unpredictable world. Clinging rigidly to them acts as a shield against exploring our deeper, often uncomfortable emotions and the fluid nature of our true selves.

Beliefs can exist anywhere on a spectrum, ranging from harmful—by creating a distorted perception of reality or a mythical conception of the non-physical world—to beneficial, by depicting reality accurately. For example, beliefs have the power to incite domination and extermination wars, or inspire transformative social movements.

Beliefs can be used as instruments for control, enforced through intellectual ideologies and emotional manipulation that disregard the self and inflict deep alienation. Humans tend to become addicted to beliefs as a replacement for something else missing or broken inside of us, and the more severe our damage inside, the more vulnerable we will be and the more vehemently we will adhere to an external belief and its possibly distorting, damaging perceptions of reality.

We internalize these beliefs when we surrender our inner self to them. Beliefs sprout from all aspects of life, including religion, mythologies, spiritual, social and political cults, and intellectual ideologies, often triggering massive, inexplicable herd followings.

Emancipation from beliefs is extremely challenging because it is not an intellectual thought process—it requires a deeply emotional process of self-discovery. It requires descending into the core of our inner selves and engaging in an existential battle between impersonal intellectual alienation and emotional individuality—a confrontation between intellect and emotion.

We conclude that, unlike emotional surrender, which stems from accepting emotional platitudes and a superficial, false understanding of our emotional nature, *emotional autonomy is the living awareness of our true and deepest emotional constitution.* It is not subject to superficial decoys and self-denials and remains steadfast as we confront challenging external misconceptions.

But why would we want to engage in such a difficult battle? When we realize how much of our emotional self has been lost and surrendered to a culture of belief, we won't settle for anything less than reclaiming our fuller sense of self, even if it requires such confrontation. This is the only route to our individual survival and self-realization, as well as the survival and advancement of humanity. This monumental, gradual journey starts with baby steps, recognizing that truths do not exist until they form within our emotional core. Truths only exist inside of us; all other asseverations are *merely socially calibrated perceptions, collective sensorial alignments.*

It is my burden of proof to demonstrate the existence of these battle lines beyond a reasonable doubt. This is probably the point where all ten people who'll read this book will make a U-turn, insisting they're emotionally sound and perfectly happy relying on intellectual beliefs born of intellectual reasoning; after all, they are deeply thoughtful humans.

Such an individual position of relative emotional sobriety still needs to be brought into a wider perspective. The counter argument in favor of dismantling belief addiction is twofold:

1. The collective emotional state of the world has reached its peak dysfunction, promoting servitude and adulation, vanity, self-interest, resentment, and hatred, all of which expose the constant lingering threat of societal collapse, which can only be averted by reducing our emotional addictions.
2. While some of us may exhibit a grounded, sober emotionality, functional within societal standards, we should consider that we still lack a deeper, fulfilling sense of self-awareness, realization, and gratification. Achieving this would grant us unparalleled autonomy for self-determination and a new understanding of an attainable emotional reality—one that unlocks endless streams of satisfaction and pleasure, coming from deeply feeling and following our emotions, one that remains to be seen anywhere in our society of pervasive emotional platitude and alienation. However, this new reality can only be pursued once a glimpse of this new possibility becomes apparent to us.

This book flows with a personal undercurrent. When I go to the streets, stopping people on their walks or runs, asking them (like a good beggar hoping for a scrap of pity) for personal examples that I can use in my book, the streets suddenly become empty, leaving me as the only soul walking, waiting for the weather to turn. It is in that solitude that I realize it is my role to offer myself as the sacrificial lamb, sharing my own examples as reflections of my thoughts.

I will not qualify this book with epithets like "funny" or "witty." Doing so would be akin to making a sarcastic remark to a friend but softening it with a preemptive disclaimer, thereby dulling its impact—living cautiously within quotation marks. Instead, I want to live as if in an open marketplace of a country far from the benevolent hand of God and the indulgence of God's country, where all the sharp comments people make about your appearance, gait, or attempts to fit in are delivered without social pretense—no quoted double-takes. Things are what they are. Or worse, things are what you perceive them to be.

Let's look through the context and perspective that I bring to the writing of this book.

I never thought of obtaining a degree in philosophy or psychology. My reasoning would have led to my departure anyway, though boredom would have driven my exit. I was born immune to the desire to elevate myself to the pulpit of intellectual discourse where these disciplines aim to exist, as doing so would have implied a tacit endorsement of their foundation, disqualifying me from speaking on the premises of this book. It had to be one or the other. Special mention goes to those pursuing degrees as psychotherapists, willing to undergo their own emotional heavy lifting as a rite of passage for the work they will ask others to do.

As a graduate student traveling on an airplane flight, I once sat next to a mother traveling alone. She revealed the higher pursuits of her family for personal growth and social awareness. Her son, a psychology student, felt sorry for those narrow-minded individuals who were immersed in science and technology (like me), believing they were deprived of the deeper meaning of life and the broader perspective offered by a liberal education. I commented that my friends and I did not find superiority in relying on a discipline that offered trite, canned recipes to teach us how to think or to give us a sense of identity. Instead, we valued the privilege of knowing that our academic formation remained distinct from our individual autonomy for social and self reflection. We had our own rogue view of the world, and academically, that was nobody else's business.

In some ways, I see myself as the prehistoric pterodactyl that got out of the cage in the movie *Jurassic Park*. Prehistoric because I remain untamed, with carnivorous voracious disregard for the civilized intellectual pursuit towards modern social virtue. I am out of the cage, and I know how to fly.

Chapter Summaries

Part I, *"Beliefs and Secularity,"* explores the nature of beliefs in correlation with secularity. If religious beliefs stem from a divine origin, then secular reasoning cannot apply, and divine decrees must be accepted as matters of faith. However, if the grandeur and splendor of the non-physical realm, such as eternal existence and omnipresence available to us all, can be understood and proven through a secular perspective, it challenges the validity of religious and mythical beliefs. This is why secularity offers a distinct perspective on the nature of belief systems.

We look at secularity from two perspectives. Chapter 1, *"A Roll of the Dice"* explores how science, primarily through quantum physics, is beginning to suggest that the non-physical realm could be governed by the laws of physics in a secular way—implying that these realms might not require religious or mythical explanations. Chapter 2, *"The Secular Avalanche,"* shows the preponderance of evidence and verifiable cases that support the idea that the non-physical realm is inherently secular. It argues that this realm is universally accessible to everyone, irrespective of religious or mythical affiliations, and that its magnificent reality is unrelated to narrow religious or mythical preconceptions.

Part I continues by assessing how belief systems are the primary mechanism for domination in our society. Chapter 3, *"Beliefs,"* briefly describes some of the ways in which beliefs are injected or internalized into our psyche through our everyday socialization. Chapter 4, "*Beliefs and Surrogacy,*" shows how the culture of beliefs permeates almost every aspect of our lives, from religion to science and social disciplines. It shows how each discipline plays its part in the propagation of belief culture. This chapter introduces the notion that beliefs rely on flawed intellectual reasoning, which is impersonal by nature and carries an intrinsic alienation of the emotional self. Intellectual reasoning, being detached from emotion, allows beliefs to take hold by disconnecting us from our emotional selves. For beliefs to be internalized, they must suppress the personal emotional aspects of our identity. In this chapter, we begin to see the epic conflict between beliefs and individual awareness—specifically, the struggle between intellect and emotion as the source of truth. This is where we begin to draw the lines for the battle ahead.

Once we understand that beliefs can bring a harmful process of indoctrination and internalization, putting our emotional integrity at risk, Part II, "*Dismantling Beliefs,*" begins to explore how difficult it is to dismantle these beliefs. Chapter 5, "*Deconstructing Beliefs,*" offers insights into this challenge, explaining that beliefs were adopted through the surrender of our inner selves, and now, to undo them, we must reclaim that very self. 5.1, "*My Beliefs, My Gods,*" takes us through a playful scenic route to the creation of our own beliefs. This is our opportunity to take liberties not afforded before to mere mortals never anointed to bring the heavens to Earth. If beliefs were created by humans to begin with, we can create our own. However, unlike recalcitrant beliefs that need to be adopted as articles of blind faith under penalty of death by the sword, we create playful speculative beliefs just to prove that sometimes our imaginative fantasy can take us closer to hidden truths. It shows a way to view beliefs as a purely emotional, exploratory and voluntary experience. Its levity might be seen with disdain, but only because we have on our shoulders 5000 years of submission to the divine, wrapped in pompous solemn gravity. We fail to realize that the path to the non-physical might be as playful as a game of hopscotch—and that is where the path to our gods becomes the path to us. For me, it is also where the grand tour takes a more personal turn, as if there is anything in the universe that is not personal already. 5.2, "*The Dance Around Fear,*" reminds us that as we begin to dismantle beliefs, we will encounter latent fear. This section shows how fear is misunderstood by society. 5.3, "*All Roads Lead to Rome,*" reminds us that the confrontation we see brewing with belief culture in order to rescue our emotional inner self, is inescapable no matter how we approach this challenge. 5.4, "*Nothing to Learn,*" reminds us that such confrontation has been waiting at our doorstep for 5000 years, and the price of the wait has been unfathomable. 5.5, "*Enormity by Invisibility,*" brings us to the threshold of the largest confrontation in our civilization's history. Chapter 6, "*Reality and Duplicity,*" describes the profound disdain with which reality has been viewed by our civilization for the past 5000 years and how no progress can be made until we understand its value.

Part III, "*Baby Steps,*" in many ways marks the entry into the subject. It's where I begin to explore a new route for guiding ourselves towards emotional autonomy and away from the crutches of beliefs that condition and control our emotions. Now that we've understood the compulsion to cling to beliefs, and have declared our intent to separate, how do we take our first baby steps on our own? In Chapter 7, "*Truth,*" we explore a new understanding of truth and its characterization from multiple perspectives. Truth must reflect reality, but now we no longer have the crutch of belief or social disciplines to tell us what reality and truth are. We are on our own. In Chapter 8, "*Life, the Personification of Truth,*" we look at our new understanding of truth within the context of our physical life on Earth. Section 8.1, "*Descent and Surrender,*" goes into some depth to demonstrate the difficulty of reaching our truths. Just with this section alone we can see clearly that this book is not meant as a motivational, inspirational piece. The process of finding truth is what allows us to dismantle beliefs and not the other way around. It might seem cleaner to dismantle beliefs before seeking truth, but that is not the natural sequence. We don't confront the dragons of beliefs simply because they exist, nor is it a goal we should aim for. It is when we are confronted with our survival, which forces us to seek our own truths, that we will inevitably encounter and dismantle the myths and beliefs we find obstructing our path. This is why Part II only lightly touches on the subject of dismantling beliefs—the heavy lifting happens here. Chapter 9, *"Present Time,"* focuses on our physical life on Earth. How do we develop an awareness of ourselves that allows us to say we have a presence in this life? Chapter 10, *"While Today is Still Forever,"* is where we say our goodbyes. We reach the end of the book and its uncharted territory. Ultimately, this chapter is about how we part ways and take our first steps independently. Now we mend ourselves. This is where we say we are done by recognizing that we have not yet begun.

Part IV, *"Addendum,"* provides full details of the reviews I presented only as summaries in the main sections of the book.

PART I, Beliefs and Secularity

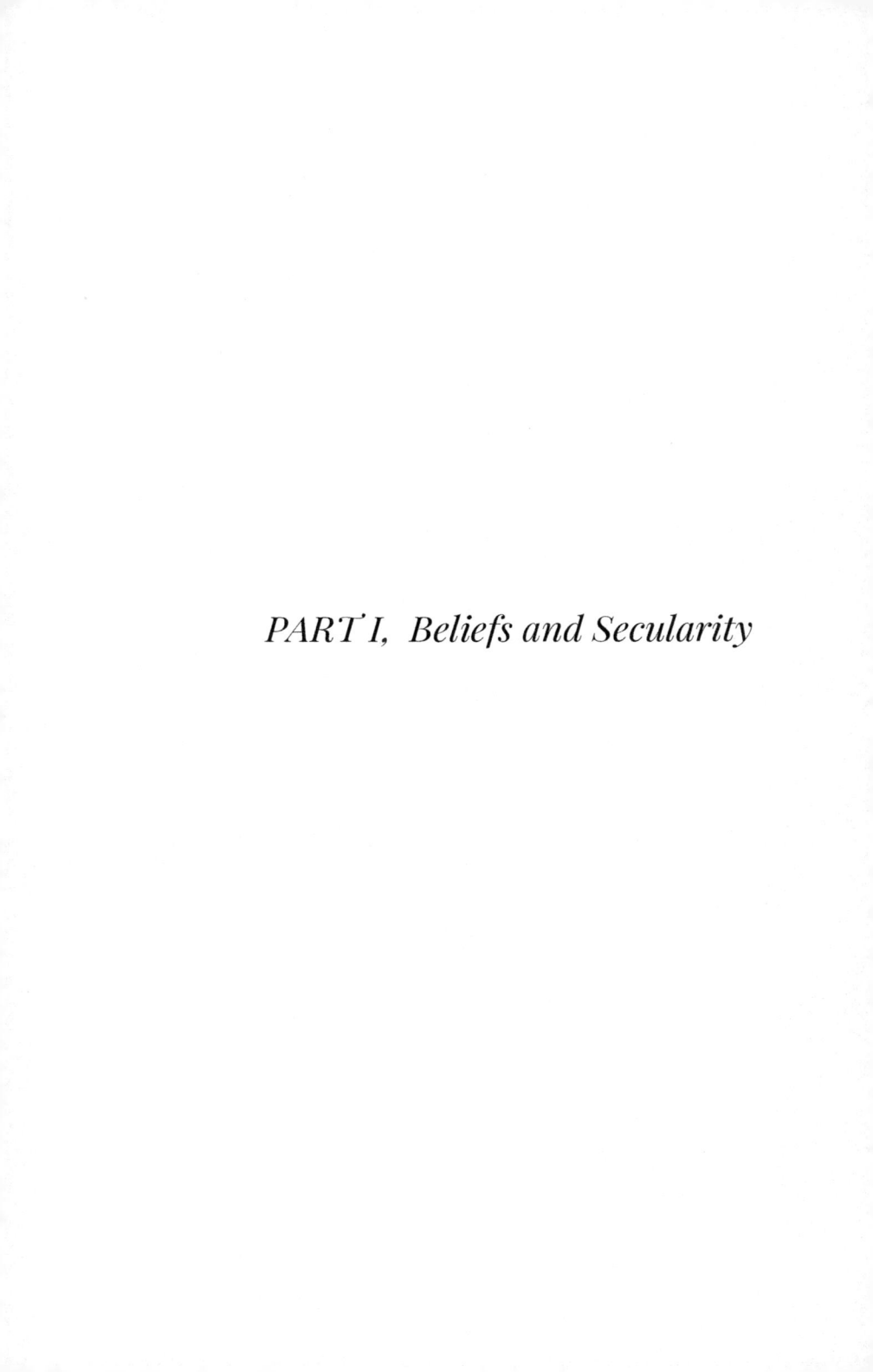

1. A Roll of the Dice

We now know about quantum physics. We can observe its behavior. And we know that its behavior is contrary to our expectations of the physical world we understand. Science has always brought to us the reassurance that it can explain the "real world" that we perceive through our senses, the world that we can see and touch. But now, for the first time in the history of civilization, after thousands of years of scientific advances, from Archimedes to Al Khwarizmi, to Galileo, we stand at the threshold of a new dawn of science. It is the new dawn brought by quantum physics, the physics of subatomic particles, with unexpected behaviors that contradict our experience and our expectations of how the physical world behaves, or how we think it should behave.

Quantum physics creates a connection between the parallels of non-physical consciousness and our emotional emancipation. Quantum physics experimentation offers plausible conjectures, explanations for evidence coming from near-death and other non-physical experiences of human beings, which provide a new understanding of the spiritual realm and our non-physical consciousness. This early experimentation offers a contrasting, human-style of "seeing is believing" approach—essential to our human nature—against a spiritual realm that has, until now, been defined solely by faith. This plays an essential role in our understanding of beliefs, religion and mundane secularity, the readily available non-physical consciousness, and therefore in the understanding of our emotional autonomy, which is, in the first place, dictated by religious beliefs. That is why this book brings quantum physics along as we seek a new emotional understanding. In other words, we cannot determine the extent of our emotional autonomy irrespective of an understanding of secularity and religious beliefs, which in turn cannot be severed from the "seeing is believing" plausibility pouring from quantum experimentation. It is as simple as that.

We now observe independent paths of curiosity, exploration, and discovery for three realms: the quantum universe, our non-physical experiences, and our inner emotional autonomy—each ultimately leading to a single point of convergence. Science will serve as the corroboration of our spiritual, timeless consciousness, while the narrowing, exclusionary proclamations of faith in classical religions will no longer fit in this reality. We will have to give secularity its rightful place in this new understanding.

We begin by offering a brief description of the behaviors observed in quantum physics.

Quantum physics brings us the principle of "nonlocality," where two particles at arbitrarily distant locations and without any communication between them can behave in synchrony, aware of each other, as if they are the same particle. It also shows that particles can manifest themselves as either energy or matter, depending on whether they are being observed, and that these subatomic particles exist without a past or future. We cannot explain these behaviors because we do not understand the laws of quantum physics. All we can do is observe and show that these behaviors are as counter-intuitive as they are predictable.

Coincidentally, survivors of near-death experiences (NDEs) describe spiritual conditions that closely resemble quantum behavior, such as omnipresence or the ability to be in multiple places at the same time, becoming a consciousness made of energy and not matter, and the ability to be in their past and future at the same time. These correlations to quantum physics may one day enable science to explain both physical and spiritual laws and remove the mysterious, magical, superstitious, mythological connotations that spirituality currently holds.

First, let's review how classical physics is governed by the mathematical laws that predict relationships between physical objects, such as how objects move in relation to each other. These are known as Newton's classic laws of physics. Empirically, we know these laws very well, because we use them all the time in our everyday life. Without our ability to predict the behavior captured in these laws, we would not be able to exist in our world. If we are playing baseball with a friend, we know that if we are right-handed, we lead with the left foot, and if we are left-handed, we lead with the right foot. This is to produce torque at the hip which will accelerate rotation at the shoulders, and even more rotation in the forearm and the hand, to impart maximum speed. If you ask an eight-year-old boy from the Dominican Republic, who dreams of becoming a big leaguer, how he generates his ball speed, he will tell you, "*Hey, it is all Newtonian physics! Don't you know you have to learn Newton's laws before you can play baseball? Yogi Berra said so."* Same when you are playing tennis. You add topspin to your groundstrokes in order to increase the curvature of the parabola to more easily clear the net, and create acceleration when the ball bounces, making it difficult for your opponent to return that ball. When you are going to cross the street and there is a vehicle coming, you can calculate its speed and time in seconds for the vehicle to reach your position, and relative to your walking speed, you can predict if you can cross the street in time or not.

By contrast, quantum physics studies subatomic particles, which, as the building blocks of atoms, are the smallest building blocks of nature and all physical matter. Intuitively, if they are the smaller constituents of the bigger physical components, we would expect them to behave the same way. But that is not the case. By contrast, quantum physics defies our imagination with totally unexpected behavior that shatters our expectations, contradicting our understanding of the world we thought we understood, and thus making such behavior difficult to believe and accept. While the scientific community does not understand the laws governing quantum physics, we now have the groundbreaking ability to conduct experiments that reveal its baffling, totally unexpected behavior—behavior that intriguingly aligns with accounts of near-death experiences (NDEs). Following are examples of experiments that have given us insights into this unanticipated quantum physics behavior.

Energy or Matter? Louis De Broglie showed in 1929 that subatomic particles can present themselves as either invisible energy or matter. As energy, a particle can be in multiple places and states at the same time. We would have to roll the dice or use probability to guess where the particle might be. But when the particle is observed, then it can be seen as one single particle of matter in one place—but only when it is being observed. This behavior seems to correlate with near-death situations where survivors experience having both a physical matter representation and an invisible energy counterpart.

The Double-Slit Experiment. Consider this experiment. You have a bucket full of balls filled with red paint, and a ball throwing machine that can fire only one ball at a time against a wall where the ball will splash. In between the thrower and the wall you place a big cardboard screen with two holes. So now, for the ball to smash against the wall, it has to go through one of those holes. When you fire the thrower, you will be facing backwards, not facing the wall. You fire one ball, then turn to see the red splash on the wall, and you see two—one for each hole in the cardboard screen. But how can that be, if you fired only one ball? You repeat the experiment, still facing backwards and you get the same result. Now you turn forward so that you can actually see the firing, the trajectory of the ball, and the wall, and you fire. Then the ball goes only through one of the holes and produces only one splash on the wall. You repeat this experiment only to see two splashes if you are not observing the event, and one splash if you are observing it. How can that be? Can the ball be in multiple places at the same time, but only if the event is not being observed? This is called the double slit experiment performed by Thomas Young in 1801, except that he used subatomic particles instead of balls filled with red paint.

The Copenhagen interpretation of this phenomenon, developed in 1925 by Nils Bohr and Werner Heisenberg, explains that a particle (or the ball filled with red paint in our example), exists in multiple states and locations as waves, according to certain probabilities. It is the act of observation that causes the particle (or the ball) to collapse into one single material representation. We do not fully understand why this happens, what purpose it serves, or how an observer can cause a particle to materialize. It almost seems as if the material world exists only through the eyes of the beholder. This idea is difficult to accept, even with consistent experimental results. Yet, it appears to align with the experiences described by near-death survivors, who report existing as both matter and energy, and as energy, being able to be in multiple places at the same time.

Non-Locality and Quantum Entanglement. For this experiment, imagine that you have one hundred rubber balls that change color to red, blue, green and orange each time you squeeze them, but in some unpredictable order. You place these balls in fifty pairs using fifty cardboard boxes. From each box you take one ball from the pair and bring these fifty balls to a city 3,000 miles away, or to the moon. Now, with the balls you kept, every time you squeeze each ball to change color, the paired ball at the distant location also changes state to that same color and vice versa—when someone squeezes a ball in that distant location, the paired local ball also changes to that same new color. These balls have no way to communicate with each other, there is no transmission of any kind at the speed of light or otherwise. So how do these balls know how and when to change state? This experiment is conducted with subatomic particles instead of rubber balls and is called *non-locality* or *quantum entanglement*.

Quantum entanglement is a bizarre, counterintuitive phenomenon that shows how the (changing) state of two entangled subatomic particles is simultaneously correlated with each other even if these particles are separated by billions of light-years of distance. As Erwin Schrodinger said, *"this is the characteristic trait of quantum mechanics that enforces its entire departure from classical lines of thought."* That is the understatement of the century. A change in the state of one particle is instantly reflected in the other, with no time lapse between them. But that would be impossible according to Einstein's theory of relativity, which states that no influence can be transmitted faster than the speed of light. It also contradicts Einstein's hypothesis that this entanglement was a form of long-distance communication between particles.

Niels Bohr in 1927 and John Bell in 1964 showed that entanglement is a process whereby two particles become manifestations of the same particle, and when located at different locations in space, their state will react as one, without influence or transmission. It is as if they represent the same entity without any sense of locality. Einstein did not have an explanation for this except to call it *"a very spooky phenomenon."* Technology is not waiting to understand this phenomenon—entanglement is already being used as a form of communication without transmission—think of the internet but without the delay of transmission times. This seems to coincide with NDEs in which individuals describe a state of nonlocality—their ability to be everywhere. For example, NDE survivors might say that they could see their past lives at the same time as their present and future lives, and that in the present, they could be in many places at the same time, listening to a conversation between physicians about their medical condition or watching a relative far away boarding an airplane to visit them.

Only present time in quantum physics. The Copenhagen interpretation also recognized the *principle of uncertainty*, which states that it is impossible to predict the location of a quantum particle based on cause and effect; we can only roll the dice and guess to a possible location. This lack of causality implies that quantum particles have no defined past or future, only a present state. This concept seems to align with reports from NDEs, where individuals experience all past and future events simultaneously.

The Higher Consciousness of the Observer? With the double-slit experiment, some thought that the observation process might affect the particles because of the instrument's own particle emissions, such as photons. They then conducted an experiment to allow the observing instrument to operate without human observation. But the particles still behaved as if they were not being observed, implying that there are some unknown characteristics of the more complex observing entity that cause particles to behave differently. It almost suggests that observation by a higher consciousness or intelligence is what causes energy to manifest as matter. It may take another two hundred years for quantum scientists to identify the laws that enable a complex arrangement of particles to qualify as an observer with higher consciousness, as well as the laws that lead to the formation of such complex arrangements.

For those of us not working to advance quantum physics theory or expecting to receive the Nobel Prize in physics any time soon, the key takeaway is that these quantum experiments reveal conditions beyond our everyday physical experience. They suggest that the spiritual state and the afterlife might also follow the mundane secular laws of quantum physics, much as Newton's laws govern daily life on earth. Put simply, the most profound value of quantum physics today is not the technological advances it brings, but rather the possibility that experiences described by near-death survivors—such as being present everywhere at once or across all past lives—may one day be explained as predictable, routine phenomena governed by quantum laws, without requiring divine favor.

As I've noted before, a day will come when science and spirituality converge, and science will serve as the corroboration of our timeless universal consciousness. When that day of discovery, ownership of our nature and greatness arrives for the human race, we will no longer be here—we'll all be long gone. But today, before we go, we acknowledge the dawn of our understanding of quantum physics as the first step toward that moment when science and our timeless universal presence unite as one. Let this acknowledgment stand as a testament to our presence—now and in the future—when we witness the most magnificent homecoming in humanity's history.

2. The Secular Avalanche

We know that we exist on this earth with a consciousness that remains with us throughout our lives. That consciousness is what allows us to recognize our existence, to think, to look at ourselves in the mirror and say *"you look mahrvelous,"* and it is what tells us that we are individuals separate from others, and better than most. But according to numerous testimonials—primarily from individuals who experienced death and were revived thanks to advances in medicine—we are discovering that another aspect of our consciousness may have existed before we were born, remains with us throughout our lives, and could continue to exist after we die. Unlike our physical consciousness, which is localized and confined to the body and the specific geospatial place we occupy, this other consciousness is nonlocal. It extends beyond the body and space itself and may even be omnipresent, existing everywhere simultaneously. Unlike our physical consciousness, which manifests as matter, this other consciousness is pure timeless energy without a physical form. This is our nonlocal or timeless consciousness, the counterpart to our physical consciousness— both integral parts of who we are.

All these experiences are secular because they take place outside the context of religion and without the influence of religious devotion, virtue, enlightenment or reward. They are not attributed to manifestations of any particular religious belief. They are also mundane because they seem to occur routinely and frequently, just as physical life on earth, and thus are experiences that cannot be deemed as exceptional, supernatural or divine miracles. They are just common everyday occurrences.

Unfortunately for those of us who would like to remain cool without a cause by the graceful blessing of agnosticism, there is sufficient evidence to nudge our reluctance towards at least considering the notion of a spiritual consciousness. If this is true, how do we know? Does this come to us as some kind of mythical superstition or divine illumination or does it come to us through verifiable, secular, mundane, routine, repeatable, personal experiences, just as the magic of physical life in this planet comes to us equally, as a secular, mundane, routine, repeatable, but often flawed experience?

The extent to which we choose to consider the existence of a spiritual realm is secondary to the essential thesis of this book—secular life without beliefs. However, in this chapter I take the liberty to explore the large volume of secular evidence pointing to the existence of a spiritual consciousness in all of us, as that might help us finetune our understanding of secularity.

The world today is awash in a tidal wave of interwoven information, enabling us to classify facts and experiences as never before. Advances in the medical sciences have also led to a dramatic increase in the number of cases where people who have been diagnosed as clinically dead according to a medical definition have been resuscitated and brought back to life. This has yielded an unprecedented volume of verifiable, secular, routine experiences that point to the existence of our nonlocal consciousness, our *nonlocal or timeless self*. Typically, this information has been collected retrospectively, recounted after the fact. Now, large initiatives are underway to collect this data prospectively, using a more consistent methodology to collect detailed data before, during, and after the experience (van Lommel, 2014; Greyson, 2013; Sartori et.al., 2006). Each such case relating to the existence of nonlocal consciousness must be able to stand on its own with externally verifiable evidence in the form of extraordinary events and revelations, which extend beyond the confines or limitations of our physical realm. We can classify these experiences in four categories which we will explain further below: near-death experiences or NDEs, the conscious spontaneous recollection of past lives, the subconscious recollection of past lives, and the conscious access to nonlocal existences.

2.1. *NDEs*

Near-death experiences, or *NDEs*, are intensely vivid, heightened extrasensorial events that transcend space and time. They occur under extreme physiological conditions—such as trauma, ceasing of brain activity, deep general anesthesia or cardiac arrest—by individuals who have begun the process of dying or have already been declared clinically dead. Under these conditions, prevailing views in neuroscience suggest that no awareness or sensory experiences should be possible.

Sometimes these events can be corroborated with facts available to us and shown that the individual having an NDE in that physical state could not have experienced them, even with a normal, fully functional brain. These events that transcend or displace through space, or that can be experienced outside a physical body or a confined physical locality, we call *nonlocal events*.

Over the past few years, researchers, physicians and medical institutions have been able to accumulate a significant volume of cases involving near-death and clinical death experiences (NDEs), many of which can be corroborated by available evidence. This has allowed them to compare these cases and find extraordinary similarities of irrefutable characteristics.

Anita Moorjani

Anita Moorjani (2012) provides a detailed account of her rich near-death experience (NDE). After four years of being devoured by cancer, she was dying of last stage lymphoma in 2006. She had tumors the size of lemons all throughout her lymphatic system, she could not breathe as she was drowning in her own lungs' fluids, her veins had collapsed and could not be used for IV insertions, and her organs were beginning to shut down. She went into a coma and was rushed to a different emergency hospital, where the oncologists gave her only a few hours to live. This is the point at which her nonlocal near-death experience outside her body begins, which I briefly summarize:

1. Unlike most NDEs, which presumably occur after the person has been declared clinically dead, it seems that her experience started before that happened, while she was in a coma.
2. In most NDEs, for which we will provide examples later, individuals describe going through a tunnel towards a peaceful light, going towards a higher consciousness, which presupposes a hierarchy. But her experience was different. It was that of herself becoming that higher consciousness. She comments that a higher consciousness is not a being to aspire to and revere, but just a state of being. A very significant difference.
3. Her experience seems to have started as a gradually expansive out of body awareness. She became gradually more aware of her surroundings. She was aware of conversations about her, some 40 feet away in the hallway. She began to feel free, light, without pain, acutely aware of the nature of these conversations and began to feel pulled away, as if there was a bigger picture, a grander plan unfolding. She understood then that we never truly die. Her body was too insignificant to house her feelings of freedom, liberation and magnificence. She felt encompassed by an indescribable pure, unconditional love. She was finally home.
4. She began to notice how she was expanding to fill every space until there was no separation between her and everything else. She felt she had become everything and everyone. She could see her worried older brother on an airplane going to see her. She felt that continued expansion beyond space and time.
5. She became aware of her deceased father and best friend, and felt incredible comfort from their presence. She felt her

father's intransigent beliefs during his physical lifetime were no longer present as they became irrelevant in the presence of this magnificent spiritual context. She could become one with her best friend and understand how her friend could then be everywhere to comfort her own loved ones still in the physical world. You find understanding by becoming one with what or who you want to understand, so that their knowledge and awareness become you.

6. Time felt different; she experienced all moments at once—past, present and future. She became aware of a younger brother in a past life, who is now her older brother, recalling how she took care of him in a rural mud hut as their parents worked in the fields. Though this scene appeared historical or from an early time, it felt as though it was happening at that very moment. This experience supports the claim by others that spiritual families form in a nonlocal spiritual space to reunite and share their physical lives across lifetimes.

7. She realized we were all connected—an interwoven unification that includes everything in the universe.

8. She expresses the unimaginable clarity with which all this awareness came to her.

9. She recounts that the depth and breadth of awareness and knowledge is indescribable. She offers the metaphor of seeing a place in total darkness and silence only through a flashlight, representing our physical life experience. Imagine suddenly switching on sunlight and seeing the entire landscape illuminated from every conceivable point of view all at once, as if you were seeing it from everywhere, from every angle, able to see it all—an omnidirectional, suprasensorial awareness. Colors, details, depth, dimensions, connections, sounds—all come into being within this new awareness.

10. She comments that our nonlocal, timeless, spiritual state transcends religion, which has meaning only in our physical life to help us understand death. Otherwise, any religion represents a narrowing or more restrictive view of the afterlife experience. Later, I illustrate typical narrowing religious precepts with examples.
11. She observes that her healing required absolutely no faith in anything but on the contrary, the complete suspension of all previously held beliefs, doctrines and dogma.
12. She also states her opinion that when we take our physical form, we are not meant to forget the magnificence of who we are, but it is just that all the misplaced beliefs make life so difficult.
13. At first, she made a choice to stay back, at which point her body died. It is unclear why there was a threshold of no return for her decision, apparently due to variation in energy levels. Before reaching that threshold, however, she changed her mind and decided she wanted to come back, fully aware that her body would then heal from cancer. Her experience is conceptually different from other NDEs where the decision to return to the physical body is made by other spiritual beings, suggesting the notion of a perhaps more contrived, confined, spiritual hierarchy. In her case, there is no hierarchy, no higher beings suggesting or commanding her what to do, just her own self expanding to reach her own decision.
14. Her healing cannot be explained medically because her many lemon-sized cancer tumors disappeared quite rapidly within days of her coming back from her nonlocal experience, and this alone represents a most compelling suggestion of a spiritual realm coming into play.

While there may be gradients of wisdom, gradual evolution, and transitions, it seems to me that fully accessible autonomy in alignment with natural universal laws might be the pure expression of beauty, simplicity, generality, and power in the universe. From Moorjani's descriptions, it seems as if all of her experience flows very autonomously into those universal laws. There is a natural simplicity, as everything stems from her expansive view of herself, into a higher consciousness, her decision to return, and her knowledge of her powers over the physical realm to heal herself. It does not come from a more narrowing concept of a hierarchy that mediates, interprets, controls and decides for the individual, as that seems to be the experience in many of the NDE cases. This is the most obvious distinction that separates her experience and alerts my curiosity. It coincides with my intuitive perception of *power as autonomy of being and becoming*, which inherently removes the hierarchy of a designer or creator. It aligns with yet another perspective—the notion of Darwin's theory of evolution and natural selection extending to the universe without a designer, as described by Richard Dawkins (2001) in *The God Delusion*. It is significant that this concept serves as such a point of convergence and fusion.

Moorjani's recount is also beautiful because of the wider secular exposure that it brings, free from the permission or ownership of religion. She states that *"Absolutely no faith in anything was required for my healing. Rather, I'd say that it was the complete suspension of all previously held beliefs, doctrines and dogma that caused my body to heal itself. In my case, the NDE was the catalyst."* In terms of her relationship to a superior being or source when she was in that NDE state, she states that she became that source and there was no source outside of her own, as she encompassed totality. Her perception of secularity is fascinating because it is nuanced, subtle, and it permeates her entire experience. Take this example: she mentions in passing that Mother Teresa's deeds (which have a religious motivation) are equally as valuable as those of a science researcher or teacher. They are all contributions.

According to Moorjani, the afterlife experience is expansive and widens our perspective on earth with magnificent, unimaginable levels of freedom and awareness, In that sense it transcends religions, and stands in stark contrast to those which represent a narrowing or restrictive view of the afterlife and its accessibility to a higher state of wellbeing—views modeled after our social experience on earth. Here I provide some examples of narrowing perspectives that might be found in some religions:

1. Individuals are required to know about the religion, profess faith in its teachings, and comply with its commandments before they can reach a state of salvation, otherwise they will fall into other much less desirable and terrifying states. Moorjani states that faith is irrelevant in reaching that state

of profound well-being and higher consciousness. It is irrelevant whether you believe that such a state exists when you are alive in the physical world.
2. Some religions describe states of punishment in the afterlife, including eternal damnation. Moorjani posits that there are no such states. Other NDE survivors have stated that because of our connectedness to others, we can feel the impact of our actions in others.
3. In some religions, individuals fall from grace before they are born, as in the concept of being born with an original sin. This notion restricts access to salvation because now we are required to know about it and make the necessary amends beforehand.
4. A religion is also restrictive when its precepts apply only to humans and not to the rest of the animal kingdom. How can there be an intelligence threshold for moral precepts to apply, and how universal are these precepts if they require an explanation and can only be understood by species above that intelligence threshold? Does this mean that the original sin does not apply to the rest of the animal kingdom? By contrast, Moorjani's expansive view suggests that the spiritual realm encompasses everything in the universe, life and non-life.
5. A religion may also be restrictive when it resembles a spiritual hierarchy similar to the domination hierarchies we are used to on earth.
6. The notion of eternal damnation is also a restriction that most of us would like to live without. It conveys such a degrading understanding of our own imperfection, and it is a conception of pain at an uncompromising level beyond any punishment emperors could conceive to inflict on us in the

physical world. So essentially, we are moving from an earthly place with limited options for attaining limited happiness, to a spiritual place that according to religion, will show the inclemency of even fewer options. Thanks to the vivid imagination of our fellow medieval Italian fresco painters, pictorial renditions of a state of damnation do not seem all that pleasant—not the place to spend a weekend getaway from the family. But add to it this "eternal" clause as a footnote and now all of a sudden it is time to reconsider everything we said about our polite religious voluntarism.

Sometimes individuals who are well-positioned to help others—either because of their wisdom, experience or public credibility—choose to set aside all of their teachings in order to leave us with one central piece of advice, in hopes that we can at least remember that and follow it, especially when they finally realize that we have the attention span of little invertebrates, and that what comes to us through one ear is likely to escape unscathed through the other one. One such individual once said, *"Only one commandment I give you: Love one another, as I have loved you."* Well, all the good that did. We can follow all kinds of religious precepts to show off our sanctimonious selves, our false piousness and humility, our sense of entitlement and moral superiority, and all that just so that we can bathe in holy water and earn the right to see others with disdain. We can do all that, but not the love thing, that is a whole different animal altogether. We haven't gone for the love thing—not for the last 2000 years. Moorjani also leaves us with one lasting thought, that the most important thing for us to do is not to meditate or pray, but instead not to take ourselves too seriously, to laugh a lot, especially at our own selves. I stare at her message with some astonishment and think: "*I choked on the blessed water of the baptismal font, I have been anointed by the infallible emissaries of God through innumerable holy sacraments in solemn ceremonies, and now I am being asked to laugh at myself? Blasphemy I say, blasphemy!*"

Mary Neal

U.S. Surgeon Mary Neal (Netflix 2020a) recounts her own NDE experience while kayaking in Chile in 1999. While another kayaker ahead of her blocked the obvious route down a waterfall, she was forced to take a more dangerous detour. She and her kayak were pulled under an 8-to-10-foot cascade of water, and trapped underwater for 30 minutes, she drowned. When her body was found, she came back to life. She had an NDE where she could see herself detach and separate from her body, hear all the conversations from above, and was welcomed into a spiritual realm by very loving individuals she did not know. Although she did not want to return, these beings made her realize that she had to go back, as she would be needed later due to an upcoming family fatality. Years later, her son was killed instantaneously by a car while crossing a street.

Other NDE Cases

Gibbs (2010), Weiss (2000, 2004) and van Lommel (2010) detail a corroborated account of a blind elderly woman who suffered a cardiac arrest at the hospital where Weiss was the chairman of the psychiatry department. She was unconscious while the resuscitation team was attempting to revive her. According to her later account, she reported that, during that time, she floated out of her body and stood near the window, and despite being physically blind, she watched her own resuscitation process. Without feeling any pain, she observed as they thumped on her chest and kept pumping air into her lungs. During that frantic process, a pen fell out of her doctor's pocket and rolled towards the window where her spirit, out of her body, was standing and watching. A moment later, the doctor walked over, picked up the pen and put it back in his pocket, then continued the resuscitation effort to bring her back to life. They succeeded.

Days later, during her recovery, she told her doctor that she had "seen" the resuscitation team at work during her episode of cardiac arrest. The doctor warmly reassured her, stating that *"No, you were probably hallucinating because of the anoxia (lack of oxygen to the brain). This can happen when the heart stops beating."* Then she replied, *"But I saw your pen roll over to the window,"* and she continued to describe the pen and additional details about the resuscitation episode.

The doctor was clearly shocked, because his patient had not only been comatose during the resuscitation, but she had also been blind for many years. In a later publication, Weiss (2004) noted that *"the cardiologist was still shaken days later when he told me [Weiss] about it. He confirmed that everything the woman related had indeed taken place and that her descriptions were accurate"*.

—+—+—

The externally verifiable credibility of each case must stand on its own. Eben Alexander, a U.S. neurosurgeon, recounts his own NDE in his best seller (2012). He has been featured in *Time Magazine*, *Newsweek*, and *The Oprah Winfrey Show*. His book was endorsed by M.D. and philosopher Raymond Moody, Jr., award-winning author of twelve books, including *Life After Life* (Moody 1975), and he is the person who coined the term NDE, as he states that *"Dr. Eben Alexander's near-death experience is the most astounding I have heard in more than four decades of studying this phenomenon. (He) is living proof of an afterlife."* Eben Alexander states he became very ill with acute bacterial meningoencephalitis and fell into a coma when he experienced his NDE.

In contrast to the typical essence of near-death experiences, he describes his NDE as very peculiar because he lacked self-awareness and had no access to his past or future. Dittrich (2013a,b), in his article in Esquire, states that Alexander's employment as a surgeon at Brigham was terminated for unknown reasons, and UMass Memorial suspended Alexander's surgical privileges *"on the basis of allegation of improper performance of surgery,"* stating that Alexander was sued for malpractice five times.

Contrary to Dr. Alexander's statement that he was in a coma and brain dead for seven straight days caused by his illness, Dr. Laura Potter, the attending ER physician, establishes in an interview with Dittrich, that the coma was instead chemically induced by her because Dr. Alexander's extreme state of conscious agitation required that he be physically restrained for his own safety. Khanna (et.al. 2018) states that he remained sedated for the first five days but that *"his medical records suggest that his coma was not drug-induced."*

There is no point in second guessing the source of the experience, be it a true NDE (comatose or not), a hallucination, or just a creative imagination, because Mr. Alexander contradicts himself, stating that in the spiritual realm, everything is remembered forever without requiring memory, yet in his own spiritual experience, he claims to have had "spiritual amnesia," no recollection of his physical identity. Yet, it was his semi-awakened physical self who called him back to his physical realm. For the reasons outlined above, I cannot offer this case as a reference. See more details of this case in the Addendum.

Omni Vision for the Blind

Ring et.al. (1997) published a two-year study describing the NDEs of thirty one blind individuals which provided compelling visual evidence during their experiences and suggests that spiritual sensorial capabilities are not limited by the condition of the physical body. This was a serious study that did not cut corners. It highlighted unsubstantiated accounts by other studies, and it gave an array of possible explanations and implications of its findings. The following observations from their study are summarized below.

They start their report by showing that the claims in many other similar studies of NDEs or out of body experiences (OBEs) of the blind appear to dissolve into the mists of hearsay, unsubstantiated anecdotes and other dead ends, and even, in one case, outright fabrication. When in 1992, co-author Kenneth Ring, Professor Emeritus of Psychology at the University of Connecticut, pressed M.D. and philosopher Raymond Moody, award-winning author of twelve best sellers and the person who coined the term NDE (Moody 1975), for further particulars about the blind person he described in one of his books, he could only remember that he had heard that account on an audio cassette provided to him by an elderly physician. However, he no longer had the tape and could not recall the physician's name.

The authors make the observation that if these claims about vision for the blind in NDEs were to be verified, they would have far-reaching and contradicting consequences for a conventional materialist view of science, and they would provide empirical support for a new perspective in science that, because of its expanded awareness, would place the nonlocal consciousness and not our physical consciousness as the primary source of reality.

The authors make the obvious statement that for these claims to be validated, they need to be corroborated through independent evidence or the testimony of other witnesses, thus establishing that these claims are something other than mere fantasies or hallucinations.

The near-death experiences of blind people coincide with the common NDE recounts found in the literature, e.g. Moody (1975). Vicky, for example, had her second NDE in 1973 when she was 22, as a result of a car accident. She recalls hearing beautiful music, going up out of her body to the ceiling, then traveling through all the floors in the hospital building and through the roof. She then discovered she had been sucked head-first into a tube and felt that she was being pulled up into it. The enclosure itself was dark, Vicki said, yet she was aware that she was moving toward an opening of light. She recalls that everybody, including herself, were made of light and there was love everywhere and came from everywhere, from the people, the grass, the birds and the trees. She was welcome by loved ones who had passed away. She was also overcome with a sense of total knowledge, as if she knew everything and everything made sense, about life, scientific and mathematical knowledge. Even though she *"did not know beans"* about math and science, she understood calculus and how the planets were made. She felt there was nothing she did not know. There was a being with great radiance that helped review her life and its repercussions since her birth and who also stated that she still needed to go back, as she knew she also wanted to have children.

Vicky had lost all eye sight because when she was born prematurely after only 22 weeks in the womb, she was placed in an airlock incubator and given excessive doses of oxygen which caused optic nerve damage, leaving her completely blind. During her NDE, as she was moving up and away from her body, she saw a thin tall body on the bed which she assumed to be hers, then saw a man and a woman discussing the potential damaging effects of the accident. But though she tried, she found she could not interact with them. While above the hospital roof, she also had the panoramic view of the city from that vantage point.

Brad had a similar NDE experience in 1968 when he was eight years old while he was studying at the Boston Center for Blind Children, and his heart stopped for four minutes due to severe pneumonia. He found himself floating out of his body to the ceiling and through the roof of the building. Then he felt himself go through a tunnel into an immense all-encompassing light, with the feeling that everything was perfect. He became aware of beautiful music like nothing he had ever heard on earth and was surrounded by beautiful tall grass and trees. He encountered a man he did not recognize but from whom emanated an overwhelming love, and who, without a word, moved Brad backward, initiating the reversal of his experience.

During his NDE, as he was moving up and away from his body, Brad saw his lifeless body lying in bed and his roommate getting up to find help (the roommate did confirm this). When he was above the roof, he noticed that he could see clearly. He estimated that it was between 6:30 and 7:00 in the morning. He noticed that the sky was cloudy and dark. There had been a snowstorm the day before, and Brad could see the snow banks everywhere except for the streets, which had been plowed, though they were still slushy. He was able to provide a very detailed description of the way the snow looked. He also saw a street car go by and recognized a playground used by the children of his school and a particular hill he used to climb nearby. He remembered being able to see quite clearly.

Not all accounts can be independently corroborated, because of time lapses, deceased witnesses, and other causes. Some accounts were accepted based on the credibility of the individuals who experienced the event. Others were properly corroborated, as in the case of Frank, who asked a friend to buy him a tie he needed for a wake. After he was dressed and laying on his bed, he had an OBE and saw himself wearing the tie—red with concentric gray circles. Later, his friend wondered how he could possibly have described the tie.

The authors point out that the NDE or OBE visual experiences of the blind cannot be assumed to be the same as our understanding of retinal vision, because the experience described by the blind, though it includes our customary visual elements of colors, shapes, distances and depth, may be the result of a far more encompassing phenomenon—that of an expanded, complex, omnidirectional, suprasensorial awareness.

This notion of seeing as a form of omnidirectional, suprasensorial awareness is also reported by Liberman (1995). During a deep meditative state, he had a very profound and startling experience. Although his eyes were closed, he could suddenly see everything—the whole room and himself in it. He wasn't seeing with his eyes or from any single point of view. He seemed to be seeing everything from everywhere. He describes how there seemed to be eyes in every cell of his body and in every particle surrounding him, everywhere. He could simultaneously see from straight on, from above, from below, from behind, and so on. The apparent escalation in awareness suggested that there was no separation between the observer and the observed, only awareness. This experience of omni directionality in the observation or visualization can be explained by the absence of separation from one's surroundings, a phenomenon which can be found in the narratives of NDE survivors, such as Moorjani's (2012).

To further exemplify this notion of omnidirectional awareness, the authors describe this account from an NDE survivor who contracted pneumonia during her second pregnancy. Upon a rushed arrival at the hospital, she lost consciousness. She left her body and could hear the nurses saying she was "dead meat," but she was already elsewhere at the time. She was hovering over a stretcher in one of the emergency rooms and knew the body on the stretcher wrapped in blankets was hers but really didn't care. The room was much more interesting than her body, because she could see everything. And she meant everything! She could see the top of the light on the ceiling, and the underside of the stretcher. She could see the tiles on the ceiling and the tiles on the floor, simultaneously, in quite detailed three hundred sixty degree spherical vision! She could see every single hair and the follicle out of which it grew on the head of the nurse standing beside the stretcher, and she knew exactly how many hairs there were to look at. The nurse was wearing glittery white nylons. Every single shimmer and sheen stood out in glowing detail, and once again she knew exactly how many sparkles there were. This coincides with the omniscient observation made by Liberman (1995) in the paragraph above, which states that there was no separation between the observer and the observed. This leads the authors to refer to it as *transcendental awareness*, defined as an awareness that transcends the limitations of the senses. In this type of awareness, it is not the eyes seeing; rather it is the mind that perceives, more in the sense of "understanding" or "taking in" than in terms of visual perception.

As we recognize that the experiences just presented can only be explained through the existence of transcendental awareness, it is worth noting that in recent years, a number of thinkers, influenced by new developments in quantum physics, have developed a variety of theories that align with this paradigm. I will illustrate two of them, bearing in mind that they are only theories, arising from individual imagination.

Dossey (1989), in his *Nonlocality Theory of Consciousness*, states that the notion of individual minds is nothing more than an illusion, a useful fiction that Dossey pointedly calls *"the illusion of a separate self and the sensation of an ego that possesses a separate mind."* He is implying that individuality does not exist because we are all inside one single universal consciousness. This theory gives us the room to say that these NDE and OBE events grant us access to this unified consciousness with expanded awareness. We should observe that individuality does exist in our physical world and is essential for us to accurately understand and interpret our physical reality, regardless of how this individuality may be transformed in the nonlocal world.

Goswami (1993, 1994) in his *Quantum Theory of Consciousness* provides the same paradigm as Dossey (1989), stating that individuality exists only in our physical world. But he provides this explanation in terms of quantum physics by stating that the unified, undivided nonlocal consciousness "collapses" and divides itself, giving rise to "actuality," that separation we call individuality.

Summary of NDE Findings

These are the typical events described by NDE survivors:

1. The sensation of going through a tunnel where at the end they find an intense white light further separating them from their physical surroundings.
2. An out-of-body nonlocal experience. Individuals experience a sensation of departure from the body, enabling them to observe the world from positions outside of and not localized near their own bodies. This existential energy, capable of out-of-body experiences, includes hearing sounds, and seeing colors and images even though this energy is invisible and lacks the physical organs that we require for these perceptions in the physical world—even when the physical body of the individual is impaired in those perceptions (e.g. blind individuals being able to see). These experiences are then recorded in the physical brain as images when the person comes back to the physical world.
3. An enhanced visual perception while out of the body (even for physically blind individuals). It is as if you were seeing everything from everywhere, from every angle, from every perspective, able to see it all—an omnidirectional, suprasensorial awareness. Colors, details, depth, dimensions, connections, sounds—all come into being within this new awareness.
4. A sensation of peace, wellbeing and absence of pain, as they have never felt before.
5. Perceiving non-physical consciousness as energy of light.

6. Moving through matter—the ability to go through matter, walls and other bodies.
7. Inability to communicate with the physical world, presumably because they are manifesting themselves as pure energy.
8. Coming into contact with non-physical beings whose intense source of energy and white light convey an immense, embracing sense of unconditional love, peace, and harmony never experienced with such intensity in the human dimension.
9. Most report that communication among beings reminds them of a form of telepathy. Others explain that communication takes place by becoming one with other beings.
10. Establishing contact with deceased loved ones.
11. Seeing their life in the past, present and future, simultaneously living their past and future lives, and having the precognition towards the future. With this, there is no perception of time.
12. No space confinement, as non-physical beings are nonlocal or omnipresent, and can be anywhere simultaneously.
13. Performing a life review and the effects of our actions in others and vice versa.
14. Most report a hierarchical spiritual relationship in which they are asked to go back to complete their human life cycle. They often refuse to come back because of the much higher quality of their existence in that spiritual realm—but nevertheless persuaded or commanded to return. In the Moorjani case, these hierarchical relationships do not seem to exist—not in the acquisition of knowledge or the expansion of consciousness, nor in decision making, such as the choice to go back to the physical realm.

Prospective NDE Research

There is now a great deal of emphasis on conducting and reporting these NDE events on a larger scale and in a formal prospective fashion, initiating the reporting and control of the event before the event occurs. This approach can be achieved at emergency hospitals, in situations of cardiac arrest, for example. These scenarios allow for the recording of these events under uniform predefined guidelines (van Lommel, 2014; Greyson, 2013; Sartori et.al., 2006). Greyson's overview is derived from nine prospective studies in four countries. He concludes there is great uniformity in the experiences themselves, with variations according to subjects' own interpretation of these experiences. Greyson and van Lommel report that *"with advancements in medical resuscitation techniques, the frequency of NDEs has increased, and thus about 9 million people in the United States alone have reported this kind of experience."*

In regard to NDEs, some approaches tend to affirm the validity of these cases on prospective evidence of subjects being clinically dead. While this classification may be essential and understandable for the characterization of NDEs, from the standpoint of revealing provable, verifiable access to the nonlocal, spiritual world, does it matter if subjects were clinically dead or just comatose, or just between blue and midnight? If the outer body experience provides evidence of information not possibly acquired in the physical life, such a case would need to be highlighted as proof of our coexistence with our nonlocal or timeless selves. Let us remember that even with the support of prospective formal studies, there will be some who will find a rationale to reject the credibility of these experiences. So while the academic approach lends formality to these findings, they still have to rely on the narrative credibility of the subjects. It is worth noting that it is a disservice to the community when academics or medical professionals who adhere vehemently to a systematic, detailed verification approach to establish credibility, such as Luján Comas (Carmelo, 2020), still cater to cases that offer zero corroborations, but quite a few contradictions, such as Eben Alexander's case (Dittrich, 2013 a,b).

But having said that about scientific conclusions, I would like to use what I call the "grand colander" approach, and let medical researchers do what they do, which is to design experiments that minimize statistical and coincidental faults to validate their findings. Our colander will retain the detailed anecdotal verifiable narratives of the experiences NDE survivors have wanted to share with all of us, regardless of the research methods used or the credibility of the researchers. These narratives add to our collective history and to our own humanity and lead us one step closer to finding who we are. This is the gift we gratefully accept from them.

Criticism of NDE Research

Positivist quantitative research and philosophical evaluation methods often serve to straight-jacket these events and to deprive us from access to the verifiable facts of these experiences. Andrade (2017) uses a philosophical approach to evaluate the validity of a certain reincarnation study. Now let's take the case of Moorjani (2012). If we were to use the philosophical methodology outlined by Andrade (2017) to review her case, we would require for this case to be predictable, so that we can establish certain parameters to predict a similar outcome, based perhaps on some statistical figures with some independent selection criteria to guarantee the independence of the results. In plain language, this would mean that Moorjani's case lacks veracity because of its singularity, and according to Andrade's philosophical methodology, nor do her assertions about reincarnation. It is worth noting the contribution of phenomenology (Husserl, 2017; van Manen, 2023) to the evaluation and validation process, which presupposes that subjectivity is inescapable and consequently accepts the singularity we see in Moorjani's case, thus validating her case.

Another criteria used by Andrade is that events that implicate a correlation between spiritual phenomena, and their somatic consequence (their influence on the physical body) cannot be accepted because no one has been able to provide a scientific explanation for how the spiritual world actually influences the physical body. According to this, the fact that Moorjani's body (with very late-stage cancer and only a few hours of life) was completely healed upon her return to her body, would also be inadmissible. In other words, if we adhere to these rigorous philosophical methodologies to seek veracity in her case, we would have to dismiss it entirely. This implies that, from a philosophical standpoint, in terms of her public voice based on her experience and testimonials, she does not exist. We must remain mindful of how these cases are evaluated and understand them in a way that allows both their veracity and the weight of their testimonials to give us a road map to determine their acceptance.

Once again, I personally apply my "grand colander" approach to filter out all positivist research statistics and look at the phenomenological value of individual cases to determine if each case alone can stand on its own feet. The colander is meant to filter the cases themselves, not the intermediary evaluator or conductor of the study. The colander also filters the evaluator's critics who dismiss an entire study on the basis of an assessed lack of credibility of the study as a whole. So the colander cleans both ways, so that we don't toss the baby with the evaluator's and critic's combined dirty waters (though we will need to bathe the baby again). This approach also has a way of cleansing those critics with a partial preconception who preemptively dismiss these phenomena, but not before bathing themselves in blessed water by hijacking the process as a whole, applying their rigorous methodologies to disprove the point, and leaving nothing standing in the wake of their rhetoric.

2.2. *Spontaneous Recollection of Past Lives*

There is also a great deal of documentation about individuals remembering verifiable events of past lives that they acknowledge were theirs. Obviously, for this to have evidentiary value, these past events and recollections need to be corroborated and facts shown that there was no possibility for the person remembering these events to have known of them in present life. This notion of having lived other lives in the past is called *reincarnation*.

Now, is it important to us that we call this reincarnation? And does it matter whether it is the same being that returns to a new physical existence? Even if we reject that these are cases of reincarnation—the same being coming to life multiple times—what is clear is that there is an energy, a nonlocal consciousness that exists outside a physical body. This consciousness is so intertwined with our physical existence that it can recollect all of our events in our physical life—an ability that we have traditionally attributed only to the retention capabilities of our physical brain—yet it retains this memory even in the absence of a brain, when our physical life has ceased to exist. This may be the most mesmerizing and perplexing condition of them all—not that there is a nonlocal existence, but that such nonlocal existence is so intertwined with our physical being that it can recall all the events, smells, emotions, traumas and glory of our physical existence even when there is no longer that physical existence. This means that there is a nonlocal presence next to us participating in everything that we do. Reincarnation or no reincarnation, it means we are not alone.

Moorjani (2012) does refer in her NDE to being able to live a concurrent life where, in some historical earlier period, she was the older sister of her now older brother, thus asserting as per her experience, the existence of reincarnation.

James 3

Tucker (2016) describes the case of James Leininger, who was born on April 10, 1998 in San Mateo, California. Early the family moved to Texas and then Louisiana. When he was 22 months old his father took him for a visit to the Cavanaugh Flight Museum in Texas, where he began to show his fascination for World War II airplanes and demonstrated a great deal of knowledge about these airplanes, to the surprise of his parents. Within two months of that first trip, James developed a habit of saying *"airplane crash on fire"* and slamming his toy airplanes nose first into the coffee table, repeating this behavior frequently. Around this time, James also began having nightmares. At first they manifested only as screams, but later he began articulating *"Airplane crash on fire! Little man can't get out."* James would shout this over and over while thrashing about and kicking his legs up in the air. After a few months of these nightmares, he began describing how his plane, a World War II Corsair, had been shot by the Japanese. When he was 28 months old he told his parents that he had flown his plane off a boat named the Natoma. One time, when his father was looking through a World War II book, James pointed to an aerial view of the base on the Island of Iwo Jima, near Mt. Suribachi, and James pointed to the photograph and said *"That's where my plane was shot down."* He recalled the name of Jack Larson, another pilot in his squadron. James began drawing scenes of airplane crashes and he would always sign them *"James 3,"* and he would state that the "3" was because he was the third James.

His father started conducting extensive research, and visiting World War II Iwo Jima veterans' reunions. He was able to verify that there was a subsequent battle in Iwo Jima, launched from the USS Natoma Bay escort carrier. There was a pilot in the squadron named Jack Larson, and the only pilot shot down in that battle was James Huston Jr., flying a Corsair airplane.

His parents later took James 3 to the waters at the site of the crash, where he cried profusely. After that, the lingering effects of the tragedy seemed to have been put behind. This case was also presented in a Netflix documentary (Netflix, 2020b). This is a compelling case because of its level of contextual, specific, verifiable detail, and because the symptoms of a past life surfaced so early through James 3's nightmares. The details in James 3's recollection are so rich that they nearly serve as a history lesson on that specific battle during World War II.

Philosopher Sudduth (2021) provides a detailed, 94-page re-examination of the James 3 case, where he raises failed objections to its veracity. His complaints include the fact that James 3's nightmares were not verified by a psychologist to be a sign of post-traumatic stress disorder (PTSD), and the fact that James 3's knowledge of airplanes could have been acquired in his present life as a child. But those arguments do not invalidate the nightmares, which by any other name are still nightmares. Nor do they invalidate James 3's knowledge about the specific events of that battle, or his signatures as James number 3 in those drawings. Please refer to Chapter A.2, "*James 3, Spontaneous Recollections of Past Lives*" in the Addendum, where I provide a detailed account of this case and a comprehensive review of Philosopher Sudduth's criticism of the case.

Other Past Life Cases

A large compilation of cases about reincarnation come from the lifetime research of Ian Stevenson (Stevenson, 2000; Tucker, 2008), but not without criticisms regarding Stevenson's research methods and eagerness for positive conclusions. Nevertheless, a percentage of his cases do show evidence that is difficult to ignore and cannot be dismissed—especially in which past-life symptoms began to manifest early, when these children were still babies not yet in command of language. He reports a case of a six-month-old baby girl crying intensely whenever she saw a bus or a bath with water, and later was able to articulate the death of a little girl who was pushed by a bus on a narrow road and drowned in the flooded paddy field by the road. This event was factual and had occurred in a nearby village before the girl was born.

Another case reported by Stevenson relates to a boy in Beirut who stated he had been a mechanic and died at the age of twenty five when he was struck by a vehicle on a beach road. Witnesses stated that the boy gave the name of the driver and the mechanic's sisters, parents and cousins, as well as the place where the accident had occurred. These details coincided with facts that had occurred before the boy was born. Stevenson in this case investigated and confirmed that it was highly unlikely that the boy could have come by this information from alternative means. Another class of cases of significant value are those where physical markings and lesions in individuals resemble the same lesions suffered by the individual they presume to have re-incarnated, and these markings are usually easier to corroborate.

Gabriel Andrade (2017), at one time professor at Xavier University School of Medicine, provides a critique of Ian Stevenson's extensive research on reincarnation using a philosophical methodology—a positivist formality that holds no relevance for this study. Andrade insists that for the validity of the research, reincarnation must be provable and predictable in the vast majority of cases. But the fact is that in order to contradict Andrade's thesis and conclude that reincarnation is a verifiable occurrence, it is sufficient to prove the validity of only one case, however unpredictable the research process may be. Under our revised criteria, we find there are verifiable cases brought about by Stevenson. By contrast to Andrade's statistical predictability approach, subjective phenomenological methodologies would allow each case to stand on its own. There is no reason why the validity of a case has to be asserted in relation to other totally independent cases.

Andrade himself shows a refusal to accept the reincarnation possibility by dismissing situations when there are the same identical body marks replicated across reincarnations, because no one has been able to provide a scientific explanation as to how and why those marks are transferred. The criteria used by Andrade is that events that implicate a correlation between spiritual phenomena and their somatic consequence (their influence on the body) cannot be accepted because no one has been able to provide a scientific explanation regarding how the spiritual world actually influences the physical body. No one in their right mind can provide a scientific explanation as to how reincarnation happens, physically or spiritually. Is Andrade saying that in order to prove reincarnation to him, there needs to be scientific discovery and proof of the certain spiritual scientific processes that cause reincarnation to occur predictably? And by this is he saying that if there are irrefutable historical independent correlations in a given case, it has to be dismissed because of the lack of scientific proof of that transfer of consciousness into a newborn?

Let us recall that the Catholic Church had accepted reincarnation until the Second Council of Constantinople in 553 A.D. At that time, a powerful group of cardinals and bishops explained that if every soul had once pre-existed with God, then Christ was not anything special to have come from God. They convinced Roman Emperor Justinian to declare reincarnation as heresy (Ebah, 2021; Utah HR, 2011) by asserting that souls did not exist before mortal conception and by banning the works of early Christian theologians, such as Origen Adamantius, who were accused of teaching the idea of reincarnation. The motivation then was to reassert Justinian's control over the Empire by convincing Christians that only Jesus came from God and that no other humans could return to God by way of reincarnation. They argued that God created entirely new souls at the time of conception on Earth, making body and soul inseparable. Consequently, they claimed that only the Holy Church could bring these souls to God. Without reincarnation, and without the protection of the Empire and the guidance of the Church, people would be doomed forever, cut off from God in hell. Emperor Justinian arrested Pope Vigilius for believing in the original teachings of reincarnation and forced him to retract. You could get so much done in those councils, at the stroke of a pen and for perpetuity. In retrospect, it doesn't matter whether there was an early belief in reincarnation or not. What is important is that the Christian religion left many voids and inconsistencies that required the formulation and promulgation of new articles of faith by mere mortals on Earth.

These new doctrines—such as the Son being equal to the Father, having existed eternally as one God despite originating from the Father, and the mystery of the Holy Trinity—had to be accepted as dogma by all under penalty of excommunication.

2.3. Subconscious Recollection of Past Lives

Santorini 1863 B.C.

One subconscious way to recollect past lives is through hypnosis. Psychiatrist Brian Weiss spent eighteen months unsuccessfully treating Catherine, a patient who had symptoms of phobia, panic attacks and depression (Weiss 1988). He then decided to treat Catherine with regression hypnosis, to bring her to the time when those symptoms started. She went back to the year 1863 B.C. when she was drowning in Crete because of the tsunami created by the explosion of the volcano on the Santorini Island. Soon after, the patient's symptoms completely disappeared. In another hypnosis regression session, Catherine stated that both Weiss' father and baby son who died at 23 days old were present in the session, and she went on to provide full details of their deaths, which she could not possibly have known. To Dr. Weiss' amazement, her description of his father and son and the circumstances of their deaths was extremely specific and accurate. It was as if through hypnosis, she was tapping into her ability as a medium.

Sadness Clouds the Eyes

Brian and Amy Weiss (Weiss et.al., 2012) recount daughter Amy's experience through regression hypnosis. When Amy was 25, she was diagnosed with a severe case of cataracts that could lead her to complete blindness. She could not understand why she would have the eyes of an old person, and after some unsuccessful attempts at regression hypnosis in the past, unrelated to her illness, she decided to give it another try, thinking, *"maybe I will have a good nap."* As she closed her eyes, she was transported to another place and time, and immediately she saw herself in the body of an old man with white hair, who was living in the Middle Ages, living alone in a hut far from a village. She observed that he was basically a hermit, *"but these townspeople thought I was a wizard and that I was doing evil."* Then she saw how the villagers came and stormed her hut, setting afire everything she owned. *"And the fire burned my eyes. It blinded me, I could feel his pain,"* she recalls. Then her father asked her to fast forward to the end of that previous life as that old man, in order to review what that life meant. And her response was that *"sadness clouds the eyes."* Besides carrying that man's blindness, it also meant that she had been carrying his sadness in her present life as well. But then, an astonishing event took place, soon after her regression session took place. Doctors told Amy that her cataracts had healed.

—+—+—

Weiss (1988) recounts the story of another patient, who as a child used to draw a map of a city with a church and a building with many windows. Under hypnosis, it was revealed that in a past life she died in a hospital while giving birth to her eighth child, and she was afraid the father would not properly care for them. Later she was able to locate the hospital, and records indicated that a woman had died while giving birth to her eighth child. Eventually she reunited her children, elderly by then, and DNA tests confirmed that they were indeed siblings.

Evidence Based?

Professor Gabriel Andrade (2017) points out that subjects under hypnosis may be very susceptible to unintended suggestions by the hypnotist, and there are well known cases where a subject has mistaken a present life experience for a past life. Even while those observations are factual and should be taken under consideration, they do not discredit the practice as a whole. Proving the veracity of even just one case under hypnosis, beyond a reasonable doubt and against verifiable events, would suggest that past life memories, while not consciously recalled, may still be available and true in the subconscious—and such cases clearly exist.

Andrade also suggests that past-life regression is not ethical because it is not evidence-based. Since religions are not evidence-based, is their practice unethical? He also states that *"past life regression therapy has the great risk of implanting false memories in patients, and thus, causing significant harm. This is a violation of the principle of non-malfeasance, which is surely the most important principle in medical ethics."* But a past-life therapist is not required nor induced to implant false memories in the patient in the same way that a psychotherapist is not required nor induced to suggest to patients false origins or assign false responsibilities to others for their patients' distresses. Is Andrade implying that the practice of psychotherapy is unethical?

2.4. *Conscious Access to Nonlocal Existences*

There are also verifiable cases of individuals who have experienced access to nonlocal or spiritual existences of past individuals. There are, for example, metaphysical manifestations of dead individuals appearing visually before loved ones, and these are secular manifestations of individuals who do not possess extraordinary virtues and are not in line for sainthood in any religion. There are a number of mediums as well as regular individuals who have provided verifiable experiences of these events, not so easy to disregard.

Oscar the cat was brought to live at a nursing home in 2005 when he was only 6 months old (Dosa 2007, 2011; Deccan 2023). Despite being rather reclusive, he would from time to time crawl on top of a resident's bed and cuddle beside them. The staff began to notice that after Oscar stayed in the resident's bed, the resident would pass away within a few hours. In one situation, when the staff knew the death of a given patient was imminent within a few hours, they saw Oscar go past that person's room and instead crawl into the bed of a healthy resident, who then passed away before the other resident who was already in agony. Oscar passed away in 2022 and correctly predicted more than 100 deaths during his lifetime. The fact that some residents soon to pass away were otherwise healthy seems to eliminate the possibility that Oscar perceived near death by some chemical decomposition of cells in the body. Oscar seemed to find comfort in the process of these transitions, almost as if he wanted to be part of this comforting experience. This reflects mediumship and a comforting understanding of death well beyond human sensitivity.

So much for religious doctrines that assert that only us humans have been created with a soul. I remember when, in my De La Salle Catholic primary school, a friend asked a Christian brother—and not just any of the younger soccer-playing brothers importing the game to a baseball nation, but the older Christian brother who taught religion in the school—the following question, *"do apes and other animals have a soul?"* The brother got quite severe and angry and with his thick gutural Spaniard accent said *"impío!, blasfemo!, tú si que eres bobo eh?, ven acá que te voy a dar un coscorrón!"* – *"impious!, blasphemous! Indeed you are an idiot, come here that I will give you a knuckle punch (coscorrón) in the head!"* Coscorrón is the kind of beautiful word that seems to warn you that whatever it means, you do not want it to happen unto you, thy kingdom come, especially when the happening is endorsed by God. All of the Christian brothers in my primary school were Spaniards. They were at that time the main Spanish export, which we found peculiar, and they proved that you cannot bring soccer to a god-forsaken country without Lionel Messi and Cristiano Ronaldo by your side. As a six-year-old I wondered if there was any evil left in the cities of Spain, as I could not conceive of vernacular language on the streets, given there was so

2. THE SECULAR AVALANCHE 73

much sainthood by way of brothers in cassocks exported to Latin America. Later I just concluded that all the righteous testosterone of the Christian Crusades in Spain must have left a lasting, multi-generational hangover that was just hard to wash off.

Many of us have probably had experiences relating to spiritual consciousness. I remember one night having a dream that I was driving the streets at night to let a friend know that her dad had just passed away. I had not been in contact with my friend for ten years. Her dad was very young and I had never met him, but it was true—that night her dad had passed away.

The night before my mom died, I had dreamt of our family doctor dressed in a white clinical robe walking a long hallway. He opened two big swinging white doors to meet us where we were waiting and nodded, resigned, to indicate that my mom had just passed. The next day, that was exactly how it happened.

I also remember a relative one day feeling the shape of a body curled up inside her blankets, seemingly wanting to be reassured, and instead of panicking, she began to caress the body gently, feeling the shape of a human body that once was, and sensing that this was what this being needed.

Another friend of mine lived as a student in a very old building at the university. He recalls seeing a boy about eight years old dressed in the style of the 1900's and wearing a French beret floating and dancing gently above his bed in soft 180-degree rhythmic swings, as if to classical music. My friend at first enjoyed the apparition, but then the boy locked eyes with him and asked with his hands for my friend to come to him. My friend got scared and the boy began to disappear from the bottom up. It was 6:52 AM in October. He was shaken by this vivid apparition, to the point that he would not accept our friendly jokes about the episode. Exactly five years later at 6:52 AM, my friend was in an airplane that crashed against a mountain and was engulfed in fire. Most passengers did not survive, but he did and was able to walk out of the fuselage of the airplane.

These private experiences are credible to me because of my relationship with the individuals involved, but likely meaningless to others outside my sphere of trust. The good news is that we do not need to adhere to these stories like a fly to a chameleon's tongue. We can let them permeate our being and consider them without feeling compelled to truly believe them, especially not as acts of faith. But if you lend some credibility to my stories above, let me know because maybe it means there is still hope for me to become a preacher and not die in vain.

2.5. *Non-Physical Individual Differentiation*

What we are still lacking is a measure of individual differentiation, which is difficult to obtain from this collection of narratives. For example, while all NDE subjects may claim that "life is better there," this does not allow us to gauge the extent of that improvement from one individual to another, nor how it varies in terms of individual self-awareness. We also do not have a sampling of NDEs from individuals who have been truly evil in their physical lifes, so that we can understand their communion with their nonlocal selves. Moorjani (2012) states that all beings, regardless of deeds, are loved and accepted unconditionally just the same, but I wonder if some beings are then somehow handicapped to participate in that interconnected unification of love, perhaps because of the pain they inflicted, which they must also feel themselves. Mediums and individuals who are able to provide a bridge between local and nonlocal consciousness do often talk about the quality and differentiation of the spiritual aura of individuals and the benefits that are thus projected to their spiritual and physical lives. If for timeless spiritual beings, coming into physical lives on earth represents a playground for continued growth, that implies that such an individual differentiation does exist in the spiritual world, and it must manifest in some ways. It must have a natural way to limit the expansion of the individual into the grand unification.

2.6. *A Foundation for Secularity*

All these experiences are secular because they take place in a context outside of religion, without the influence of religious devotion, virtue, or enlightenment, and not as a result of religious reward, and without the adjudication of these events to manifestations of particular religious beliefs. They are also mundane because they seem to occur routinely and frequently, just as physical life on earth, and thus these are experiences that cannot be deemed as exceptional, supernatural or divine miracles. They are just common everyday occurrences.

By definition, secularity is the absence or separation from religion, and thus, from religious beliefs. But what happens if this separation is not precisely from religion but from a form of divine spirituality, such as new age spirituality? Or from mythology and superstition? Or from cult veneration—not to a deity but a political figure? Out of necessity, we want to bring secularity to its most conceptual, generalized, and essential connotation—*the disaffection for ideological fabrications*. Secularity is then the separation from beliefs that might become internalized in a human being, whether these beliefs are religious, non-religious, spiritual, philosophical, or political. This broader and deeper definition also encompasses the separation from our own individually created beliefs—those private constructions we develop to support our personal delusions.

So, if secularity means not being attached to any beliefs, where do secular thoughts and notions come from? They have to be innate in ourselves, and therefore the singular foundation of secularity has to be that these notions come cleanly and directly from our inner selves. In order to come from ourselves, they have to be void of any residual beliefs filtered externally through the cracks of our consciousness; otherwise, we just fall again into the business of the re-interpretation of external beliefs. This also means that in order for us to express secular innate thoughts and notions, and for those thoughts to be truly ours, we would need to have a clean path to our inner selves, and that is not an easy accomplishment. Throughout the course of our civilization, we have never accomplished this form of separation from beliefs individually or as a culture, just the opposite. No culture has even identified such a separation from the consumption of beliefs as an issue or goal.

Outside of secularity, we all accept factual events that are routinely verifiable and do not require interpretation. Whether and to what extent we can accept experiences from others, particularly spiritual ones, like the ones described in this chapter, depends on our individual thresholds for measuring reality. These thresholds are often connected to our emotional constitution, as well as our acceptance and acknowledgment of credibility, which stands in contrast to blindly surrendering to a belief with absolute servitude. While it is useful for us to speculate about the veracity of the spiritual experience of others, we do the speculation merely anecdotally and not with the intention or prerequisite that they have to be accepted. These experiences are peripheral and independent of our own life process, which focuses on gaining access to our inner selves. After all, our salvation does not depend on what we believe or don't believe awaits us, but on what we know we leave behind, as we depart looking back at the footprints we have left.

Secularity provides a more powerful natural understanding of the world, physical and otherwise, because it means that the secular reality is just there and everywhere, explicit and equally accessible to all, not subject to narrowly constructed beliefs that require coercion via indoctrination, interpretation, man-made initiation or vetting ceremonies and rules to manage membership, such as baptism in Christianity or being excommunicated for professing heresy. These beliefs are not intuitive like mundane facts are. Moorjani (2012), the survivor of the best known and richly detailed NDE case, confirms secularity in the spiritual world as the general, equalitarian, autonomous form of engagement. It does not make sense that something as mundane as being with ourselves would require mediation or interpretation of an external belief. Accepting a belief is just a way of lending our power to a promise that will never be fulfilled. Spirituality has to be just as available to all beings. It makes sense that if we remove ourselves from the claustrophobic domination of internalized beliefs, religious or otherwise, we can open up a clear path to our inner selves, granting us unparalleled spontaneity, creativity, awareness, and an outward outlook, all of which are impossible when we are submissive to externally imposed beliefs.

To the extent that we lend credibility to these secular spiritual events, like the ones presented in this chapter, and which after all, are extremely numerous and well corroborated accounts, we can say that we have gained enough insight to infer that there is a mundane, secular, routine understanding that we exist as a physical temporal representation of our own nonlocal, timeless, omnipresent consciousness. This is a mundane and secular understanding because it does not require the creation of a narrow belief system with obscure human-made rules in order to reach this understanding. The wealth of clinically substantiated near-death experiences (NDEs) brings these cases to us on a silver platter.

And now that we rest on a wide fabric of spiritual evidence that we may accept as a secular routine condition similar to the way we accept physical life on earth, what is next for us? The time to fabricate reason about reasoned fabrications is over, and with that, a time to move forward. Because of what we know now, we can exclude ourselves from creating trivial recipes that will bring only temporary instamatic inspirational motivation to our lives, and from demeaning and trashing our physical human condition in order to pay servitude to spiritual myths. Without the falsely protective crutches of beliefs, we can begin to think about what will bring congruence and synchrony to our lives with our presumed timeless existence. Now we have to find the secular pillars that will sustain us and provide an understanding of a world that just got a bit wider and exists close all around us but just the same outside our physical existence.

3. Beliefs

What is a belief? And do beliefs just affect us individually, or do they affect the entire civilization as a whole?

In this chapter we are going to explore the concept of beliefs and the process by which they permeate both the collective, and, more importantly, the individual self—ultimately leading individuals to adopt these beliefs as their own.

3.1. Beliefs

Beliefs are deeply ingrained socialized notions that we often internalize, shaping and often dominating our sense of identity. Beliefs provide structure, certainty, and a misunderstanding of who we are in an unpredictable world. Clinging dependently to them acts as a shield against exploring our deeper, often uncomfortable emotions and the fluid nature of our true selves.

Beliefs can exist anywhere on a spectrum. *Unfounded beliefs* are harmful because they create a distorted perception of reality or mythical conceptions of the non-physical world. *Congruent beliefs* are beneficial, because they depict reality accurately. For example, beliefs have the power to incite domination and extermination wars, or inspire transformative social movements.

Beliefs are often used as instruments for manipulation, control and domination, because humans tend to become addicted and fanatical to beliefs as a replacement for something else missing or broken inside of us. And the more severe our damage inside, the more vulnerable we will be and the more vehemently we will adhere to an external belief and its likely distorting, damaging perceptions of reality.

Beliefs can act as mechanisms of profound alienation and control, sold through intellectual ideologies and enforced through emotional manipulation by disregarding the self. We internalize these beliefs when we surrender our inner self to them. Emancipation from beliefs is extremely challenging because it is not an intellectual thought process, it requires a deeply emotional process of self-discovery.

Any idea can become a belief once it is deeply internalized by an individual. When beliefs are internalized en masse, they just become institutionalized beliefs, the law of the land, of God's country, take your pick. Let's take a look at some notions that come into play when traditional religious beliefs become institutionalized in our cultures:

1. That the highest representative of a religion, chosen through voting by their peers, becomes infallible when making statements about God and religion.
2. That all humans are born with the original sin and therefore subject to eternal damnation.

3. BELIEFS

3. That a secular person who presumably communicates with spirits is evil and must die.
4. That one race is inferior to another and therefore subject to dominance.
5. That one sex is superior to the other and therefore, the presumed superior sex has the right to exercise dominance over the other.
6. Accusations of political adversaries made by political leaders are turned into capital faults, which would make these adversaries immediately subject to punishment.

These ideas could simply remain harmless floating notions, innocent and even entertaining, if they stayed that way. But when they get baked in, perpetuated in society, and when they become internalized by individuals who accept them as unquestionable dogma, their implications can bring daunting real-world consequences.

A belief is typically sold by using a carrot and stick approach. It offers an appealing model of the world while attributing unreachable superiority to the belief's actors or gods in order to establish a contrast with our doomed inferiority, therefore manufacturing the need for subservient reverence to these beliefs and actors. For example, in some interpretations of Christianity, God commands an unreachable superiority because only he has the power to judge and forgive. Humans are inferior since they have to be redeemed from original sin, and it is outside their faculties to do it themselves. The carrot and the stick come in the form of heaven and hell. This easy sell has misguided and continues to misguide our civilization into the constant practice of mythological fabrication. An unfounded belief system is typically an ideology or a set of precepts that are to be accepted as absolute dogma, contrary to our own personal intuition, understanding and limitations. Consequently, such an internalized belief represents a negation of the self and a loss of the bigger reality—our coexistence with our presumed non-physical, nonlocal consciousness. This negation is internalized by faith, which provides the unconditional acceptance of what we ourselves find unexplainable.

For example, let's consider the belief that humans are inherently good. If we look for the answer inside of ourselves, we will find it to be either true, false or simply unknowable. However, if society enforces this notion as a belief requiring our acceptance and we capitulate, it will undermine our intuition. Our intuition might warn, *"this person means harm and poses an immediate threat."* But if we've surrendered to the belief, it might override our instincts, persuading us with rationalizations such as, *"contrary to our intuition, the greater truth is that people are inherently good, so just smile."* This creates doubt, alienating our own sense of reality, and stopping us from relying on our own judgment. In essence, we lose our autonomy and cease to exist as freethinking human beings.

I had a friend who was walking to her bus in the early morning, and she saw an individual walking towards her who radiated malice and consequently scared the wits out of her. But pursuant to her belief that people are intrinsically good and they ought to be given the benefit of the doubt, she did not cross to the other side of the street and just kept walking. This person beat her to the ground and stole her purse. She had a brain aneurysm that could have been ruptured from the beating, so she put her entire life at risk.

Adoption and Internalization

Internalization is the process of unconscious assimilation of a belief. As such, it implies that awareness of the self has been lost, alienated, and relegated by this take over. *Indoctrination* is the process of persuasion or imposition to internalize a belief—the process by which a notion is sold to us to suppress our intuition and access to our inner selves. In other words, *indoctrination is the sale tactic used to get us to buy into and internalize an ideology as a belief.* Once this happens, our connection to our own sense of self is replaced by an external belief system, depriving us of individuality and dictating our thoughts and feelings in accordance with its principles.

A belief can be adopted without it being internalized. But either an unfounded or a congruent belief can be internalized—it depends on whether or not the belief is disseminated by indoctrination. There are different mechanisms used in society for the indoctrination of beliefs. The imposing force of these mechanisms go hand in hand with the level of subservience, faith and loyalty required by the given belief, as well as its comprehensive, all-encompassing nature.

I emphasize that the most consequential impact of a belief on ourselves and society is not the truthfulness, relevance, or factuality of it, but whether it was internalized blindly by individuals without full intellectual and emotional consciousness. Unfounded beliefs are almost always internalized fanatically via indoctrination.

Indoctrination and internalization are the prevalent mechanisms for belief adoption which have carved the course of herd alienation and submission for the last 5000 years of society life, enabling constant takeovers, mass domination and licensed cruelty and leading to the unspeakable stagnation and repetitive destruction of the entire human civilization.

It should be noted that the state of individual awareness of the self in our societies has not needed the imposition of beliefs in order to succumb to alienation. Individual alienation is not an issue looking for a culprit, because it is too deeply entrenched within ourselves. Its eradication is essential to the eventual emancipation of human nature because of its fundamental role in the stagnation of civilization.

Capitulation

How does a belief get internalized? We like to believe that in a world of emotionally developed individuals with a clear sense of autonomy, there would be no room for vulnerabilities that make us susceptible to submitting to beliefs. Instead, we would much prefer to be left alone, free to think and act independently, no matter how imperfect our reasoning may be. This means that in order for us to accept and internalize a belief, there has to be a form of *emotional capitulation* to the external pressure that might come in the form of inspiration, motivation, persuasion, manipulation, denigration, imposition, isolation, doom, or death.

But what makes such herd-oriented emotional capitulation so easy? None of us in our right mind would surrender our sense of self as a result of a casual intellectual exchange on a walk in the park. However, it is often the case that at an early age we are exposed to sustained oppressive alienation that pushes us to a breaking point. This forces us to surrender our sense of self, leaving the door open for the easy subsequent imposition of beliefs into what is now a fractured or absent sense of self. A classic example of early oppression comes in the form of parental authority reinforced with religion, such as when a child is forced to unilaterally accept the will of a parent in the name of God, under threat of isolation, punishment and removal of love. In order to survive such alienation, a child has no choice but to abandon their sense of self. This example reminds us that even though the wounds of oppression memorize their specific event signature, relationships of domination spill over and become inherently impersonal. Parents enforcing obedience inadvertently establish a pattern that, once internalized by the broken child, will later manifest indiscriminately—even toward individuals whom the parents may dislike even more than they dislike themselves.

This capitulation results in the irreversible distortion of our autonomy and identity, leaving us unrecognizable to ourselves. We can see now that it does not matter if a notion or ideology is true; what matters is that it was externally imposed.

When we capitulate and become addicted to a belief, we become delusional in our internalization of it, and this process is irreversible unless we admit the delusion. Belief addiction is internalized emotionally and cannot be reversed with intellectual reasoning. When we justify our reasons by rationalizing the merits of our beliefs, we only show our dislocated point of view as we ignore our potential addiction. This emotional delusional deadlock explains why our civilization has remained stagnant for 5000 years.

Internalization, by any other name, is an assault on our sense of self, leading to our capitulation. It is similar to the hostile takeover of a fortress culminating in the tearing down of its gates. Once that breach occurs, the gates will remain open for subsequent takeovers—no force is needed; they can simply walk right in. Often that first most damaging assault may take place through personal forceful alienation in family, school, work or social settings, but primarily family, since that is the circle closest to us. A classic example is the mix of parental authority and religion forced unilaterally upon a child, as in the example I mentioned earlier. For a parent to deny love to a child to force obedience in the name of religious virtue is a profound violation of the child's self. This act of coercion renders the child emotionally vulnerable, setting the stage for a lifetime of susceptibility to future intrusions on their autonomy.

As irrational as it is, this process of internalization and capitulation can lead entire segments of the population like herds into submission under these beliefs. This submission is often total and praised by the belief enablers as unwavering faith, overriding the individual's own intuition. If we were to arrive on this planet as impartial observers, we might mistakenly assume that such mass submission is impossible. Afterall, these humans are strikingly beautiful, capable of speaking and reasoning eloquently for hours as if they know what they are saying, and they stand upright—a posture often associated with intelligence. Yet despite these traits, it would be difficult to see why they freely and voluntarily kneel in submission to the unspeakable.

The Flip

When we speak of capitulation, we might be referring simply to the act of submission to a belief. There is no dishonor in accepting defeat and bowing your head before overwhelming external forces. However, what often happens is that, in order to mask a humiliating defeat, we may attempt to regain control by flipping—becoming someone entirely different, someone we are not, once again fully in control of but likely aligned with the belief that was imposed upon us. This behavior is more difficult to accept. Why? Because it is turning a false behavior outward to the detriment of the surrounding society. It is a flip. A flip is a violent undertaking. A classic example is the preacher who proclaims the word of a kind and merciful religion but whose voice carries an undertone of hatred and superiority. That ain't love they are preaching. If we were taught how to read in kindergarten, we would be able to read in the preacher's voice, words and demeanor, if his resentment is with his father or mother, if it was because he was abandoned and left to die or because he was straightjacketed all his life, if he is angry with his sister for not abiding by the morals he advocates, and so on. But we would only see this if we were taught how to read in kindergarten. With such a flip, the belief system just gained a lifelong, zealous advocate. When that flip happens, the person is lost to themselves, alienated from their own identity, and essentially becomes a different person unrecognizable to themselves, with little hope of return.

This is further compounded by society's inability to prevent these flips, repair them, or even recognize their existence. There is no awareness that those individual personality failures highlight essential clues to our collective survival. How can there be when society itself is often the direct or indirect enforcer of those beliefs? Society gives you air to breathe, teaches you to spell your name so that you can claim literacy on a job application, and provides some health care so when you die your family can be told, *"Oh well, we did our best."* But what it never does is return your true self to you. Once society takes your self, your identity, it's gone for good. Oh well. The good news is that, as part of your newly acquired alienation, you will never know that your self was ever taken away to begin with. So, how are ya? – Oh, me? I am fine, thanks for asking.

A Belief in Superiority

A wide array of symptoms can signal capitulation to beliefs or the structure of the belief itself. One of the most telling is a sense of superiority, placed either in the belief and its adherents, or in yourself, if you successfully completed your flip. I therefore contend that whatever the nature of the belief, however generous and humble in appearance and goals, there will always be an embedded sense of superiority in any belief, either explicit or hidden, simply because that is the way to transfer into a belief that is not yours. And where there is superiority, there is always a causal undercurrent of inferiority. This in turn tells us that superiority is a lure that dwells outside ourselves, it is never ours to own. This underscores the argument that well-founded, self-centered secularity is the only way to exist in separation from these false hierarchies of superiority and inferiority. Both are symptoms of a deeper issue: the failure to recognize and honor the self. They simply reflect a state of being off center. Self-centricity, by contrast, is not about selfishness; it's a reminder that everything about us begins within us. We are our own center. Even airlines understand this principle when they advise passengers to secure their own oxygen mask first before that of a child or others.

It should be noted that, in recent years, a number of thinkers, influenced by developments in modern physics, have elaborated on a variety of theories of transcendental consciousness—a consciousness that transcends or exists outside our senses. For example, Dossey (1989) in his *Nonlocality Theory of Consciousness*, states that the notion of individual minds is nothing more than an illusion, a useful fiction that Dossey pointedly calls *"the illusion of a separate self and the sensation of an ego that possesses a separate mind."* This would imply that individuality does not exist because we are all inside one single universal consciousness. Even if this is the case, such individuality does exist in our physical life on earth, and therefore, self-centered introspection remains the only mechanism to reach our own physical individual self, en route to any sustainable universal truths that might exist in our nonlocal consciousness.

Belief Sublimation

We tend to deify or glorify what we sense to be superior to us, and we elevate them gratuitously to ungranted levels of perfection and power. That is how creeds, mythologies and superstitions are created, extended and perpetuated. Our 5000 years of history has been written, more than anything else, on the consequences of beliefs. Consider Moctezuma II, emperor of the Aztecs in 1519, residing in the city of Tenochtitlán, with an estimated 200,000 to 400,000 inhabitants and an empire capable of fielding up to 700,000 warriors. Despite this vast power, the Aztecs fell to the Spanish conquistador Hernán Cortés, who commanded only a few hundred soldiers. This was a consequence of Moctezuma's hesitation, caused by his initial belief in Cortés' divinity. This hesitation allowed a turn of the tide against the Aztecs, creating a momentum that even his successors, first Cuitlahuac and then later Cuauhtémoc, the Diving Eagle, could not overcome. When Cuauhtémoc and his companion the Chief of Tacuba were being tortured by the Spaniards, tied up with fire under their feet, the Chief of Tacuba said to Cuauhtémoc, *"my emperor, my pain is too great to withstand,"* to which Cuauhtémoc famously replied, *"and do you think I am in a bed of roses?"* Cuauhtémoc, under barbaric torture, never uttered a word of betrayal to reveal where the Aztec treasures were hidden—not even on the day of his death. Spiritual beliefs almost always polarize good and evil, presenting divinity as superior, perfect, and incapable of wrongdoing. A secular view that dares to question the nature of a spiritual existence is rarely embraced. The Aztec emperors, for instance, saw the Spaniards as divine beings and did not question their motives.

Faith and Trust

For most, *faith is the proactive, unquestioning acceptance of an entire internalized belief in advance of any future proof or personal verification in the afterlife.* It is a way to maintain our surrender to a belief on autopilot. Faith is the unconditional loan of the self to an unproven belief, made on the promise of its forthcoming proof, which will then restore the sense of self which was given in loan. In the meantime, this sense of self is replaced with stoicism and a tormented self-denial, caused by accepting unproven beliefs, carrying inherent anxiety. For example, in Catholicism, faith may include accepting the precepts of the immaculate conception of Virgin Mary, the infallibility of the Pope, or that all individuals are good, all without corroboration of their veracity.

However, for some, faith may reach the state of an unbreakable bond with the spiritual realm or a higher sense of well being, bringing with that, a source of peace. Some may achieve this by bypassing the restrictive negative impositions of their own religion, in essence creating a secular private tunnel that gives them independent spiritual access despite their religion's attempt to suffocate that passage. We recognize that most faithful, if not all, will claim to have reached such an unbreakable bond, as opposed to the insecurity generated by surrendering their sense of self. After all, who are we, if not the masters of the universe in self-denial?

By contrast, *trust is the repeatable corroboration of an intuition that already lives in us without surrendering or lending out our sense of selves.* For instance, trusting a friend to overcome his defeat, after he lost his sense of self in a damaging romantic relationship, is fueled by your confidence that he will find his center again—not because of blind faith, but because you know his character and have seen him navigate emotional challenges in the past. You have seen him find himself before, and you know him. In other words, you trust him. Next time we are in a situation we can ask ourselves, are we acting by faith or trust?

3.2. *Blanket Beliefs*

Blanket beliefs are internalized notions or ideologies that cover all aspects of our entire relationship with our own selves. Many of these blanket beliefs are also viewed as unfounded beliefs when they do not reflect a verifiable reality. Blanket indoctrination is the process of internalization of these all encompassing beliefs. The classic examples are spiritual cults like some which emerged in the 1960's in the U.S. and even led their members to commit horrible crimes; ancient Greek and Viking mythologies; and some religions which require servitude and obedience in all aspects of our lives, encompassing spiritual, social and political dimensions. For adherents, no significant action can be taken without conforming to the dictates of the ideology or religion without seeking permission from its enablers.

Because this type of internalization is such a big imposition, a spiritual or religious wholesale approach may require four conditions for it to be successfully adopted: universality, exclusivity, condemnation and faith. Because religious beliefs cannot always be imposed by blunt force, at least no longer in modern times, its internalization needs to heavily rely on these four pillars of intellectual and emotional manipulation for the successful internalization of a blanket belief:

1. *Universality*. The belief will postulate that its truths, powers and actors are universal, which will maximize the power, authenticity and entitlement of the belief. For example, it is easy to see how most religions and mythologies claim that their gods are universal, that they rule over the entire universe.

2. *Exclusivity*. In order for the belief to attract lifetime followers, it has to offer an exclusive relationship, by way of its unique authenticity. This prevents followers from following other similar sects or religions simultaneously, therefore dismissing any other competing doctrine as non authentic. For example, Vikings considered it a crime for Christians to say that their gods were not true deities. Conversely, Christians proclaimed their god as the only true god of the universe.
3. *Condemnation*. The belief has to offer an "*unaffordable downside*," a spiritual state that we cannot possibly afford to fall into under any circumstance. For example, eternal damnation prescribes that if you reject the given belief and its precepts turn out to be true, you will face eternal damnation. So you'd better not pass up this belief, just in case. For example, in the case of some interpretations of Christianity, damnation by eternal fire in hell is a proposition we may not be so eager to test, so why not become an obedient Christian in case that turns out to be true.
4. *Faith*. As I said before, faith is the process by which followers unconditionally accept present and future precepts of a belief system without question. Once the belief has been internalized, faith allows the belief system to run in automatic mode. For example, in the Catholic religion, you would blindly accept all articles of faith, past and future—whether they include the infallibility of the Pope, the acceptance of reincarnation before the condemnation by Emperor Justinian, or its subsequent rejection. Faith demands unwavering adherence, regardless of changing doctrines or contradictions.

3.3. Selective Beliefs

Some beliefs only affect specific aspects of our lives or personality, and I refer to these as *selective beliefs*. For example, a political ideology could be considered a selective belief if it primarily requires us to accept or assign moral values to monetary ideologies or theories, or racial and gender stereotypes, while leaving other areas—such as belief in a specific god, or views on promiscuity and celibacy—unaddressed. When we have already internalized a blanket belief system, the adoption of selective beliefs becomes easier. This is because the individual's inner defenses—the boundaries protecting their sense of self—have already been compromised. Additionally, selective beliefs often appear as natural extensions or derivatives of blanket beliefs, making their adoption feel seamless or justified.

The mechanisms for selective indoctrination do not have to be as forceful as those in blanket beliefs. But what typically happens is that the selective belief is positioned as a derivative of a blanket belief in order to leverage the incredible power of the already internalized blanket belief. Usually, the promotion of selective beliefs consists of the creation of creeds, similar to those in religions, that focus on discrimination or division in cultural issues—such as race, gender, economic status and others.

Work is usually the most time consuming activity in our lives, and for that reason it can become a distraction from exploring our true selves. It is ideal when the work we do aligns with our passions and life goals, but that is not the reality for everyone. While work itself may not typically involve belief systems that are imposed on us, our time is still subservient to causes deemed by others to be more important than anything we are, such as the financial interests of an institution, which take precedence over our individual priorities. As a result, it deprives us from seriously pursuing our own inner interests. Work becomes a form of submission we endure to secure basic needs like food and shelter, all in the hope of someday becoming independent—only to then realize that life may have already passed us by. It is impossible to truly find yourself when you are constantly preoccupied with responsibilities that don't align with your authentic self.

Blanket beliefs demand your soul, not your time. Conversely, selective beliefs usually demand your time and not your soul. But what good is time when you don't have a soul? What good is your soul when you don't have the time to own it?

3.4. Inspirational Motivation

Many well-intentioned individuals aim to inspire and motivate others to achieve great goals by showing the colors at the end of the rainbow, a light at the end of the tunnel. That is admirable because sometimes an uplifting vision can even rival the fun of a good movie. And this is the gist of the inspirational sermon—to present an alluring reward at the end of the journey—a promise of wonderful states of being that will embrace us in love and happiness yet unknown to us. It is also its limitation because it acts as a softer form of indoctrination meant to appeal to a collective audience without taking into account the individuals' unique starting context. But this form of collective motivation rarely works. It might work to trigger a stampede, such as in get-rich-quick schemes or to launch attacks and insurrections when hate and resentment is already festering inside. But for genuine, lasting transformation, it falls short because it fails to meet us individually at our starting point—a starting point that's not easy to find, as we may deny it, and which, in itself, may be the longest journey.

If someone is stuck in a mud pit where it keeps raining, making the mud softer and more difficult to escape, an inspirational ray of sunshine peeking through the clouds may bring a brief smile, but it won't solve the problem when the rain continues. What they need is someone willing to sit with them in that mud pit, find their own individual starting context, and work with them to devise a way out. Without a starting point, roads to take us anywhere do not exist.

I also want to recognize that sometimes, inspiration emanates from the need of the motivators to project their own beliefs for self appeasement, injecting the process with adrenaline-charged methods and toxic positivity. In other circumstances, inspiration and motivation are used as a hard-sell tactic: showing the colors of the rainbow while wielding the threat of dire consequences for failing to pursue it. At that point, it's no longer inspiration and instead falls into the realm of intimidation and manipulation.

Luján Comas and Anji Carmelo (Carmelo, 2020) wrote a book called *Does Death Exist?* Comas, a physician from Barcelona, Spain, specializing in reanimation, reviewed the validity of innumerable cases of near-death experiences and the testimonials these survivors gave about the afterlife being such a beautiful expansive place well beyond our imagination. They offer this motivational thesis for their book: *"If we change our view of death, we will change our way of living."* With this slogan they are attempting to create a motivational narrative from a collective, inspirational end goal, which is the eventual transition to the afterlife. We can evaluate their thesis to demonstrate that inspirational and motivational narratives are often riddled with more flaws than a colander has holes. Comas and Carmelo fail to understand the fundamental fact that every personal emotional journey must begin at the starting point, uniquely identifiable by each individual. Inspiration never comes as an orphaned, isolated piece of advice. It comes from a personality trait in a deluge of impersonal distortions with no relevance to the recipients. Comas, in her book, invites her readers to believe, asserting that if they believe in something magnificent, that perspective alone will make them magnificent. Just how manipulative and meaningless is that statement? How many times have we heard the essential trigger point of inspiration, *"Just believe!"* Her slogans keep coming, a dime a dozen. The pervasive nature of inspirational indoctrination should illustrate the understated damage to society.

Even at a very pragmatic, extrospective level, there must be some notion of an individual context. For example, if I am overwhelmed with responsibilities to feed my family and put my children through college, and I feel like an absolute failure because of my inability to respond financially, I probably don't even know what death means and I don't care. Give me death or give me life, it is all the same. I am past death because I only care here and now about allowing my children to reach their goals. I must first reach an understanding within myself that what I have already given my family holds lasting value and significance. Once I get to that point, I may be able to stand tall, raise my head, and gaze at the emotional horizon where my death awaits—seeing it within the context of my purpose on this earth and the mark I have left behind. Even if I start from my beginning and manage to move emotionally toward gaining the perspective of death, it is likely to be understood in the context of the value of my life. It would not align with the cotton candy notion that I get to throw away my life's earthly contextual meaning just because when I die there will be a big homecoming celebration awaiting for me. This motivational narrative fails in at least three respects:

1. It provides a collective end and not an individual beginning.
2. It denigrates the context and value of the physical life in favor of the afterlife by saying, "hey, never mind your physical life, your hungry children you leave behind, because upon your passing we are throwing for you the biggest homecoming celebration you ever saw."
3. While it is true that what is new about this understanding of the afterlife is its secularity and that may appeal to a new population segment not persuaded before by religious beliefs, it is also true that this is not the first time that an afterlife has been described as a beautiful place to be, well beyond anything imagined on earth. Every religion and mythology, such as the Vikings' Valhalla, have described the afterlife in glorious flying colors. But this depiction has not seemed to promote substantial change on Earth. On the other hand, it is noteworthy that while the value of the NDE survivor testimonials compiled by Luján Comas (Carmelo 2020), a physician from Barcelona specializing in reanimation, and by Dr. Manuel Sans Segarra (Segarra 2023), surgeon

from the University of Barcelona, both recognized experts in NDEs, lies in the intrinsic secularity of the experiences, they still go out of their way to cater to all religions by blindly endorsing them with equal validity. This occurs even though these same religions contradict each other and, with their exclusionary approaches, directly oppose the very principles of secularity. They further assume that the teachings in these religions are consistent with these secular experiences, thereby undermining and discarding the entire secular premise that justified their interest in NDEs in the first place.

Demeaning the Starting Point

Another way to manipulate an inspirational message is by making the end goal more attractive by demeaning the starting point. That is also a worrisome trend promoted by NDE advocates to provide an inspirational and motivational approach to overcome our defenses by recognizing a new beautiful reality at the other end of the spectrum of life, at the expense of demeaning our physical selves. While these are beautiful discoveries, outside the initial enthusiasm, they may not do much for providing the necessary advancement through our defenses. It is great to look at what lies at the end of the rainbow, but to get there, the motion forward still has to start at the sinking muddy pit we are in. Segarra (2023) trivializes this proposition, contradicting himself. On the one hand he states that life is wonderful. We can agree and attest to that. Life gives us so much, and it is all around us— it gives us music, Beethoven's Piano Sonata No. 14, Barber's Adagio for Strings, and the Soggy Bottom Boys (2008). It gives us colors and some limited awareness of ourselves. But on the other hand, Segarra states that the Freud-style "ego," which is according to him who we are in this life, the physical representation of our timeless or nonlocal existence, is vile, petty, egotistical and self serving, and with that, in one swipe of the tongue he completely undermines our value in this life—wow, *"thanks, I needed that,"* said the man in the Mennen Skin Bracer aftershave commercial after being slapped hard on both cheeks. But nevertheless, Segarra comes up with the obvious solution, which is to simply discard the ego, toss it like toxic waste, and bypass it in route to our beautiful celestial nonlocal or spiritual self, essentially denying any value or purpose to our physical existence. We understand his reverence for Freud because he is a big name, but since when has Freud been given a pedestal in the pantheon of the emotional? To trash our physical self is to deny our history and purpose. He continues with the dismissal of our physical value in servitude to our own higher master, our very own spiritual or nonlocal self. So we haven't even started to look outside of ourselves and we already have a master inside, reminding us that our physical life has no value. I hate to think what would happen if, when we pass, an entire celestial hierarchy seeks us out to remind us of our place at the bottom—perhaps due to our lack of wisdom and awareness, but the bottom nonetheless.

3.5. *Collective Internalization*

Beliefs, originating from predefined notions and ideologies, are obviously impersonal, they are also collective—applied to groups of individuals. For a notion or understanding to be singular and individual, it has to be borne from within that individual. If we assume that our internal comfort is bound to what is ours, then it is borne from our individuality. It is easy to infer that internalized beliefs will always cast a level of inner discomfort within ourselves, simply because they are foreign notions to us.

There seems to be a proportionality in that the more collective and impersonal the belief, the more forceful its imposition, the more uncomfortable our inner self becomes upon adoption, and the stronger our need for appeasement of that discomfort by urging the propagation and even imposition of that belief unto others. Conversely, the more personal our descent to our inner selves, the more comfortable we will be with our findings and the less likely they will require appeasement by dissemination unto others. What is yours stays with you and does not need to be sold; while you may want to share reflections of who you are, there is no agenda of appeasement.

3.6. *Beliefs and Exclusivity*

In the natural sciences, we give merit to laws that apply more generally, or even universally, and we see generality as a testament to their validity. The beauty of conceptualization is in achieving such generality. Similarly, a belief disconnected from nature and that applies only narrowly under artificially constrained conditions—limited to specific situations, contexts, or groups—becomes exclusionary and is less likely to retain its credibility. This narrow application also necessitates more aggressive means of enforcement for its acceptance. For example, a belief that states that one race is superior to another, as an absolute, is artificially exclusionary, making it less credible and requiring more forceful means for its adoption. It also exposes itself as a human invention, not a principle born out of universal norms.

Some religions have assigned the physical apparition of deceased religious individuals as a sign of sainthood or divinity exclusive to that faith, deeming it heresy if similar apparitions outside their religious frameworks are reported. Nevertheless there are plenty of secular, private credible events of that same nature that have happened to many of us, such as deceased relatives appearing and speaking to us to make announcements or to warn us of imminent danger.

When we look into the reach of a religious belief, we need to think, does it apply to just one culture or country? Does it apply to all humans? Does it apply to all living beings as well, like gorillas and orangutans? Is there a vetting process or an entry criteria? Is the entry criteria voluntary in the sense that there is no penalty or condemnation for refusing to enter, or are we doomed while we exist outside the religion? For example, with Catholicism, we are off to a bad start, because we are all born with the original sin. This forces us to accept the religion to redeem ourselves or else face eternal condemnation.

4. *Beliefs and Surrogacy*

Powerful blanket beliefs—such as religion and mythology—when adopted, deprive individuals of their own sense of self. They also create a general blanket of repression over the entire culture to condemn and stigmatize as taboo the notion of individuality and reliance on the inner self for answers, as individuality poses the greatest threat to the societal order established by such belief. These whole beliefs have the power to internalize such adoption with extreme forceful methods. This control is so absolute that there is no aspect of society left where the individual's sense of self is allowed to prevail.

The imposition of individual self-deprivation or self-denial is also applied in society by less comprehensive or selective beliefs that are applied to only certain aspects of our lives, such as political cults, self-help philosophies and scientifically originated beliefs. These selective beliefs act as surrogate sources because they replicate some ideologies, and with that, the impositions of the more comprehensive blanket beliefs.

The purpose of this chapter is to illustrate how this pervasive approach in civilization, which denies our sense of self, has been practiced for thousands of years. This denial does not stem from a single source, such as religion, but also from other influences, including philosophy, psychology, psychiatry, intellectual fabrications in science and medicine, as well as political and social movements which collude with each other to gain strength and perpetuate this deprivation.

4.1. Religion, the Mother of Blanket Beliefs

Blanket beliefs exhibit the extraordinary characteristic of controlling every aspect of an individual's thinking and actions. In this case, no action can be taken by members outside the precepts and guidelines of the ideology. We showed in the previous chapter the basic characteristics required for a successful internalization of these beliefs: universality, exclusivity, condemnation, and faith. The classic examples of blanket beliefs are spiritual ideologies, mythologies and religions, but there are other examples. In the 1960's in the U.S. there were non-religious social cults that exerted full domination of every conceivable aspect of the members' lives, to the point of driving their agenda to capital crimes. Some theocracies or religious military dictatorships enforce the associated religious belief that alone permeates every aspect of life for the entire population, compounded by the political and military power of the dictatorship, which allows the theocracy to further extend its dominance into the workplace and enforce these beliefs with physical punishment, such as jail, torture and death.

4. BELIEFS AND SURROGACY

This book is not in the business of making assertions or denials about the existence of deities promulgated by religions. From time to time, it is useful to expose certain religious idiosyncrasies as mythological fallacies or exclusivity claims about non-physical phenomena that cannot necessarily be adjudicated (exclusively) to a particular religion. Instead, the purpose of this book is to expose the emotional addiction of believers to their religions and its devastating effect on our civilization.

Dawkins (2001) in his book *The God Delusion*, discusses a number of arguments adopted by believers justifying the existence of the God of their religion. As is the case throughout history, our emotional constitution is largely ignored, and he refers to the adoption of religion as a byproduct of primarily rationalized behavior, overlooking the fact that it's made possible by an underlying emotional isolation and surrender. For example, he characterizes children as naturally inclined to follow their mentors in pursuit of religion, ignoring their natural fierce independence except when forced to surrender to emotional alienation as a preamble to religion subservience.

In many religions, the faithful worship and pay tribute to the religion's deities, god or gods. Worship is designed to create the most significant distance possible between a deity and their faithful followers. The faithful must show subservient respect, complete servitude, a recognition of inferiority, a negation of autonomy and their sense of self. The faithful do not have any self-determination over their growth into enlightenment, except for what is voluntarily granted by the deity. The deity, on the other hand, is seen as superior in ways that the faithful can never achieve. This creates such a disunity, such an abysmal chasm between deities and their followers. Because this requires that followers accept such unnatural relationship dynamics, denying their sense of self in subserviency to deities, it follows that these dynamics can be internalized only by very forceful coercive external imposition.

It seems inescapably obvious that some religions have created their deities in the image and likeness of hundreds of years of imperial bondage. Worship and adoration, this form of relationship to other beings, is nothing more than a replay of our relationships of domination here on earth. Apart from our own millennial training into human-style submission, there is nothing, no logic or intuition that tells us that a relationship to a superior being has to have a form of surrender and blind obedience. It is that man-made style of domination that religion has transposed to our relationship with presumably superior spiritual beings. I am also surprised about our lack of imaginative options. When we had total freedom to design our gods, we decided to create them in our own image and cultural likeness, but more specifically, the likeness of those emperors and rulers who had all the power, zest, creativity, pleasure and inexhaustible fountain of energy for oppression.

Richard Dawkins in his book *The God Delusion* (Dawkins 2001) describes the God of the Old Testament as *"arguably the most unpleasant character in all fiction: jealous and proud of it; a petty, unjust, unforgiving control-freak; vindictive, bloodthirsty ethnic cleanser; a misogynistic, homophobic, racist, infanticidal, genocidal, filicidal, pestilential, megalomaniacal, sado-masochistic, capriciously malevolent bully."* In other words, just an enhanced edition of the emperors, genocides and dictators we find on

Earth. Thomas Jefferson described the God of Moses as *"a being of terrific character – cruel, vindictive, capricious and unjust."* So, we did not gain anything on the down side, we went from being burned at the stake in ten minutes by emperors on Earth, to being condemned to eternal fire in the afterlife, with the "eternal" footnote having that special meaning well beyond the capabilities of our emperors, but fire either way. On the upside, we did much better with some rewards at the end of the road. In between the upside and downside, we did not fare any better; the voluntaryism in the saying *"give God what is God's and Caesar what is Caesar's"* does not quite apply, because it was meant to say *"surrender yourself to Caesar and surrender yourself to God, just surrender either way."* There is not that much of a difference either way. The good news was that with our extensive practice in surrendering and living in misery, we did not have to learn anything we did not know before. In addition, if we begin our relationship with God under an obligation to give to Him, that can only showcase a petty, miserable man-made depiction of superiority and alienation, which could not possibly reflect the autonomy beyond measure that we would expect in the spiritual realm.

Contrary to all this religious creationism of gods, relationships to superior beings could be more naturally presumed under the opposite set of premises. For example, these superior beings may come from the same peer evolutionary process as we do, and serve to provide a foundation of perspective that accentuates our innate ability to do as we wish, when we wish and for our own individually conceived personal purposes.

In a given religion, we may find that most of its articles of faith are not self-discoverable, but quite the opposite. They are based on very contrived imagery and artificial rules. How can a religion exist if it is not self-discoverable? If a religion's articles of faith are self-discoverable, then such religion would not have reason to exist, nothing to teach or preach, and thus would not have a claim to exclusivity. If it is not self-discoverable, the only way to its adoption would be by internalization via humanly-conceived indoctrination and coercion.

Religion in most cases represents an inherent duality. If Christianity, for example, is imparted as the exclusive means of salvation, as shown in this Christian statement, *"I am the way, the truth, and the life. No one comes to the Father except through me,"* does this mean that anyone without access to this religion will perish? This statement is a tough proposition for individuals who devote their life to science, to the prosperity of their communities, thousands of years before that one religion was created, or for individuals that live outside the sphere of accessibility of such religion, such as in inaccessible jungles. Part of the construction of a religion requires the manufacture of answers for everything. For the statement above, one exit from the uncomfortable dilemma could be to say that the statement is absolutely true, but not enforceable—when it comes to verbiage, we humans can get away with anything.

Exclusivity by any other name excludes animals that spend their lives surviving and strategizing to feed and protect their packs in the wild. Are we saying that these religions are so cruel that they can deprive these animals of salvation regardless of their virtues

4. BELIEFS AND SURROGACY   111

in this life? This notion of exclusivity does bring a most uncomfortable undertone to the predicament of coexistence in modern society, because if on the other hand, a given religion is non-exclusive, this means that it advocates that salvation can be attainable through other religions or means that contradict and negate the validity of this one religion's own imagery and precepts.

Some religions are unequivocal in their exclusivity as commanded by divine providence. If the faithful have a contrarian understanding of their religion, they can always disassociate these commands and just give to God what belongs to God and give religion what belongs to religion.

As an exercise, we may want to define our favorite religion as the path to God through ourselves—essentially, the path to ourselves. This then becomes our own personal path. But even in this case, religion is still dictating the terms that define our very own path to God. Do we have an idea of how utterly alienating it is to have that path, our own path, proactively mediated, imposed, dictated, blocked, punished and threatened by these mortals, infallible emissaries of God that know nothing about us but in their infinite wisdom do not need to know in order to dictate our path for us? Any idea how alienating that is?

A religion is typically defended in two moral realms: first, the "supernatural" spiritual realm, through the assertion of its outerwordly claims, and second, the mortal realm, by justifying the implication of this spirituality into the physical world. From our perspective, the moral values associated with religion, even if they coincide with our own, are irrelevant, because they are still mediated and prescribed to us externally, and are therefore depriving us of our own relationship with ourselves just the same.

It is important to continue to review the mechanisms whereby a given religion can inject itself as the mediator of an individual's sense of self. For example, some interpretations of Christianity recount that all humans are born with the original sin, to no fault of ours, but just the same it has now been awarded to become our fault in need of intervention just to stay morally afloat in this life. This is another example of the unaffordable downside of not accepting a religion.

It is safe to assume that a significant segment of the religious population in the Western Hemisphere have adopted their religion by first understanding the historical context in which these religious events first took place. For example, we are first introduced to Christianity by learning details of the birth of Jesus in a manger in Bethlehem to Mary and Joseph, a carpenter. We hear that he was visited by three wise men, and angels announced his birth to a group of shepherds. Further historical accounts provide details of his life, his sermons and his death by crucifixion. It would be rare for a Christian believer not to know that Christmas commemorates the birth of Jesus and Easter commemorates his crucifixion and resurrection. It is fair to say then that such religious adoption first happens through a historical context. Additional historical records provide timelines of the writing of the gospels and articles of faith after his death. As such, wouldn't it be appropriate and of natural curiosity to validate and find corroboration for such historical events? Ehrman (2014) provides an in-depth historical recount of how and when the articles of faith cementing the pillars of Christianity were first annotated and how they were aggregated to the body religion. These historical records would be very important to the faithful in order to assert the veracity of the religion because they reveal sources, contradictions and timelines of when certain articles of faith were first promulgated, often not by Jesus himself and long after Jesus' death. Ehrman's historical accounts are quite detailed, and they include these statements:

1. That the earlier three gospels are so called "synoptic" (meaning providing a common view) because two include the same ad verbatim copies of a single third common source, so therefore were not independently created as originals,
2. That all these gospels were written anonymously, without known authorship,
3. That it was not until the year 180 AD that Saint Irenaeus assigned authorship to four of the many gospels written to that date which were then included in the Bible, and it is unclear how he came to such conclusions of authorship, given that these gospels were written in Greek and not in Aramaic, the original language of the apostles,
4. That there were no proclamations of the divinity of Jesus in the early writings, and as time passed, these divinity proclamations were assigned to earlier and earlier in the life of Jesus, so there was a sequence in the timing of these writings, such that in the earliest documents, there were no statements as to his divinity and his resurrection, then in later documentation, resurrection was seen as the moment Jesus became divine, then in subsequently later documentation, it was earlier during his baptism that he became divine, then in further later documentation, it was during conception, and

finally, that he had been divine all along and therefore before he became human, thus creating the mystery that he was divine without a beginning, the same as his father, even though he was his father's son, created by his father.

Ehrman's historical revelations can be and must be contested on historical grounds first, to reach factual conclusions. Individuals may then still choose to adopt a spiritual perspective based on religion, but such a decision should follow from an informed understanding of the historical evidence. Since religious beliefs are often rooted in historical events said to have led to divine illumination on Earth, why would religious individuals not be curious enough to engage in this historical verification process? By exploring the historical and gradual composition of the Bible, compiled from diverse sources written in different time periods, it becomes possible to assess whether it constitutes the literal Word of God or a human narrative attempting to capture the presumed divine revelations. For example, in Catholic mass, the reading of the gospel is prefaced by saying, *"the gospel according to Saint Mathew,"* but the reading concludes with the affirmation, *"the Word of God."*

The Bible's New Testament was first assembled from documents by contributors and authors writing in different languages such as Koine Greek and Aramaic over three centuries, most of whom did not meet Jesus. The fully assembled Bible became an article of the faith in the year 1382, when it was considered the literal unified voice of God, grave and solemn, much like it was spoken to Moses in the Mount Sinai scene of the movie *The Ten Commandments*, where actor Charlton Heston, a.k.a. Moses' alter ego, takes upon himself to interpret the voice of God as the Gun

Whisperer, anointing him to the deliverance of a country longing for the unquestioned assertion of divine providence entrusted to hand-held repetition artillery.

Many individuals and Bible scholars wish to disassociate themselves from the literal interpretation of the Bible, which exposes the vulnerability of the religion to assert its specific divinity claims. The interpretation of the Bible seems to lead to two different avenues of adoption. To the extent that we take the Bible only for its inspirational content, the Bible becomes a secular source. But to the extent that we take the Bible as the Word of God, we are then pressed to accept the literal interpretation of the Bible.

The moment you accept the Bible, the gradual collection of documents by multiple authors over time, as the Word of God, that becomes the crucial pivotal surrender to the traditional Christian religions. Once that acceptance has been made, you are bound to all the present and future articles of faith professed by the religion, regardless of their source, such as the infallibility of the Pope for Catholics. There is no turning back.

I wonder how filmmaker Cecil B. DeMille chose the voice of God in his *Ten Commandments* movie: old, grave, cavernous, solemn, taciturn, lethargic, lingering, severe and unrepentant, ready to come down big time on Sodom and Gomorrah. God hasn't tried that again recently, like in San Francisco in the 1960's, but His chances are getting better with the prevailing winds of the 21st century. That was a voice you would not want to double cross. When I saw that movie I was expecting the high pitched playful voice of a little bird tweeting and going from branch to branch.

Isn't it a contradiction to look so old and be eternal? And they still say that we did not create God in our image and likeness, not to mention in our misconceptions of wisdom, gender and authority.

If we are able to surrender ourselves to blanket, all-encompassing beliefs, then we are more easily able to subsequently surrender to other selective beliefs with limited scope, especially if we see them as complementary and more assertive than our original beliefs. In addition, we may be inclined to proactively defend and justify our terms of surrender to a belief, by propagating and imposing that belief on others. Furthermore, if the surrender to a belief brings a great deal of discomfort to our sense of self, then we can imply that our intent for propagation of that belief may just be the reflection of that discomfort and downright hostility unto others. It is then of no surprise that a large portion of the historical armed conflicts in the western hemisphere have come with strong overtones of religious domination.

Anita Moorjani (2012), given her well-deserved prominence and credibility in the field of NDEs, often receives the question in her seminars of why she never emphasizes the role of religion in her transcendental experience, and she answers by stating that it is because she sees religion as a "narrowing" of the wider conception of spirituality, what I would interpret as the exclusionary nature of religion.

There is a deeper reward when our actions are secular, truly owned by us, and not the result of a belief, but rather, the result of our natural desire emanating uncontested from deep inside ourselves. For example, it may be our goal to be kind to others, to forgive them for their transgressions, and not to harm anybody or anything around us. But if these behaviors are not coming from the depth of our own reality, and instead come from a sense of guilt, obligation, seeking of approval or the avoidance of a good old fashion confrontation, then our deeds are not genuine. They become meaningless to us, pulling us deeper into the quicksand of hypocrisy. In such moments, we lose touch with ourselves, failing to achieve the satisfaction, fulfillment, and joy that come from living in alignment with our true sense of self. The action may therefore lack the staying power to give it credibility, even though it may have marginal value to others.

Fast-track contrition is another example of a quick-fix recipe. In a more open setting, we would be willing to recognize that we do mean to take certain questionable actions, and find pleasure in them, admitting our lack of remorse. As we explore subsequent emotional layers, we might dismantle the beliefs and superstitions about ourselves that created the motivation for those actions. Only then we may feel regret, as we own a better reality. Our society is a quick-fix, feel better society—religion and society do not grant us the slack to own those intermediate layers. Instead, they ask us to live in self-denial about our intentions—not the best way to create any form of universal synchrony.

This is what religion may be taking away from us—the opportunity to synchronize with our authenticity and the true state of our emotions. That would be a narrowing of our vision and of our access to satisfaction.

Our relationship with our physical and non-physical selves, or, for that matter, with anything of a larger scope, is intrinsically secular and private. The idea that access to ourselves—who we are, what we hold inside, what we feel from day one, what we see the first time we open our eyes or what we think when we breathe—requires an intermediary is profoundly alienating. This alienation operates at such an all-encompassing scale that other forms of marginalization based on race, culture, gender, or sexuality, seem minor (and easier to impose) compared to the sweeping alienation imposed by blanket beliefs. No wonder the pulpit of blanket beliefs often becomes the most fertile ground for discrimination. Some of the most insidious forms of prejudice come from those looking to appease the blanket belief they have accepted.

Religion has surrounded us throughout history, and we cannot help but admire and feel our hearts ache for the countless heroic sacrifices so many individuals have made in the name of their religion and beliefs. For example, St. Peter was crucified upside down because his love for Jesus was so great that he felt he did not deserve to die in the same manner. What kind of love was that? How can our hearts ever be large enough to embrace such love, commitment, and heroism? It is too much. And the saints clearly did this for what they saw was essential to paving a path forward for humanity. As I write this, bathed in tears, I assert that we do have the option to choose a different road to salvation and to recognize that we are not bound by the weight of their sacrifices.

4.2. *Scientific Beliefs*

Scientific beliefs arise not as religious perspectives, but as intellectualized extensions of scientific discoveries. Beliefs can fall from grace not only because of their heavy-handed systematic internalization processes, but also because of their lack of objectivity. It is appropriate to review them for their factual merits and showcase their contradictions, as that serves to expose our society's rushed addiction to the constant fabrication of beliefs. As we confront our addiction to beliefs in a false quest for knowledge, it is crucial to distinguish between knowing and *being*. This distinction allows us to find peace in accepting that we don't know what we don't know and that we don't need to rush to seek knowledge where it does not exist.

The best way for us to be less susceptible to internalizing these beliefs would be to have an emotional back bone—a clear connection to our inner self that provides us with our own sustainable individual intuition. But alternatively, we can also engage in reasoning about the logic of these beliefs in order to see their foundations crumble, and that would give us a form of immunity from accepting these beliefs. That would be a cheap immunization that comes from simple reasoning and does not require us to have that emotional back bone.

In this section, I explore the two prevalent approaches where science is used as a tool to reason about the spiritual realm. One approach involves using scientific concepts as a foundation to extend unproven pseudoscientific theories with no basis in scientific reality, leading to the creation of elaborate speculative fantasies reminiscent of superhero comic books. This is exemplified by the belief system of the supra (or spiritual) consciousness purportedly based on quantum physics and fantasized by Dr. Manuel Sans Segarra, as described below. An opposite approach is to use scientific reasoning to guard us against accepting mythical beliefs based on speculation that cannot be proven by science. The down side of this approach is that the inability to scientifically prove a spiritual condition does not necessarily make it untrue, nor does it mean we cannot embrace it with our intuition. This case is illustrated further below in reference to an article by astronomer Carl Sagan.

Hyper Extending into Pseudo-Science

Experimentation in quantum physics shows properties of subatomic particles which contradict our expectations of the physical world, such as the fact that a particle can manifest itself as energy but turn to matter only when observed, or that two particles can behave as one regardless of the distance that separates them. NDE survivors describe similar behavior at the level of their own spiritual being, such that they are the pure energy counterpart to their physical bodies and that they can be in any location at the same time. Those are similarities worth noting. However, one happens at the subatomic particle level, while the other pertains to the spiritual essence of a complex consciousness, such as us, human beings. To assume that the subatomic particle behavior in quantum physics can explain the properties of complex spiritual beings is an unproven fantasy turned into mythical belief.

4. BELIEFS AND SURROGACY

However, there are those who make grandiose unsubstantiated claims about the spiritual realm, derived from baseless assumptions about the implications of quantum physics—a theory whose rules we still don't understand. While it is encouraging that quantum physics does not inherently contradict spiritual concepts and may offer explanations in the future, we are far from that point. To make those inferences pulled out of our sleeves just contributes to the proliferation of new baseless beliefs and mythologies.

There is a worrisome trend among researchers and proponents of NDE experiences in relation to quantum physics implications (Segarra 2023, 2024b; Carmelo 2020), to "certify" their fantasies with references to individuals of celebrated renown, such as Nobel Prize winners, best selling authors, classical ancient philosophers, and renowned psychiatrists, notwithstanding that their contributions 1) may be outside their level of expertise, 2) might have become obsolete and proven wrong centuries ago or have been untrue since inception, 3) may represent archaic patriarchal intellectual views that should have never been given a place in societal discourse, or 4) may have been produced by their own eagerness to turn speculation into intellectualized dogma. Their fabrication of mythologies is only accelerated by "certifying" these beliefs in the name of unity with all religions and by trivializing their fantasies with superficial slogans easily swallowed by an addicted population.

Medical doctors, because of their proximity to NDE situations, are in a unique position to compile, compare and catalog these cases, which unfortunately gives them license to hijack these results to create myths and unfounded beliefs about the afterlife and our current relationship with our spiritual selves. Being medical professionals (practitioners without engagement in basic research) does not qualify them to build a belief system out of their observations. They fail to understand that it is not the pomp and circumstance of Nobel prize recipients, nor the celebrity status of individuals in any one discipline that will qualify them to provide a certification of these beliefs. On the contrary, it is the individual emotional growth into autonomy, driven by curiosity, that will provide the understanding of our place on Earth and offer the perspective needed to observe the secular spiritual life around us.

To illustrate these intellectualized beliefs and mythologies, consider the narrative offered by Dr. Manuel Sans Segarra (2023, 2024b) regarding the correlation of quantum physics to the spiritual realm. Dr. Segarra is a Spanish physician and surgeon, former chief of digestive surgery at the Bellvitge University Hospital in Barcelona, Spain. He has been a researcher of NDEs and the originator of an unsubstantiated made-up belief about the properties and behavior of the nonlocal (non-physical) self, attempting to correlate NDE narratives primarily to quantum physics, as well as with any other discipline on the horizon, such as medicine, psychology, psychiatry, religion, and philosophy. In doing so, he draws false conclusions and revives theories that have long been debunked.

We must be careful with the conclusions that Dr. Segarra pulls out like a rabbit from his sleeve, because they lack foundation and harbor many contradictions, and with that he has created his own brand of "quantum mythology."

1. Dr. Segarra validates quantum physics by stating that its language is math and its properties are proven, and therefore they can be applicable to his anthropology. But there is no mathematical model that explains quantum physics, only probability to guess its behavior.
2. Dr. Segarra asserts that there is a "first intelligence," which he equates with the same god referenced in numerous unrelated religions. In doing so, he attempts to establish the veracity and equivalence of dozens of man-made, often contradictory religions, in one single sweeping statement.
3. Some cosmologists believe that based on the principle of "quantum uncertainty," which allows energy to emerge from nowhere, an infinite number of universes may exist. If intelligence is energy, and if we were to make the colossally unfounded assumption that organized intelligence is created instantaneously, and not gradually by random evolution, wouldn't there then be one "first intelligence" for each universe? How can Sans Segarra possibly know that there is only one first intelligence?
4. Dr. Segarra claims that we are eternal beings because energy is never created nor destroyed. But this assertion might be contradicted by the assumption that energy itself was created with the Big Bang which brought the universe into existence. Also, even if all energy existed at the beginning of the universe, it could have simply been rearranged and connected in ways that gave rise to intelligent beings only at later stages.
5. If we have existed forever, as he claims, how did this first intelligence who created all of us, exist before us? Richard Dawkins in his book *The God Delusion* (2001) contends that

> *"any creative intelligence of sufficient complexity to design anything, comes into existence only as the end product of an extended process of gradual evolution. Creative intelligences, being evolved, necessarily arrive late in the universe and therefore cannot be responsible for designing it."* In addition, it would be odd that the physical realm, which is only a projection of the spiritual realm, abides by gradual evolution but not so the rest of the spiritual realm. How does Segarra know that Dawkins is wrong? Segarra seems to be filling in the blanks with good old Christianity at a frantic pace. For Segarra, where does this compulsion for certainty come from? We are just grateful he is not a politician.

6. There is a quantum physics experiment called the double slit experiment that I described in Chapter 1. The experiment shows that a particle behaves as energy when not observed and only materializes when it is being observed by a consciousness. This experiment leads Sans Segarra to state that we are all "co-creators" of the material universe without even defining the term. There are no words to describe the magnitude of this leap into quantum mythology. While there is evidence of spiritual control over the physical world, does he mean that we co-created the universe, matter, laws of physics in unison with our peers? If we are co-creators, how is it possible that we all agreed to produce a single, unified materialization of reality that we collectively share and call our universe?

Sans Segarra does not stop at borrowing from quantum physics to create physics-based myths; he takes his mission further by drawing from Freud, Jung and classical philosophers to create a moral myth. He attempts to design the moral profile of what he calls the *supra consciousness* (the non-physical consciousness), assigning completely baseless and arbitrary moral characteristics to separate the local and nonlocal consciousness. He claims these characteristics are derived from "universal" moral values. He claims that the local consciousness is egotistical and materialistic, while the nonlocal (spiritual) consciousness is altruist, generous, and loving. His recipe is intellectually seductive because it ties Freud's problematic conception of ego structures directly to the physical and spiritual selves. He states that local consciousness (our physical self) is ruled by Freud's "ego," while the nonlocal consciousness is guided by the "superego" and by Plato and Carl Jung's "universal archetypes." He further claims these archetypes represent universal norms that dictate morality for all humanity, making his correlation look seamless. However, this alignment falters under scrutiny. Freud and Jung's patriarchal archaic theories were defunct on arrival, produced by intellectuals with no awareness of their own emotional composition—an essential factor for true understanding and self-awareness.

Segarra's belief in the inherent worthlessness of physical life represents a gross alienation, because it dismisses the significance of our physical personalities—what he condescendingly calls the "ego." This perspective overlooks how deeply intertwined our personalities are with the complexities of our Earthly experiences: our interactions, consequences, dreams, pursuits, goals, actions and failures. So his belief proposition is dead on arrival. Segarra would state that physical life is wonderful, but his contradiction in no way dismisses his original premise. He states that anything of value in our physical self comes from our access to the nonlocal self. But why then would the nonlocal or non-physical self invest in lesser, worthless physical life experimentation without subsuming any gain from it? Couldn't the mediocrity of our physical life be directly implied by the mediocrity of the nonlocal or non-physical self in its quest for evolution? If that mediocrity, or imperfection, includes elements of evil, wouldn't the universe strive for progress toward repairing such disunity?

In crafting a belief system based on quantum physics, Segarra's approach is reminiscent of the Christian religious paradigm where the physical self is born doomed and hopeless under the weight of original sin—only this time it's in the form of the irredeemable indelible Freudian ego. Who needs 2000 year old Christian precepts to help in the fabrication of the most modern quantum religion when Freud will do just fine?

Segarra has created a cult based on the nature and relationship of the local and nonlocal consciousness. He states that there are ways for us to reach the nonlocal, or *supra consciousness*, while we are still in this physical life. One way is through a crisis that causes the emotional scaffolding to collapse, and with that, a brand new shiny individual will emerge from within the ashes like a phoenix. While the new behavior may be radically in opposition to the old, the substantial changes are always gradual, marginal and microscopic. Segarra states that meditation is another way, but (Moorjani 2012), the person with the most enriching, detailed, lived account of an NDE, suggests that contrary to meditation and prayer, the best way to remain close to ourselves is by not taking ourselves too seriously and being able to laugh at ourselves.

Segarra states that becoming altruist and generous with others is also one sure way to move closer to our nonlocal self, but nothing could be farther from the truth. This form of preaching is how dangerous, misguided cults are born, because Segarra is selling a recipe that will only result in more alienation and separation from the self. Segarra needs to understand that the Spanish cultural obsession with certainty, pursued through quick fix slogans, has only fueled holy wars and conquests for the last 2000 years—and these outdated approaches are not serving him any better. As he clings to any historical icon to add to his slogans, he claims that access to our nonlocal self can be achieved by blindly following Mother Teresa's advice for altruism. He needs to be reminded again that the autonomous emotional stature of a person cannot be measured by their commitment to altruism, as that can reveal the opposite: an extreme sense of guilt and subservience to religion.

Provable by Real Science

Science and scientific reasoning can also be used in the opposite direction, to prevent us from falling into mythical beliefs. However, it can also deny access to our intuition, preventing us from the free flowing exploration of our emotional and possibly spiritual selves, since that would fall outside the rigor of the scientific method or the current knowledge of science. We can observe this in an article by Carl Sagan discussed below.

Great U.S. astronomer and philosopher Carl Sagan, who brought to us such an existential perspective of our life in the universe, and who died too soon in 1996, published in 1987 a short article called *The Fine Art of Baloney Detection* (Sagan 1987). In the article, he presents a series of guidelines for recognizing myths and frauds in tales of the supernatural and existence after death. He mentions how much he misses his dead parents, and how much he longs to believe they still exist somewhere, however "childish" that desire may be, and how sometimes he is seized by the overpowering realization that they really didn't die. He is concerned that claims about the departed are rife with fraud and lack credible evidence, and individuals like him, or those with "dissociative psychiatric disorder," are easy prey for these beliefs. Unfortunately, all his reference choices point to the most transparently fraudulent and unbelievable afterlife schemes with no correlation to reality. He wonders, if life exists after death, *"Why don't Sophocles, Democritus, and Aristarchus dictate their lost books? Don't they wish future generations to have access to their masterpieces?"*

He quotes philosopher David Hume, U.S. revolutionary Tom Paine, and biologist T.H. Huxley for their very similar statements about the dangers and consequences of believing or pretending to believe in unsubstantiated beliefs. They, like Sagan, advocate intellectual provable logic as the mechanism for protecting ourselves from falling into such obscurantism. Sagan proposes a series of pragmatic guidelines to help us discern fraudulent beliefs, such as seeking independent confirmation of the facts, engaging in substantive debate on the evidence, avoiding undue reliance on arguments from recognized authorities in the field, and fully examining the entire chain of reasoning.

It is undeniable that using logic to uncover the fallacies in beliefs holds intrinsic value that should never be dismissed. Sagan has confined the dialogue to the realm of intellectual arguments, where facts can be proven, debated, defended and contradicted—a process we as humans do very well. But there may not always be enough facts or physical laws to achieve the provable conclusions that he seeks.

What happens when proposed notions transcend the governance of intellectual facts or natural laws? By confining these dialogues to the scientific and intellectual arena, Sagan, along with references such as Hume, Paine and Huxley, overlook an essential point. Intellectual reasoning is always subservient to the emotional composition of human beings in their quest for truth. They also miss the profound reality that the most magnificent truths—those that transcend the physical world— are those that emerge from ourselves out of nothing, born subjective. With this perspective in mind, I would have liked to have asked Sagan his subjective opinion. As he longed for the possibility that his relationship with his parents would have endured after death and felt the reality of that connection, what did those feelings mean to him? How much weight should such feelings have carried in his life? And as he resigned himself to a worldview devoid of transcendental purpose and enduring connection, did that perspective make sense to him? How much weight should he have credited to that as reality?

Sagan wonders, as do I, why didn't Sophocles, Democritus, and Aristarchus, dictate their lost books after passing away? We would still like to read them. There is speculation that the non-physical realm is also imperfect and that communicating with the physical world is an art which most non-physical beings are not able to master.

Sagan approached life through a narrow slice of reality—one dominated by the relentless, unwavering logic of the mind and the scientific method, with only cosmetic emotional adornments. In doing so, he missed the boat of life. He misread it. He fell for the seduction of the articulated word, which he saw through his precocious scientific bent, and he used it as a kind of fortress from which he rarely ventured. It seems that Sagan's personality left little room for the value of emotional exploration, or credible assertive intuition. Sometimes science can act as an armor against the fear of being seen as foolish, but if we accept that we are already fools, we are free to make space for that sliver of intuition and credulity we all need. With the death of his parents, the limitations of pure intellectual reasoning became evident, leaving him emotionally adrift in their absence—a void that reason alone could not fill. In the end, the emotional reality came to demand its due. There is always next time.

This happens to many of us, that when the passing of a loved one occurs, we are tormented by not knowing where they are, or if they are anywhere. This is compounded by our adherence to only provable facts and our hesitation to give substantive credit to our emotional intuition to guide us to a sixth sense of comfort and confidence about the state of all of us, departed and living.

4.3. *Philosophical Joe*

We can define philosophy as a discipline that seeks to understand fundamental truths about ourselves, the world in which we live, and our relationships to the world and to each other.

4. BELIEFS AND SURROGACY

Philosophy acts as a kind of surrogate discipline for the propagation of rationalized beliefs about our inner selves and, in doing so, it deprives us of the personal, exploratory experience of forming emotional truths. This dynamic will be illustrated through several examples in this section.

1. Philosophical reasoning, rooted in intellectual discourse, is distant, detached, impersonal, and proselytic—contrarian qualities to emotional truth formation, essential for understanding fundamental truths about ourselves. This patriarchal process, unchanged for 5000 years, has hindered progress towards our exploratory paths to self-discovery.
2. As an intellectual discourse, philosophical reasoning relies on *"self-evident truths"* that must be bootstrapped from the discipline itself, creating a hermetic inbred framework that leaves no room for emotional truth formation. Because these self-evident truths are not rooted in sources beyond the discipline, they lack their own foundation and are necessarily, arbitrarily defined.
3. With reasoning comes the creation of rigorous evaluation methodologies that can be applied to arrive at predictable, if not arbitrary conclusions. Conclusions obtained with these methodologies, by virtue of their adherence to that given formal or scientific process, are expected to be accepted and internalized as proven facts.
4. Because the intellectual reasoning process carries so much formality, it becomes heavily persuasive in the argumentation and internalization of those conclusions, depriving us from our own emotional truth formation experience.

We are caught between a rock and a hard place. Unfounded blanket beliefs will attempt to force us to believe notions that are simply not believable, and philosophy, with its encapsulating, heavily rationalized formal methods will attempt to persuade us to disbelieve notions that are actually quite believable.

The Bouncy Floor of Self-Evidence

Let's look at an example of the artificial encapsulation of philosophical thought within intellectual confines. Dr. Segarra (2023, 2024a,b) in his lectures about NDEs, in discussing the role of the physical self in relation to our nonlocal, spiritual or non-physical counterpart, draws correlations from any discipline at hand, including classical philosophy. For irrelevant reasons unknown to the world, he keeps quoting Aristotle, *"thought conditions action; action determines habits, habits form character, and character shapes destiny."* Heads or tails? Where does this sequence really begin—in the middle, or at the end, or does it go backwards instead? While this seems like a very logical consequential statement, it is based on the monumental assumption that thought is the innermost engine starter that drives human behavior. Though Segarra embraces this statement as having withstood the test of time, it was flawed when first enunciated by Aristotle because of his complete unawareness of the complex emotional constitution of individuals—an aspect that philosophy ignores in favor of the illusion of reason and thought.

Thought is conditioned and subservient to our emotional foundation, where wounded trapped emotions are hidden behind a defense mechanism that protects and perpetuates the entrapment. Therefore, in this case thought is not pristine or free flowing but tainted, compulsive, repetitive and produced by the chronic conditions of such entrapment. It is this compulsive thought emerging from the entrapment that gives birth to habit formation above all else, suppressing original or creative thoughts before they can emerge.

For example, a deep wound producing an inferiority complex may produce thought, but underneath lies the repetitive nature of a chronic defense mechanism—creating compulsive habit, which precedes the emergence of thought. In this case, habit did not build character; it only perpetuated the compensatory behavior of becoming, say, the best scientist, in order to keep feelings of inferiority restrained. This is not a showcase of character building but a compulsion hiding behind a facade.

While original creative thoughts have occasionally driven human pursuit, we cannot ignore the profound role our emotional constitution plays in shaping those thoughts. This calls into question Aristotle's perspective, which diffuses the necessary scrutiny of our thoughts, essential to guiding us towards a sense of individual reality. Instead of being helpful, these philosophical slogans are a disservice to those who would like to eliminate noise and establish a connection with our inner selves. This exercise also exposes the thin layer of semantics that philosophy rests upon. It exists within a patriarchal rational thought process where logic is rapidly fabricated. If philosophy were to incorporate the rich, thick, emotional layer into its framework, the self-evident truths it relies on would no longer be available, and philosophy itself would cease to exist.

There are countless ways to define emotionality. In contrast to our engagement with philosophy and thought, we can define *emotionality as the creative reverberating engine of thoughts not yet conceived.* By this, I mean that truths are revealed only when we tap into the erupting magma of our emotions. When you are disconnected from your emotions, truth remains elusive. In other words, the emotional and philosophical processes are at odds with each other. In philosophy you start with self-evident truths and then proceed through reasoning. In the realm of emotion, you start by exploring the raw, irrational currents of your feelings. Then after discovering the source of those emotions, truths can spontaneously begin to form within you.

Let us now look at a couple of popular maxims. Socrates' *"know thyself"* turns out to be an oxymoron, or a catch-22, because to know yourself you have to first be yourself, and to be yourself, you first have to know yourself, and this is impossible within the confines of philosophy. This creates an unsolvable riddle because it requires abandoning the quest for the dry, sterile, rationalized, and prefabricated "truths" of philosophy, to find the greener, more fertile pastures of truth formation, where truths do not yet exist. To do this, you have to embrace uncertainty, risking your sense of sanity, and as you do, you will never again define yourself in terms of philosophical "self-evident truths." Without those presumptive self-evident truths, there is no philosophy left. The philosophical experiment is over for you.

Socrates also coined the phrase *"all I know is that I know nothing."* On the surface, this slogan seems quaint—a philosophical statement of humility and a reminder to acknowledge the boundaries of knowledge. However, there is a gigantic underbelly to the slogan, because to reach the point where you understand that you know nothing, you must first endure a solitary emotional descent into the depths of your own nothingness, your own void. It is the place where the make-believe superficial reality you thought you knew, does not exist. This descent brings you face to face with the edges of your sanity, where disorientation and bewilderment overwhelm you. Nothingness is not the place where superficial socially consumable humility can exist. It is the place where truths will be formed—slowly, like nebulae form stars. It is not a world of words but a gateway to life where you pay the price of entry. Philosophy trivializes and ignores this emotional layering all together. It is the place where our insanity dwells—a destination that now demarks the beginning. In this context, I don't refer to insanity as the unaware clinical madness where bizarre, destructive behavior is unleashed unchecked and disconnected from reality. On the contrary, I define insanity as a void state of heightened awareness, where our life-time superficial make-believe fantasies crumble, confronted by the revelation of our deeper, sobering reality never before exposed. It is a state where this dichotomy results in unbearable anguish. Without this context, Socrates' slogan looks like a neon sign on Broadway, stripped of its haunting implication. This is another example of how, for so many thousands of years, our civilization has largely remained oblivious to the deeper human condition, replacing it with a caricature of belief consumption.

The Closing of the American Mind

I want to review the philosophical book *The Closing of the American Mind* written by Allan Bloom in 1987 for the following reasons: 1) to show that the philosophical discourse has remained stagnated for 5000 years and remains intellectual and aloof from a nuanced, intertwined reality, and 2) to show the dominance of intellectual discourse over emotion, as evidenced by the great popularity and praise the book received upon publication.

The Closing of the American Mind, a #1 New York Times National Best Seller written by Allan Bloom (1987), comes from the realm of classical philosophy and received a great deal of attention and overwhelming reverence because of its criticisms of the modern culture of the second half of the twentieth century. Bloom's thesis of the book is a criticism of higher education in the United States, arguing that it has failed to teach students of the 1960's and 1970's how to think and therefore has impoverished their souls. He claims that U.S. universities have been taken over by moral relativism, the notion that morality is entirely subjective and depends on individual perspectives, rendering the concepts of right and wrong undefinable. According to him, this has led to a decline in intellectual curiosity, exacerbated by a lack of religious upbringing, which he also sees as a contributing factor to the spread of moral relativism. As I illustrate below, Bloom's book fails in fundamental ways.

In 5000 years, with respect to the search for truth, it has never been the role of education or philosophy to teach people how to think, as Bloom claims. No one can teach you how to think, let alone how to feel. To believe otherwise has been the false existential premise that erases philosophy from the face of the earth as a credible pillar of society. By enthroning himself in the realm of education which Bloom says is the solution, he is naming himself as the root of the problem.

Bloom's book is an example of how intellectual judgment of an entire generation can be forcefully imposed by flooding the thought process with seemingly related but otherwise unfounded, disparate philosophical arguments. Unfounded because they are unrelated and do not apply to the generations in question. Unfounded because his examples do not showcase the moral virtues he wants to exemplify. This process is designed to alienate a generation by isolating them from the underlying realities underscoring their experience. This observation is particularly relevant in the context of belief systems because it shows how philosophical argumentation can be used as an intellectual surrogate for religion and myth to block our access to individual emotional realities. Heavy argumentation is a way of imposing intellectual views that block a more pensive, reflective access to emotional understanding.

At the heart of the failure of *The Closing of the American Mind*, lies the gross misunderstanding that human depth is found solely through intellectual pursuit. Bloom attributes what he perceives as the failure of the 1960's and 1970's generations to the sudden and surprising failure of the educational system. But education has nothing to do with it. Throughout 5000 years of civilization, education has never served or had an understanding of the essential emotional composition of humans. Bloom's misstep lies in his unquestioned adherence to the principles of classical philosophy, which command intellectualism over emotional understanding—principles entrenched in the framework of educational pursuits. This blind allegiance to ancient philosophical ideals undermines his critique, making classical philosophy itself a key contributor to the book's colossal failure.

If we want education to provide a paradigm shift and become a protective emotional space for truth formation—a space where truths cannot be taught but discovered—it must become entirely different from what it has ever been in the history of civilization, and certainly nothing like the intellectual philosophical predicament Bloom wanted it to be.

Another major failure of his book lies in Bloom's eagerness to showcase his superiority and pass a condescending judgment on an entire generation. He encapsulates the turmoil and imperfections of the generation but fails to acknowledge or explore the causes for this generation's predicament as a natural evolutionary consequence of prior generations, whose values and structures had reached their limits, were showing their cracks and were destined to collapse. The more incisive and nuanced the reasons behind this historical continuum, the more insightful our future, and the more clear our generational continuity, so essential for this understanding. The problem with searching for underlying causes as I advocate, is that it completely undermines Bloom's stance: instead of preaching from the comfort of a pulpit, he would have had to step down, sit side by side with his students, and engage as a peer to understand their perspective. Instead of starting at the end, giving conclusive professorial summations about his findings, he would have had to start at the beginning, at the perspective from which his students view the

4. BELIEFS AND SURROGACY 139

world. He would have had to immerse himself in their experiences, to the point of forgetting he once stood in the pulpit. But what is the point of writing a book if you have to abandon the pulpit altogether?

Another failure of Bloom's book is that in an effort to remain loyal to the philosophical predicates of 2000 years ago, he offers no insights that reveal and identify the unique signatures of these modern generations in question. You cannot unleash your criticism of a generation before you can establish a profile that uniquely identifies it in place and time. Reading this book, you might think you are reviewing generations from the ancient past, nothing to do with today's world.

If Socrates had reviewed the 1960's generation, he might have used the same language to establish his predicaments, because the philosophical discourse has not changed since. He probably would have been more coherent in his correlations, but at this intellectual level, coherence or incoherence are both inconsequential.

We cannot criticize Bloom without showing how a review of these same generations could be done. To provide a contrast to the outlined criticisms of his book, let us indulge in a micro exercise to provide our own review of these generations from the 1960's and 1970's. In this exercise I want to illustrate generational continuity stemming from these modern positions. From my own observations, let us look at intuition and the fear of intimacy across these generations, which more than anything else reflect our modern era because they are heavily conditioned by the prejudices and liberations of the times—yet topics for which

Bloom completely omits to offer a comparative perspective. At the risk of oversimplification, let's define the fear of intimacy as the fear of entrapment, and love as merely emotional exploration. Intuition, which is the entry to our Inner Sanctum, serves as the lens through which relationships are entered and explored. In the 1950's, intuition was hardly at play because relationships were quickly dominated by social norms and expectations, which destroyed any possibility for individual autonomy—the very condition required for intuition to flourish. Emotional intimacy was so out of the question that a woman requesting it from a husband would have been construed as an assault to manhood and dominance and lead to compelling grounds for divorce. As we moved into the 1960, 1970's and beyond, the concept of intimacy began to come into play. Individuality and autonomy in the relationships led to the emergence of intuition as the guiding compass. This became the hallmark of generational differentiation. Today we see how intuition can play a role in emotional exploration, and with that comes the fear of exposing our emotions based solely on intuition.

But given that our trust in our own intuition is still fragile and underdeveloped, the symptoms observed in new generations—continuing into the new century, is that the bolder the intuition, the quicker the backlash, as it crashes against the fear of insecurity, doubt and exposure. This fear leads to the vilification of our own intuition, a defense mechanism against the perceived threat of entrapment. The only way to escape this perceived threat is by rejecting and vilifying our own intuition. This fear of entrapment is often reinforced by an individual seeking seclusion in religious and moral beliefs. Thus, the new cultural symptom emerging in generations after the 1960's is the failure of intuition and exploration to reach full realization. This fragile sequence typically consists of intuition, fear of entrapment, perception of threat and vilification of intuition, all while preventing true exploration. This suggests that the most insightful individuals in these generations are those who face the greatest obstacles, being affected by fragile intuition and seeing their sense of exploration crushed. This generational loss is unsustainable. It calls for the next generations to provide a new cultural foundation where individual autonomy and gender emancipation grow so that options are expanded to support the realization and coexistence of these emotional explorations.

This direct emotional exposure to the effects of intuition is also deeply cultural—a beautiful trait in prevalent U.S. culture that is absent in many other cultures. In those cultures, rigid cultural roles often permeate and diffuse direct interpersonal interactions. Beautiful trait and all, partly because it reveals, with full transparency, the reverse effect caused by vilification: how our fears perpetuate isolation by confining us to immobilizing entrapments.

See *"Chapter 9.3., Intuition, Transparency and the Blink of an Eye"* for more details on intuition and entrapment. See *"Chapter A.3. Joe and the Closing of the American Mind"* in the Addendum for my more detailed review of the Bloom book.

The Context in the 1950's

My comparative reflections on the 1950's leaves me wanting to revisit the way cultural changes demarcate time. I have always wanted to time travel to the past, and my first stop would have been the 1950's, partly to visit my parents and grandparents, and partly to just gloat on how the culture has changed in such a short time. I would revel in incredulity, observing the gender roles of the era, so blatantly rooted in insecurity. Young heterosexual white males, exuding transparent arrogance, seemed so blissfully unaware of how pathetically obvious their posturing appeared to an observer. Yet this was the valuable culture that Bloom saw decaying alarmingly in *The Closing of the American Mind*.

Then I would visit further back into our past. The rare moments I have encountered real, unrestrained entitlement, arrogance, hatred, and venom in contemporary civilized society—moments that sent shivers down my spine—make me realize how little we understand the sheer built-in pressure in the personalities that sustained the cultural structures of centuries past. Those traits, when fully unleashed, are something to see. Our imagination of such personalities is often shaped through movies, where actors portray these historical archetypes, earning Oscars for roles mimicking these characters without understanding what it took for those personalities to form. Occasionally a performance might give a tiny tingle of a hint of that reality—like Wes Studi's portrayal in the movie *The Last of the Mohicans* or Gerardo Taracena in the movie *Apocalypto*.

Because of how dramatically the culture shifted from the 1950's to the early 2000's, I wouldn't mind also time traveling into the future, say some two hundred years from now. In our current culture, there is a pervasive lack of ownership of the self. The self often feels absent, disconnected, and unclaimed by its very owner. This lack of self-ownership is so pervasive that it has become the norm. We don't even question it. That unnecessary servitude we encounter—an endless cycle of offering ourselves, only to be reciprocated by others doing the same—defines life as we know it today, built on the assumption that everyone means well. I would like to walk and mingle the busy streets, universities, nightlife and markets two hundred years from now, assuming there are still such busy places then, to see how that self-ownership and servitude has evolved and how it is reflected in people's faces compared to today. I would walk and walk until my toes bled, driven by the hunger of someone who has never eaten, determined to take it all in—to grasp where we might be as a society two hundred years from now. I would make sure I can absorb that experience, capturing it as mine forever. As toddlers say, "*mine!, mine!*"

4.4. *Doodling and the Rabbit Hole*

Defense mechanisms are rigid, inflexible behaviors, thought processes, and viewpoints that often stem from an unaware or unconscious origin. They are developed within the individual to block access to the inner self, where unbearable painful emotions are kept. In this sense, defense mechanisms act as *emotional guardians* to the more genuine inner self. The more emotional guardians the inner self is forced to create to protect itself, the less genuine our behavior and emotions become, resulting in a subsequent loss of quality of life.

The range of behaviors a human being can exhibit—including personal tastes, opinions, strategies, moral decisions, and actions—can originate from a free flowing emotional and intellectual process within the individual or from the constrained rigidity of defense mechanisms designed to guard the inner self against vulnerable, painful exposure.

In different situations, individuals may demonstrate incredible flexibility in their behavior and thoughts or, conversely, total inflexibility because of the constraints imposed by defense mechanisms. For example:

1. Individuals may exhibit full flexibility in expressing a preference, such as for an ice cream flavor or for certain colors, or even in changing those preferences.
2. They might exhibit limited flexibility in career choices, where pursuing a path like dance could be constrained by defensive mechanisms guarding against the vulnerability of expressing the body in a more gender fluid manner.
3. They could display zero flexibility in accepting the mere existence of gender preferences in others because of the rigid stance provided by their internalized religious belief, blocking their access to their own fresh individual perspective.

This highlights the existence of behavioral ranges that are inaccessible or unavailable because of defense mechanisms acting as barriers. Consequently, *socially available behavioral ranges* are those limited behaviors offered by individuals without requiring them to confront and bypass almost impenetrable defense mechanisms, those emotional guardians. This creates what I call an *emotional state of decoy*—behavior enacted by defense mechanisms to obstruct and disguise access to our essential human nature. This state of decoy, the observable human behavior, has nothing to do with our essential emotional human nature.

Approaching human behavior solely within socially available behavioral ranges and therefore perpetuating the emotional state of decoy that hides the more impenetrable defense mechanisms is the pervasive approach in psychology, which only highlights its uselessness. Grant (2023), states in his book *Think Again* that *"This book is an invitation to let go of knowledge and opinions that are no longer serving you well and to anchor your sense of self in flexibility rather than consistency."* This is an invitation to superficial, conversational change, unlikely to be adopted by most humans. You can pick any population segment for a test run, let's say personalities in the business of political coercion, select your favorite U.S. politicians ranked by highest venom concentration in foamy saliva, and have them play a round of musical chairs for flexible thinking. You'll quickly confirm that no change will be forthcoming from Grant's recommendations.

We recognize that emotional accidents or wounds sometimes pierce these defenses, puncturing the self and resulting in what is often termed a mental health issue. In psychology, psychoanalysis and psychotherapy have been the disciplines tasked with addressing these issues within an individual's personality. Psychoanalysis aims to help patients understand how their unconscious mind influences their behavior, in order to heal from past experiences. Psychotherapy aims to help patients improve their quality of life and strengthen their relationship to social norms and regulations.

Sigmund Freud was the first to look at issues of mental health by creating an arbitrary profile of the individual personality or psyche and using psychoanalysis to bring about mental healing. Freud never saw a mental disease that he did not recognize nor an emotional state that he did not label a new mental illness. This is also how he proved to the rest of the world and to our full satisfaction, that he had no clue about the existence of humans as emotional beings, and their emotional depths as the true ignition of awareness. His focus was aimed at bringing so-called ill patients back to the status quo—a modest goal at best. Essentially, he facilitated a shift from socially unacceptable compulsions to socially acceptable ones—a horizontal transition, rather than anything vertical or meaningful. Because he had no perception of emotional depth, illness often meant an emotional variation outside the norm that he could not justify. There was no concept of an emotional constitution as the source of truth formation. Because the acceptable social behavior of the mind was the goal, he saw no need or value, nor did he have the abilities for depth exploration as the source of undiscovered truths. This is understandable because emotional precociousness is not found nor granted in intellectual pursuits like Freud's psychoanalysis. Freud did not have the emotional capacity to see the inner self's full potential and value because he did not have such inner access within himself.

This limitation in the perception of the inner self also exists in psychotherapy because it is founded under the same guidelines used to bring mental health back to social normalcy. In this context, when a defense is pierced and the inner self is exposed, psychotherapy tends to view it as requiring only the minimal intervention to "suture" the wound and return the individual to normalcy. This is widely acknowledged in the literature, where successful cases are measured by the individual's return to socially acceptable life—no more than that.

The creation of psychoanalysis and psychotherapy to repair mental illness exposes a deeper limitation in their understanding of the self. Illness, as a framework, limits engagement with the self because it is defined primarily as an externally perceived pejorative divergence from socially acceptable behavior. This approach is limiting, because if there is no such divergence, there is no illness and no cause for subsequent exploration of the deeper layers of the self and its defenses. Conversely, if there is divergence, it is viewed with contempt. Thus psychology has no reason nor motivation to find what lies in those deeper layers; it wants nothing to do with the autonomous pursuit of the self because there is no recognition of the intrinsic value of the self beyond the pejorative mental illness. It is outside its charter. So for example, the internalization of religious or political beliefs would be classified as normal behavior, not warranting repair or further growth, and would be considered outside psychology's domain. From this perspective, psychology fails to engage with individuals who deviate from society's norms yet have never experienced mental illness. I would argue that psychology has nothing to do with us if in our discrepancy with society we chose to never have been mentally ill for a day in our lives.

Psychology has diversified quite a bit, and there are other areas within the discipline, including cognitive, organizational, business and educational psychology. However, they all relate to the individual in terms of their *already available behavioral range*, meaning behavior available without having to pierce the defense mechanisms, such as the behavior depicted in (Grant, 2023), #1 New York Times Bestseller. With the exception of psychotherapy, these areas of psychology do not attempt to exert influence or bring about behavior beyond the inaccessible layers behind the defense mechanisms.

Pinker's Rationality

Cognitive psychology explores the processes behind human thought. It examines how thinking, emotions, creativity, and problem-solving interact to shape our mental functions. The problem is that psychology is a passive intellectual observational discipline collecting behavioral data. This passive approach leads to a misunderstanding of human nature by interpreting behavior at face value, rather than recognizing it as superficial dramatizations that serve as decoys to conceal deeper emotions beneath defensive layers. By remaining purely observational, psychology becomes ineffectual, accepting these behavioral dramatizations as definitive and leaving no option to proactively uncover the true essential behaviors hidden deep within. Let's consider an example below.

Steve Pinker is a cognitive psychology professor at Harvard University and has been a psychology professor at MIT and Stanford. He was named one of Time's 100 most influential people in the world in 2004. In 2023 he was awarded the 15th Edition of the BBVA Frontiers of Knowledge award for his contribution to rationality (BBVA, 2023).

In his New York Times bestselling book, *The Blank Slate: The Modern Denial of Human Nature* (Pinker, 2003), he argues that human behavior is shaped by both evolutionary adaptations to life experiences, and innate traits we are born with. This contrasts with the theory that the human mind is a blank slate at birth and solely shaped by external social factors such as education, environment and experience. He argues correctly that the blank slate theory negates our natural individual differentiation, and I would go further to say that the notion of the blank slate acts in collusion with religious beliefs in their sale of equality.

Because I am not a psychologist, I can offer my intuitive perspective on the subject without relying on complex prefabricated theories or social research studies. It seems obvious to me that we are born with a complete and holistic individual nature, not with a blank slate. However, this innate nature lacks context and remains undeveloped. Society plays a dominant role in shaping our nature, either by nurturing, promoting, overpowering, or destroying it.

Our pre-birth traits may include a predisposition for specialization, such as the innate ability to become a concert pianist at a young age, or conversely, an open and adaptable, generalized flexibility that allows us to develop abilities not immediately apparent. The blank slate theory, already challenged by Pinker, can be further challenged by evidence suggesting that some of our predispositions may come from previous reincarnations (Stevenson, 2000).

The question is, does it really matter for our understanding of human nature, if we start with a blank slate or not? If Pinker's book is aimed to deepen our understanding of human nature, his approach—merely proposing a better observational perspective by considering behavior as possibly innate—misses the point:

1. We remain unable to determine if the presumed innate behavior is innate behavior.
2. We are still unable to determine if the presumed innate behavior is only superficial dramatized behavioral decoy and not an underlying essential behavior.
3. Our passive observational vantage point does not improve from these speculations.
4. Our understanding of human nature requires the incisive ability to identify and bypass layers of behavioral decoys to uncover our true essential nature—something that is not on Pinker's radar.

Watching a baseball game from the 5th floor or behind home plate, a curveball strike remains a curveball strike. We still don't know the cellular density or any other characteristic in the pitcher's wrist muscle that allows him to drop the curveball four inches more than any other pitcher in the league. We are just observers and remain observers. We are there for the good times and a hot dog. Pinker so completely misses the mark because he comes in as an observer buying what he sees, and because psychology is a passive, observational discipline, unequipped to offer any incisive authoritative insights into human nature.

4. BELIEFS AND SURROGACY   151

Pinker corroborates this depiction of psychology when he states *"We ought to use every intellectual tool available to understand what it is about the human mind and human social arrangements that leads people to hurt and kill so much."* He fails to propose any such intellectual tools, because there are none. He also fails to understand that this is not an intellectual proposition. It is not the human mind that we need to understand, and it is not through intellectual tools that any understanding will be forthcoming, because it is the deeper emotional engagement driving the mind we need to understand.

Pinker suggests that his new understanding can help parents avoid self-blame when a child deviates from their upbringing, implying the child was innately flawed. However, except in rare cases, his assumptions about a child's innate state are largely baseless and purely speculative. Does Pinker think that the mere speculation about the innate state of a child will be enough to appease the pre-dated colossal sense of guilt that parents brought to the table? Is that his reading of their human nature? It could also be the opposite, that parents' self-blame and overwhelming guilt might be the real cause, all landing squarely on the child's lap.

Observation alone does not provide insights, allowing us to identify further shortcomings of Pinker's approach. We cannot determine, for any specific behavioral trait in an individual, whether it is due to nature, nurture, or a combination of both. Moreover, we cannot conclude whether such behavior is intrinsic and unchangeable or a superficial decoy subject to resolution by descent into deeper emotional layers.

For instance, a boy's extreme and unexpected volatility in a calm family setting does not necessarily indicate that this behavior is essential or innate to his nature. A deeper understanding might reveal that it is merely a superficial protective facade for the immense love he is capable of giving—something that cannot be discerned through observation alone without mining deeper into his more perdurable essentials.

Pinker fails to acknowledge the point that true human nature is fundamentally emotional and lies captive beneath observable, dramatized behavioral decoy; thus Pinker's observations are misleading and irrelevant, leaving the reader without access to the underlying human nature. His view remains trapped in an intellectual unidimensional or "horizontal" perspective of human nature that does not provide insight on the emotional depth of our true human nature. Therefore, Pinker's observations find nothing and remain the blind denial of the real human nature his book was meant to criticize. To rephrase, the conversational, anecdotal and statistical comparative stories offered by Pinker fall within what I coined earlier as *socially available behavioral ranges*, perpetuating the behavioral state of decoy or disguise that hides the more impenetrable defense mechanisms.

Because the intellectual-emotional dichotomy is so significant to our state of affairs, let me go back to the well again. In Ambrose Bierce's *The Devil's Dictionary*, Pinker cites the entry for the mind: *"...Its chief activity consists in the endeavor to ascertain its own nature, the futility of the attempt being due to the fact that it has nothing but itself to know it-self with."* It was never the endeavor of the mind to ascertain its own nature. That is the unidimensional intellectual view of the last 5000 years, where our emotional self, the essential source of our human nature, is ignored and obliterated. When I read Pinker, my first reaction was to reflect on the unidimensional intellectual entrapment in his narrative. And this serves to illustrate once again the largest confrontation in civilization, between intellect and emotion.

Pinker's book becomes orphaned content in search of a thesis. He settles the controversy over a blank slate with a couple of sentences in his preface, leaving the remainder of his argumentation untethered to a central purpose. The opportunity to advance a new understanding of human nature remains unfulfilled, with no clear outline of the path required to reach that essential concept. The reason that the new understanding of human nature is never fulfilled in Pinker's book lies in his adherence to classical intellectual psychology, which falters by remaining merely an observational discipline. Pinker attempts in vain to unravel this understanding from new angles of observation, but human nature is not to be found in statistical observation of behavioral decoys. It lies inside the emotional process of individual truth formation, hindered by a civilization still too primitive and reluctant to move beyond its current reliance on intellectual beliefs.

Pinker's understanding of human nature, as presented in his 2003 work, is governed by the mind and centers on rationality as the manifestation of reasoning. This perspective is not an intellectual accident caused by gravitational pulls in celestial realignments at the turn of the century. In his more recent book, *Rationality: What It Is, Why It Seems Scarce, Why it Matters*, Pinker (2022) doubles down on the irrationality that rationality must be cultivated and learned through an intellectual educational process, such as the use of probability, to characterize human nature by statistical means. With this, Pinker has found the bottom of psychological intellectual dementia, ever more astray and elitist.

These views align with philosophers like Bloom (1987), who see intellectual education as the path to enlightenment. Pinker asserts that there are *"major tools of rationality that we are not born with but that we have to learn and cultivate,"* including logic and probability theory, which he believes *"every educated person should understand but no book has explained all together for the general reader."*

Pinker's stance can be seen as advocating educational elitism, narrowing the understanding of human nature by depriving it of its rightful intrinsic access to emotionally-sourced rationality. He overlooks the idea that rationality is found within our inner emotional selves, where intuition and common sense, though mostly dormant, always exist in their purest form. Instead, he claims rationality should be discovered through learned observational disciplines, applying tools such as probability and statistics. The tools of our trades are not extensions of our rationality. Even if rationality were to come to us through endless layers of intellectual mediation flanked by descending custodian archangels with higher degrees in probability theory bringing enlightenment where none existed before, why would we then want to be rational, if what we want more than anything else is just to be ourselves? The fact that these ideas can be accepted by the entire intellectual community is astonishing. On the bright side, premedieval obscurantism is about to get a jolt into the future if Pinker writes a new book about rationality delivered through humanoid robotics.

4. BELIEFS AND SURROGACY

Nothing like a statement from Pinker to illustrate the battle lines between intellect and emotion. In an interview for his *Frontiers of Knowledge Award in Humanities* (BBVA 2023), he is quoted: *"When rationality is deployed in service of maximising human wellbeing, that is what can drive progress."* This begs for a few observations:

1. This accentuates his perception of rationality as something external to human beings—something you have to fetch externally and "deploy," thus implying it is a collective by-product, further away from emotional individual essence. Is Pinker suggesting that there are contrarian cases when rationality is "deployed" against human wellbeing? And why would that be called rationality?
2. Does this deployment come with a user manual or a probability course prerequisite?
3. He implies that rationality is not really ours, not part of our essential emotional complexion because its "deployment" can be severed from our actionable emotional selves.
4. To summarize, rationality is an intrinsically individual emotional trait, without a collective alignment for approval, as he seems to suggest.

These two Pinker books are a disservice to society because they do not help us understand the essence of human nature. Instead, they occlude our intuitive understanding. His works exemplify the institutionalized damage caused by relentless intellectualism moving further and further away from the essential reality of human beings.

Our cultural world thrives on diversity of pursuits. One example is immersing ourselves in the fashion world and setting your goal to create the most beautiful designs. After all, we all want to look like Liberace on New Year's Eve. However, when the goal is to deepen our understanding of human nature—a crucial survival pursuit—our reasoning must align with this aim. If a thesis contradicts its intended goal, it's time to abandon ship; otherwise it just steals ownership from the essential emotional self to give it, in isolation, to an intellectual elite.

In his quest to understand human nature, has Pinker ever proposed how we can discern between behavior decoys, like genocide or spiritual redemption, and the true essence of human nature? How many hundreds of years do we need to continue in these hyperbolic intellectual glorifications before we can flee in reverse stampede and abandon these evenings of empty award ceremonies?

Why ask about human nature if we lack the purpose to find out for ourselves? This requires navigating through the emotional labyrinth of complexities, self deceit and pretense, descending to the dungeons where the answers lie for ourselves, and consequently, for others. Human nature is not what is left when you remove all the personality aberrations for crime, violence and others; rather, it is what is still hidden, inaccessible beneath, after these aberrations and polarized influences have been removed.

For 5000 years we have been observing human nature through a detached, intellectual lens, often influenced by biased observers who have secluded their emotions in order to preserve their intellectual theories. Meanwhile, institutions like MIT, Stanford, and Harvard continue to invest significant resources in perpetuating these intellectual pursuits. They invite elite scholars to lead future generations in endless blurry circles without resolution. At a time when liberalism is under attack in our society, liberal education can no longer continue to showcase that such criticisms are well justified and that the priceless value of time and human resources continue to go to waste. It is time for new liberal institutions to prove they exist to favor not the elitist liberals and their self-indulgent conversations about a superior world over endless hours at a coffee shop, but the raw, individual emotion that sits in every human being's gut, turned into a Gordian knot.

Steve Pinker is indeed a celebrated sacred golden calf in the world of psychology, inebriated in the bacchanalia of rhetoric fabrication. However, for the reasons outlined above, his books do not have innovative relevance and may become obsolete shortly after publication. Yet, Pinker has finally achieved immortality by way of a less-than-effusive review in my book, which will linger for a while as it gains traction in the hands of a few generations to come who will still see their future as a blank slate not yet lost in the pit of intellectualism. Can't get too picky about immortality.

Gatekeepers of the Self

Psychotherapy is the only area that examines defense mechanisms with the immediate goal of suturing the wound and bringing the individual back to the surface. Typically, these other areas do so by associating psychology with statistics to establish and justify generalized, impersonal stereotypes. This allows them to infiltrate other areas, often adorning them with colorful visuals like pie charts and bar graphs, such as in business strategies and education. They forsake and betray individuality in favor of a herd-oriented statistical mentality. These other areas in psychology outside psychotherapy would be more properly called "behavioral statistics."

Psychology could steal a page from phenomenology (Husserl, 2017; van Manen, 2023), the study of the lived experience, which with courage and conviction has done the opposite. It has taken social grouping trends and evaluations—until then the exclusive domain of quantitative statistics—and framed them within an individual, subjective framework. Phenomenology makes the unequivocal statement that everything is subjective, which becomes the sociological counterpart to my claim that everything is personal, and that the impersonal is in fact, personal. However, because the psychology charter was never originally meant to pursue individuality beyond the "suture and flee" closure mentality, we must excuse these other psychology areas from this betrayal.

Because psychology ignores the true essence of the self in favor of a "suture and flee" mentality, as we have reviewed above, it serves as a surrogate, satellite discipline of the more powerful blanket beliefs which perpetuate the alienation and obliteration of the inner self:

1. Psychology pursues individual normalcy by rushing individuals into modest contentment with their relationships in society. It does this by advocating an action-oriented "closure and healing"—essentially a "suture and flee" mentality. This involves closing the coffin on emotions trapped in trauma,

leaving them behind in order to advance to some form of normalcy. This approach is incompatible with one that seeks full restoration by bringing individuals to reside permanently inside their wounds, thus allowing them to descend into deeper levels of their inner selves. Such a gain in perspective would likely lead to social advancement, as it could bring about fresh perspectives for justice and accountability in issues like sexism, racism, and other forms of oppression.

2. Psychology hijacks the psychotherapy process under a veil of exclusivity, assuming that being a therapist requires knowledge of the self that is unavailable in the mundane world. This presumption creates an intellectual hierarchy, with therapists position as gatekeepers to the self. In this way, psychology mirrors the exclusionary traits of religions where absolution and penance can only be given by ordained priests. While psychology has the right to control its own discipline and licensing, the process of truly reaching the inner levels of the self will inevitably need to take place outside of formal psychology. The effort must include an unlicensed egalitarian effort that honors full individual autonomy.

3. Well within the natural boundaries of its discipline, which is to seek social normalcy, psychology actively foments a ready-made recipe culture for feeling good and trivializes any hope for real growth. Consider the following example, as one of many. CNBC, the reputable U.S. financial television network, published on the August 1, 2024 edition of their website, along with other news about the Ukraine war, the Israel-Hamas war, and the Venezuelan elections, an article by #1 New York Times Best Seller author Adam Grant, psychologist at the Wharton Business School of the University

of Pennsylvania, about exercises to know yourself better (Grant 2024). The exercises Grant describes are based on an activity created by researchers from the Harvard Business School and the University of Michigan's Ross School of Business, designed to help you see yourself "through the eyes of others." What does that tell us about our culture when, on CNBC, a presumably sober financial channel, this topic occupies the same real estate as globally impactful news? This is an example of the recipe-oriented nature of psychology, which admittedly provides value in helping people navigate work and social environments. While it is fine to bring the circus to town from time to time, and more fun than playing charades, its negative impact stems from the fact that these ready-made solutions reinforce psychology's superficial mission of social normalcy, completely obscuring what should be its mission: the recognition of the urgent importance of the individual's true encounter with the innermost self. This urgency is glaringly evident when juxtaposed with news headlines, side by side with Grant's psychological gospel on CNBC. The real damage is the distraction itself—the circus—and the implied presumption that there is nothing of essential, urgent, or deeper value to occupy our minds and souls, other than the immediate gratification of ready-made recipes. This is the true harm to a consumption-driven society.

4. What then is the essential, urgent and deeper value in which to occupy our minds and souls? One example is the systematic dismantling of defense mechanisms in individuals statistically classified as "normal" according to multi-page psychological tests—a game played through the eyes of others.

4. BELIEFS AND SURROGACY

> This other example exempts us from immediate action, because, given our current emotional limitations, there is little we can do—except perhaps to briefly consider what that superior level of awareness would look like for individuals who could successfully reach their deepest caverns of insanity, coexist, and survive. And what might the world look like if we all could reach that place?

This psychology perspective remains in sharp and opposite contrast to the view of descent to the emotional self, where the emotional constitution is seen as the revelation of an inner self that exists beyond and outside the confines of pejorative mental illness in psychology. This incursion into the notion of the self highlights and contrasts the sempiternal damage of the limiting intellectual pursuit that has allowed psychologists to claim ownership of something they never truly understood. Freud and psychology have created a false interpretation of the mind's function, hijacking and binding emotion within that framework, thereby reducing the self to an invented subservient model of the mind. In doing so, they have claimed ownership of the self and a personal relationship to it—one that they are neither equipped to possess, nor qualified to substantiate. To distance the field from everyday, intuitive concepts, the social sciences tend to overemphasize intellectual pursuits, often when there are none. Psychology has become the modern equivalent of witchcraft, producing intellectualized recipe books for the mind, while a publication like *Psychology Today* remains entrenched in dire competition with *People Magazine* for what enquiring minds want to know: recipes lightly peppered with a psychology vocabulary, yet with a full omission of the first premise of the human condition—that joint, unlicensed, equally shared emotional submersion is prerequisite sine qua non for human understanding and for giving voice to the human experience.

To demonstrate that the "suture and flee" closure approach is too superficial to bring healing, it is important to understand that repairing emotional damage does not simply return an individual to their prior state but implies a betterment of their being. The rationale for this is as follows: if emotional damage has occurred, it is likely in part because a portion of an individual's self has not yet been fully owned and appropriated by that individual. Any repair would require the individual to acknowledge and embrace that portion of their self, allowing them to contrast it with the distortion causing the damage. This process would then enable healing. The implication is that, through this process, the person then would have grown by exposure to a previously unknown aspect of their reality, ultimately becoming a more complete and self-aware being.

Many clinical psychologists are able to recognize mental illness on the spot except when they see it in the mirror: "*Ahh, content*," they exclaim in the morning, as another word for depression. After all, if depression took you away from unbearable anxiety, what is there not to be content about? And when you are back to normalcy and being dismissed from therapy, your psychologist brings success to the closure, as the assessment of your contentment. But why should you not be content if you are getting out of therapy?

But there are among them one or two rogue heroes who have been there, done that. They will gently blow a couple of lazy leaves off the ground, just to uncover the rabbit hole where your insanity dwells deep inside. They will see you go in, and follow beside you, gently inspecting each discovery along the way, both face up and face down, seeing them for what they are, unaffected by the uncharted truths that lie beyond your place of insanity. They will witness your first glimpse of human wisdom the moment you are free at last, on the other side. They are heroes, not because they seek recognition, but because the truths they carry live within the comfort of their individuality and privacy. These truths are not the uncomfortable, mediated beliefs that need constant validation and appeasement through preaching. It is from this place of private inner comfort that they shall remain anonymous. Their heroism is borne of anonymity. I mention it as a formality, and out of context, because the role of the rogue hero who ventures into the rabbit hole was never part of the charter for this discipline. It never was.

Psychology has claimed an intellectual ownership of the self. It has appropriated by intellectual means the term "self," which only exists in the emotional realm. With respect to the emotional composition of human beings, psychiatry has traditionally played an opposition role. It has not exactly been an advocate of humans as essential emotional beings, because humanity has been criticized intellectually as irrational. Psychiatry is a surrogate for belief, intellectualizing our human experience and distancing it from any genuine human touch. To any of you who are preparing the creation of a new religion, I will ask you to add a new commandment for me: *"Thou shalt not pronounce the words 'psychology' and 'self' in the same sentence."* However, psychiatrists can be excused, because they do not have to relate to the self. Psychiatrists have the advantage of being able to medicate you into oblivion if they spot even the slightest sign of a self emerging from the numbed, amorphous block that you've become. Psychologists, on the other hand, are left to deal with that self—your self—using their intellectual potions to bring closure, ultimately letting out a sigh of relief when they close their door behind you for one last time.

4.5. *Democracy and Self-Combustion*

Democracy is an indulgent, fragile, and self-destructive political experiment in which the inalienable power of individual liberty, combined with the certification of imaginary realities, sets the table for inexorable, spontaneous self-combustion—an outcome that can only be defused with individual emotional autonomy and a firm grasp of reality.

Let's take a look.

Democracy gives power to the individual, relying on their strength and integrity to sustain it. A democracy is built on the individual rights of its citizens, but in practice, it acts as a surrogate ideology, relying on blanket beliefs, like religion, to transfer religious precepts into political doctrines that shape individual indoctrination. Religion and democracy (and political power in general) act in an ideal surrogacy relationship. Religion has for millennia bent the population into submission, but in modern times, it no longer enjoys the forceful mechanisms to do so. Political (totalitarian) structures offer those enforcements, including financial punishments, incarcerations, and death.

Democracy, as one specific political structure, implements surrogacy in a number of ways. One way is by enforcing otherwise unenforceable religious precepts. Another way specific to democracy is by enforcement of individual rights stemming from religious doctrines, such as equality and individual liberty—rights that religion itself lacks the power to enforce. While some of these enforcements take place under the umbrella of democracy's (expanding) individual liberty, they can only be accomplished by actually restricting these liberties and depriving individuals of their rights. It is the narrowing of religion enacted through surrogacy. Democracy is built under two premises: a presumption of a common reality upon which democracy will abide by its rules, and the resulting individual inalienable liberties.

During the course of our entire human civilization, reality has never been duly accredited or given any respect or value, and it exists primarily only to be distorted, changed, dismissed, destroyed, and recreated as something else. Democracy is built on the power to sustain a set of premises under an existing set of commonly accepted realities which can be objectively assessed. Obviously, without a sense of accreditation of these realities and the logic stemming from them, common premises do not exist; democracy crumbles and sets the democracy experiment in peril.

What sets democracy apart from other political forms, such as political dictatorships that suppress the individual perception of reality, is its reliance on an understanding of reality and its accreditation of that reality through the liberties granted to individuals. This is what sets it in a particular collision course with individual emotional autonomy as the eventual guardian of our rational perception of reality. This is why emotional autonomy is of foremost importance to the guard railing and evolution of democracy.

When the common understanding of reality has already been destroyed, democracies are left vulnerable and exposed. They are forced to rely on the madness of misunderstood individual liberty—*the inalienable unchecked right to arbitrarily invent, distort, trash, neglect, manipulate, circumvent, retract, ignore, destroy, and recreate reality.* This inevitably elevates herd mentality citizens above the laws of reality, conferring upon them the status of gods. In doing so, they align their self-assigned rights and liberties with their exercise of the vote, making them the sempiternal forever-sweet targets for herd manipulation.

Reality is a big deal. If you can defy reality, such as by walking on water or floating through the air, we will promptly call you a god. And so, by the individual power that democracy invested in you, and by your inexhaustible ability to distort and recreate reality, you can proclaim yourself a god. There you have it. But there is logic to madness, and if your newly crafted reality is unable to jive above the logical foundations of yours and our democracy, we will need to conclude that you have just lost your marbles, have no sense of reality, and our humble glossary will

4. BELIEFS AND SURROGACY

have a term just for you: you are an idiot—something you get to keep for posterity.

So this is all good news. Gods are being created or discovered, we are now in a human procession, making newly unchecked decisions as we move into an unchecked future—one that is our own, cleansed from the burdens, constraints and responsibilities of the past. But here is the hiccup—reality is what reality is and not what we say it is. Having the power of liberty combined with distorted realities at our fingertips, is the prime formula for spontaneous, colossal self-combustion. This may happen so quickly that the originators may not have the luxury of time to see consequences. We saw this hiccup in Germany in 1945—it led to the interrupted mass suicide of that country—that would be a hiccup.

In a democracy, unchecked individual power and the corruption to distort, destroy, and recreate realities, forms the prime recipe for spontaneous self-combustion. This unstable state of self-combustion will remain brewing in democracies for the foreseeable future. Two things need to happen before this self-imploding volatility can be defused. First, the value of reality must be fully accredited: a new understanding and its role in society needs to lead to a full respect for the natural logic laws of our surrounding realities. Second, societies must adopt a perspective that allows individuals to emotionally immerse themselves in a path that breaks through the armoured defenses blocking our emotional states, enabling them to reach their long-sought emotional autonomy, no longer subject to manipulation and herd mentality.

Without emotional autonomy, democracy is impossible—it will never be a reliable, consistent social movement. Without emotional autonomy, the quest for a new accreditation of reality will never be reached. Emotional autonomy is the only name of the game.

As we are exposed to a zoological array of personalities in politics—narcissistic, grandiose, vain, self-serving, subservient, opportunistic, revengeful, merciless, heartless, criminal and genocidal—we could over-simplify and say that above all those traits lies ignored one fundamental trait that feeds all others—being an idiot. In our attraction for oversimplification, we can just say that an *idiot is simply a recalcitrant individual with no sense of reality*. And we learned in third grade geography that idiocy is a swampy, soggy islet in a big toxic lake of ignorance and self-denial.

With a new understanding and respect for reality, if and only then, we will be in position to make a case as to why idiots can no longer be allowed to vote. And so, my fellow citizens, as the torch shall have passed to countless new generations ahead, ask not why you are not allowed to vote, but how you can bring reality to bear.

Equality

It is obvious that blanket religious beliefs, as well as surrogate disciplines like philosophy, have served as the foundation for developing derivative beliefs in other areas, such as politics. For example, out of necessity, democratic politics are built on the notion of presumed equality. Without equality there is no democracy.

If someone listened to a conversation of mine with a friend about the existential risks at stake for us as we accept the challenges of a deeper reality, that listener may think that our understanding of life and reality is superior to what they would even consider. Conversely, if I were to listen to someone else's conversation, I could be left speechless, as the issues at stake in their life would dwarf the comparatively trivial and superficial nature of my own life playground. So that is the thing, we are not all that equal. Call us all equal if you want, by whatever platitude you choose, but we are not all that equal, especially in what matters—not in terms of our emotional stature and subsequent understanding of reality. Equality is oversold.

I look at equality not to prove that it does not exist, but to understand it as the surrogate, trickled down construct from religious and philosophical beliefs.

Inequality

So that brings us to inequality. After 5000 years of civilization, we are still unable to understand that inequality is not an implied reason or justification for oppression, domination or exploitation. The only natural way of relating to inequality is by fostering our desire to complement each other to form richer, longer-lasting, mutually rewarding relationships. There is nothing more beautiful than to know you can contribute as no one else can, and that for someone else, you are it. Therefore inequality is not an instrument for oppression or domination. Such a social misconception has been very conveniently created with perversion for the purposes of massive, pervasive exploitation.

We see politicians in democracies act as circus contortionists in their public speeches, convincingly proclaiming that we are all equal. Yet, in their next sentence, they negate this by exalting the fact that we are all different, we are that melting pot with different and unrelated contexts, backgrounds and struggles. But thankfully, a third sentence soon follows to relieve our discomfort, declaring that we are still all equal "under the law"—that magic end to the dissent. Perfect cue for a pause, an applause, and a gulp of water.

Richard Dawkins (2001) notes the intentional secularity of the founding fathers of the United States, but their reasoning and wording still demonstrated the opposite—their inescapable perception of the world as created by God. How can our equality be granted to us by their promulgation of "self-evident truths"? Where did these self-evident truths come from? They did so by passing the buck to God, under the presumption that it was God who created us equal, but maybe not so equal if one species exists to take advantage of another, like orcas making a living by feeding off seals. I fail to see the self-evidence of God-conferred equality here. And why would a higher consciousness bestow such a notion of equality? This assumes that there is a creation of consciousness by another consciousness as a deliberate artisan process of hierarchical governance, carefully calibrated so that despite some apparent differences, we could all come out equal at the end, thus recognizing that this is no longer an autonomous spontaneous event. Furthermore, we assume that this equality is very selective, like being accepted into a private country club. Humans are equal to humans and only to humans. "But what about gorillas and orangutans?"—sorry guys, just keep scratching your backs. Can we please relieve the pressure of feeling domesticated by equality and take it to the animal kingdom and just say that we are at least superior to other animals? But how could the founding fathers, these wise patriarchs of any country know that? And be so smart in simplifying the process by leaving women out—just for the time being? Their understanding of equality could only come from an implied belief in the religion of a God, despite their futile attempts at intellectual secular emancipation as noted by Dawkins.

When countless future generations watch the political speeches that today make us cry, they will not help but be embarrassed for us for the primitive way in which our intersocial political relationships needed to be defined to prevent society from collapsing.

Living in a world of mythical beliefs encourages the fabrication of "self-evident truths," passed down to us from birth, providing the convenient relief from what is not to be questioned. After all, we are a consumption society, and that includes, above all, myths and self-evident truths. They pop up everywhere—philosophy would not exist without them, religion has claimed many, and politics has done its best to mix and match religion and philosophy as needed. Self-evident truths are the roots of any discipline, ideology, or religion—and you get to take them all out at the knees—enjoy.

As long as we misunderstand inequality as an implied reason for oppression and domination, the concept of equality will remain a caricature, under unbearable pressure, burdened with the overstressed responsibility of bringing about a peaceful reductionist collectivization.

As inequality needs to stay in the closet, we can say that as long as we lack a collective respect and understanding of reality, the notion of equality—at least as we pretend to understand it—becomes an oxymoron: how can it be self-evident that we are all equal under each person's disjointed, non-intersecting, fabricated pseudo reality?

Why do I bring this up? For one, it highlights the pervasive nature of our process of internalizing beliefs. All we seem to do in this life is open our mouths and swallow. But more importantly, it underscores a deeper issue: after 5000 years of civilization, we are unable to recognize the intrinsic value of just being ourselves. If we recognized it, the notion of equality or inequality would be irrelevant. That is why the notion of equality is such a derogatory, uncomfortably demeaning term that we all have to swallow. Our civilization does not recognize that inside each of us there is a home that we are meant to own and inhabit, and it is from that home that we are meant to live our lives and not from an external collective layer of equality. This example shows how far away our civilization is from making that concession and allowing us to live in emotional autonomy.

This is also an example of how blanket beliefs permeate surrogate beliefs, which in turn permeate every facet of our life. Concepts like these must be deconstructed as we navigate this intricate jungle, guiding us to an understanding of the self yet unknown.

Should we just abandon the notion of equality all together? We cannot because the world will self-destruct. Besides, we have the perfect excuse to hold on to it: equality, as we know it, hasn't even been fully realized anywhere. First, we must see it firmly established throughout the entire planet. First things first, and that buys us a lot of time. Once reality gains traction, standing on its own without reliance on mythological beliefs as the driving force of our civilization or being subject to disdain or manipulation, we will finally be able to exercise reality as a way of life.

Politics of the Herd

As we look at inequality in the context of politics, we might fall back on the idea that everyone is superior and inferior in different ways to everyone else. But if we break down those attributes in more detail, we may find that they can often be explained by more subtle reasons that encompass different contexts and perspectives. This may lead us to better classify individual traits as less comparable differentiators. However, we don't want to abandon the notion of inferiority altogether. It is important that, in some respects, we allow ourselves to view others as superior in order to de-stigmatize the idea of inferiority and remove toxic implications like denigration and condescension.

This would help us establish a clear distinction between natural inferiority and a so-called inferiority complex, which is a unstable self-image that seeks constant appeasement and plays a fundamental role in herding the masses towards the indoctrination of beliefs and political cults. Our connection to our inferiority complex is never straightforward or transparent. Because this complex has been forcefully imposed, it travels inwards with a thirst for retribution, manifesting as anger, control, unforgiveness, domination, and superiority, all complemented by reality distortions needed for these emotional aberrations to take root. This understanding of herd politics suggests that a political exchange fought on objective reasoned facts will unlikely be won, because it is instead decided within the inner substrates of the psyche. Thus, the politician who exploits these substrates instead of objective realities is the one who can persuasively dominate these masses. At the end of the day, we can then see that such political outcomes are the direct result of the populace's lack of emotional autonomy.

It is clear that for a herd with a common, ingrained complex of inferiority, the political intention is to create the mirage of a false compensatory narrative, which is by its collective nature manipulative and needs to be assimilated by indoctrination.

All these cultural gaps can create self-conscious, inner instabilities that need to be appeased by exporting these insecurities into external, fabricated realities, and this mechanism is a classic example of herd manipulation. Consider, for example, the education front. When we have experts in the field of public health, they bring their well educated knowledge and experience as a form of expertise—superiority if you will—that others do not possess. When this expertise gap is accepted naturally, the value of their arguments can be evaluated more objectively. Otherwise, this gap stimulates the inner discomfort of a pervasive inferiority complex requiring massive authoritarian appeasement to bring an unexisting equality to the table. This can be accomplished by dismissing everything these experts say and overriding the dialog with overpowering control.

4.6. A Paper-Thin Unidimensionality

I want to redescribe another differentiator when comparing the intellectual world with emotionality, as we find in intellectual psychological literature when advancing insights in human nature (Pinker, 2003), or when mining for "self-evident truths" in philosophy. This intellectual approach is intrinsically unidimensional. By that I mean that it does not advance the state of deeper emotional insights beyond what is literally stated. It seems deep emotionality is neglected by the intellectual process, and nothing will be offered at a deeper level because of its stagnation in the flatlands of statistical findings and results, which are only collective regurgitations of the narrative coming into the system, so no deeper insights will be forthcoming. Therefore, the narrative stays flat, unidimensional, and "horizontal." The arguments intended about the self, remain caged within that unidimensionality, with no option to escape. The reason for this intellectual approach is obvious. Our sense of self is alive and emotional, and intellectuality is trapped in the confines of neglecting our sense of self, which is purely emotional, out of reach. It is therefore impossible to move into emotional territory. I illustrate this unidimensionality later with an example in the section, *"Truth Formation."*

PART II, Dismantling Beliefs

5. Deconstructing Beliefs

The fact that beliefs have stayed with us for thousands of years is a testament to how difficult they are to eradicate. Let us now consider what lies ahead if we entertain the possibility of living without beliefs.

5.1. My Beliefs, My Gods

This section takes a scenic route through the process of creating our own beliefs. This is our opportunity to take liberties previously denied to mere mortals, unordained to bring the heavens to Earth. If beliefs were created by humans to begin with, we can create our own. However, unlike recalcitrant beliefs that need to be adopted as articles of blind faith under penalty of death by the sword, we create playful speculative beliefs just to prove that sometimes our imaginative fantasy can take us closer to hidden truths. It shows a way to view belief as a purely emotional, exploratory and voluntary experience. Its levity might be met with disdain, burdened as we are by 5000 years of solemn submission to the divine, wrapped in pompous and grave reverence. Thus we might fail to recognize that the path to the non-physical is, above all, playful—like a game of hopscotch—and surprising—where the path to our gods may hide the path to ourselves.

Given the irreparable damage of our millennia-long addiction to archaic mythical belief systems, consider this alternative: rather than continuing to exalt ourselves through grandiose myths that once again subordinate our free will and intuition to external absolutes, or resting complacently on the apotheosis of well-worn philosophical "truths," let us instead find time better spent creating our own soft, speculative, and private belief systems—lackadaisical and whimsical. These beliefs will not bring back external absolutism into our inner selves, but will allow us to play with our free-flowing intuition, desires, fantasies and imagination about everything timeless, rewarding and beautiful. This detour would allow us to play out emotions with the sublime value of having been created with abandon, in the most whimsical and spontaneous fashion.

Gods Without a Cause

Most religions, and certainly traditional Christianity, make the adherence to their beliefs and practices obligatory, under the misperception that we need their gods in order to attain a false perception of autonomy in our physical lives. This creates a contradiction. Such an obligation is compelling, but it robs us of the freedom to think independently about the non-physical world.

Who needs God when you have Elvis Presley on a poster inside your wardrobe door and the best looking guy in town as your best friend, too cool to surrender a smile, not even to your mother as he takes you away from her on the road to perdition? My mother's youngest brother by fifteen years came into this world to disrupt the family harmony of live music played at my uncles' house where we spent our summer vacation—the lazy syncopation of Antônio Carlos Jobim's bossa nova (1962), occasionally interwoven with the love of God, Sunday mass and the morality radiated by church sermons. These gutsy sermons signaled that the status quo of dressing chic to parties were soon to be over. For my youngest uncle—the classic rebel without a cause—life began every day at 6 PM with the ceremonial combing of his hair to create that high greasy panache, trembling but never coming undone at the rhythmic snap of a finger. He wore his leather jacket in city heat that would melt street asphalt at 3 PM every day, signaling that the night would revive itself from the night before, while the rhythm of the day slipped into a lazy sleepy intermission. Hair done and he would vanish without notice from the universe that we kids called our household.

Our other two uncles would go at it with him after another late Saturday night proved once again that the road to perdition is the road of no return. Their faces, stern with moral indignation, would be met with his sarcastic mockery, irrepressible laughter, and clever, incisive name calling—exactly the kind of retaliation designed by the devil himself. La Mimi, my grandma, such a boisterous happy person, now speechless, would nod her head in disapproval and terminal resignation. For us kids, watching these exchanges was more fun than the 5 PM cartoons of Heckle and Jeckle on TV. All we needed to do in life was to take sides–easier to do without the compromising moral investiture of sacraments yet to come.

My sister and I met my uncle's sarcasm with sarcasm, his name calling with name calling, and an eye for an eye. We mocked the morality of the family with disdain, replaying intonation, inflexion and exclamation phrases, laughing at him and vilifying his immoral prowesses, trashing him with his own dose of sarcasm. Sister and I still celebrate the fact that the nicknames he inflicted on us never percolated to the ranks of our high schools. We ridiculed him because he was not a true follower of the gods of rock and roll. It was well understood by us that the mean streak these gods dramatized on stage was meant to be reenacted for real by their followers in the streets, and my uncle did not have that mean streak—too nice without a cause, and for his own good. All he had was idolatry for his gods, aimed at preserving the purity of cool and providing a feast for us two kids—but it was true idolatry nonetheless. There are some laws in the universe you are not meant to break—there is no crying in baseball, and there is no drooling in cool. You cannot go around showing too much admiration, or repentance for that matter. One time my uncle was beaten up and kicked somewhere out in the streets. He didn't defend himself because he was holding a little bag of flower seeds he was bringing to his big sister, a second mother to him, and first mother to us. He didn't want to lose those seeds—way outside cool. And so, he carried them with him, bruises and all. Still no moral mercy from the older uncles. We kids guessed that God's morality moved in a straight line.

We understood at an early age that the only way to award equality to another human being was through irrepressible sarcasm. It was like jumping in the mud to make it splash in somebody else's face, until we all end up covered in mud. Dust to dust with mud in between. My sister and I share our identity with the generation of my mother's extended family, inheriting many idiosyncratic traits that became signatures of their last name, with virtues like generosity in the face of adversity standing out most of all. As a physician, my grandfather, upon arriving in a beautiful rainforest coffee town in the mountains to live near his brother, had flyers announcing his practice: *"5 córdobas per consultation, and free for the poor."* There! That was our family signature. But my sister and I also had an understanding as kids that you could only truly become a member of our family and deserving of our last name by relating to our uncle with that two-way sarcasm—equality, equality to all. If you treated him with false distant respect and well disguised moral condescension, not able to sarcastically ridicule him as an equal, you were not family—not one of us. And so it was that nobody ever became a member of our private family club. By our standards of entry, only my sister and I were deserving of our last name, which came to die with the two of us.

My youngest uncle had subversive plans for me, wanting me to grow up in his image and likeness—a godless plan easy to devise, as it simply ran counter to anything else the family had forged. One time, when I was still a little child, probably five, he took me to a neighborhood cinema, with no air conditioning and thick pillars supporting the second floor, which you had to avoid if you wanted a clear view of the screen. We managed to sit within the first few rows. Then, a screen message appeared from the cinema owner: *"May the culture of our people be the exponent of our race."* It was a futile attempt to calm the restlessness of the crowd of savages and prevent them from enacting their daily repertoire of bad behavior—couples in the back seats taking out their bubble gum to make out like there was no tomorrow (and there wasn't), or kids in the upper floor pouring their drinks on the crowd below who couldn't pay the higher fare for upstairs seating. But the announcement served only to incite the true exponent of our race, and elicit objects to be thrown at the screen. The movie started—it was an old movie in replay—and on the screen, bigger than life in black and white, there came Dion and The Belmonts in their suits with thin ties walking towards you, snapping their fingers and singing *The Wanderer* (Dion, 2024). My jaw dropped to let the flies in, and I never spoke a word that night. Rock and roll was born.

My uncle and his friends did prove that rebels without a cause all die young. My uncle never got his wish to see me raised in his image and likeness and get from me what he wanted. I grew to be pulled in by everything math and science, too proper to follow in his steps. But when it came to rock and roll—then he got from me everything he wanted. But yet, the razor sharp sarcasm with which we treated each other, beyond the confines of proper family cordiality, set for me the perspective with which I would see life inside and out. The love of God never came to me. To this day, I have never been compelled to speak of the love of God and the love for that raspy voice of Little Richard (1958, 1995) in the same sentence.

Sarcasm made room for my identity. When I saw confining morality rubbing elbows next to me, it reminded me that I was from another world—a rebel without a cause of sorts, in black and white. It gave me wings to fly to places where my own sense of self could take shape.

And with that secular sarcastic equality, we broke that generational obligation to be at the service of God's morality. We conferred ourselves the freedom to shop around for our own gods and beliefs, or live in the earthly paradise of their inexistence.

As rock and roll came to me for the first time, I understood, walking back through the urban streets and hearing voices and music playing through the open doors, that for us children, it was a promise of becoming something ahead that we weren't yet. For me, rock and roll gave birth to music—the rest of it. So many Latin American and U.S. cultures came all through my pores as mine, through music. Music followed me and nourished my introspection. When I came to the U.S. for graduate school, the cultural separation was abysmal and the isolation vast and inhospitable, like an infinite lunar landscape perched on a black celestial space with an unreachable horizon. Oddly enough, it made that entire space mine. It became prime ground to stand on my own and walk alone for the first time. Through these fields of landmines and magma eruptions came realizations about myself—who I was before and who I might become. I left my uncle and everyone behind, as music became mine in a way that only mine could be, because now I was walking alone where only I could walk. In season, I was both hunter and hunted, and music was my only sustenance. Every landmine, every realization and discovery of myself was brought home with music and bathed with rivers of tears, sometimes until dawn. Through my new understanding, the blessed beauty of wisdom was becoming mine. This lunar landscape was a blessing in disguise, because it was an entire planet inhabited only by me, and impossible to have experienced without the cultural crossing I was walking through. But it was that old gift of music that carried me.

Fusion of Essentials

We could make the assumption that the more powerful our made-up notion of the divine, the better chance it may contain a grain of truth. If it turns out to be true, then our life will be less in vain and we will be rewarded with more seamless synchrony in our transition away from this life. Conversely, the more delusional we are and our imagination more irrational and misconstrued, the more of a price to pay when we make the transition at odds to more natural and encompassing realities. So if we are delusional and we go out on a limb with our own incongruent made-up beliefs, we will pay the price later in our transition. But then we are already delusional, and whether we venture into our imagination or not, we are already paying that price in advance. Really the only real shame of it is that we are oblivious to what that price actually is.

While spending many years at a U.S. university graduate school, most of my friends were Latin Americans and Europeans, and they did what foreigners do. They left God's country for a better place—maybe a place where the word of God is not backed by guns. The only U.S. male friend that I made at school was in the Ph.D. program with me. I had not seen him in a very long time when recently, he came over to stay at my house for a couple of days. Then I realized that he had become a god. Just that—he is now a god. And how did I come to such an atypical conclusion? Why is he a god? Primarily, because that is what I thought. I see his attributions and facets of himself as indivisible, no longer fragmented or scattered; there's no need to transition from one to the other: his intellectual precocity in computer science, his practice and teaching of martial arts, his unhesitant sarcasm towards anything that moves—including the idiotic thought processes of tech celebrities in his path—his love of family, and his mastery of espresso coffee preparation.

He has an ingrained non-US-centric global view of the world which is more meaningful and rare than we often concede, especially for U.S. men who never venture outside their control zone. U.S. women have a broader view of the world which comes from their ability to lend their emotional selves to uncertainty, just to satisfy their curiosity. The word curiosity does not quite jive with U.S. men the same way, as it often implies the opposite, a zooming, narrowing intellectual focus and hardly ever a widening emotional one. Just look at the population that has the emotional malleability to learn and speak a new language like a native, and you will hardly find a man in that count.

In the U.S., the individual global view of the world is misconstrued by misunderstanding our privileges as false superiority from which we create a bubble to relate to the rest of the world. These privileges in our consumer society buy us comfort, personal isolation, and a distorted social naivete that keeps us disconnected from essential direct human connectivity, creating a personality stereotype that is both apparent and laughable abroad. When your view is confined to a narcissistic need for self-centeredness, then your global view decays to nothing more than a parasitic, inward-looking form of permanent evasion. It shows a false superiority inbred from privilege, and it does expose you to the laughable stereotype that it showcases.

My friend's non-US-centric global view counters this stereotype. It is an understanding of privilege and skill that is not rooted in comfort or education, but in more natural, intrinsic human values, way down at a common bottom of equality. It represents quite a free fall from the heights of encapsulated false superiority and it remains a rare human trait to possess. For my friend, all of his facets come with free, visible access from the outside. All of this is indivisible in him; you can no longer separate one from the other as you could before. And as all these essentials have come together, his inner self has become denser, smaller, lighter. As a result, he looks like he could walk on air. Given that I have no experience in the materialization of gods, my conclusion was that he is a god, and I began to treat him as one. And on top of that, he does not age, remaining bony and lean like he did in yesteryear. Sometimes I think I am too cool to fall for anybody, but I guess I am a sucker for someone who fuses their essentials. My jaw drops in amazement, letting the flies in, and in my defense, even nuclear physicists will tell you that fusion is a big deal. I would not say he is perfect, and I think I can offer a helping hand here and there, but he is still a god.

—+—+—

When I am in a social gathering with friends, absorbed in my own thoughts, living in my own form of non-centric global perspective, I just imagine the free fall that people around me have to endure, to land at that common bottom of equality, a place where they are able to socialize in a world that is way down the line, not first or second. This thought sends shivers down my spine because I am so afraid of heights. Sometimes I see in my wandering imagination, their bones already crushed from the fall, just to realize it was a free fall they never took and never will, as they are still enjoying a drink.

If you take that fall into that common bottom, and find yourself surrounded by an unrecognizable world with unfamiliar realities, you are bound to come across someone perhaps having had enough grandchildren, without a cell phone, not a dime to her name, illiterate with no shortness of eloquence, no concept of subservience and no loss of autonomy for the vast financial divide surrounding her. Then you can either retreat into a world that is all about yourself, or just look at her, pause and see what she means by life, and how she owns her own world. Without your weight of superiority, you may get to think "Oh I get it." You will give a little wink, a little smile, and like in the Irish movie *The Commitments* (1991), show a little tenderness. Then you get your three minutes of introspection and wonder, *"what is it that I have given up that she hasn't?"* You will have arrived to ponder your own questions to yourself for which you don't have an answer. You have arrived at something yours, that little piece of unanswerable void that is yours and only yours, your own little piece of nothingness, all without breaking a bone in the fall.

But at the bottom, a little void sits on a big void: the big vast raw underbelly of civilization. Bigger than all the layers of choreographed and counter choreographed civility in a well elaborated world. Bigger because it is the bottom. A wedding cake is always bigger at the bottom, not at the top where the plastic figurines of a happy couple lay staring at you forever. And for you, the bottom is this new culture that in some ways you despise and spit on for its traditions, its values and its conditions. There is no authenticity in it or any culture because authenticity and culture disintegrate each other, and the worst you can think is that you can submerge and be one with it. But if you stay outside, you can see its autonomous power to generate life bonded in eternal individual isolation camouflaged by the culture's internal overpowering context. One day something may click in you, and you will say, "Oh I get it." You will remain outside a culture that now rubs elbows with you and that you don't mind; yet that raw, vast underbelly of unchoreographed life will now stay with you, leaving you better for it. But that place is reserved only for a few individuals who have eyes that take their time transitioning slowly from place to place, not for the rest of us.

—+—+—

Let's not let go of sarcasm, where the shallow see-through crystalline waters of irreverence which beautifully reflect cloud and sun, turn into a mud pit. Sarcasm is the cleansing of false respect. Sarcasm is an art—the roundabout art of encircling a person before deciding to relate. It is also the art of cutting the mustard to strip away layers of unearned respect. If it is not poignant, it is not sarcasm. If it is toxic, it is not sarcasm. Sarcasm also serves a social function. The sarcasm in my high school was explosive, merciless, funny, and off the charts. The time for that brand of sarcasm is gone, and we will not see it again. It should have been used by sociologists to predict the level of seismic social changes to come. I think sarcasm was so pronounced in our high school because we knew we were all on our way to hell, and laughter was the fastest way down the spiral. Sarcasm is an art to aspire to. If you do not have sarcasm, you do not exist, or better said with the help of Robert De Niro ("Bobby" to his New York italian friends), as Al Capone in the movie *The Untouchables* in 1987: "*You got nothing, nothing, you are nothing.*"

—+—+—

If you have an issue with my approach to creating gods, you can always voice a complaint. You can even sue me. But you will have to do it in the afterlife, where my creational approach can be proven wrong. You will have to find me. I will not be next to those angels and archangels with their tender, softly twisted chubby little hands reaching out to the skies, so beautifully painted by Botticelli and Michelangelo. But you will find me.

A note of sobriety about my friend. His personality now draws my attention because of how cohesive it is. It signifies progression for him and will fare well in his transitions and his future. What is important is that, at the end of the day, my intuition and emotions are probably quite fitting. Not being confined by the way I describe his progression gives me free rein to amplify my emotions, though they will still fall short of doing justice to the physical and timeless being he is. So if we are going to fall short no matter what, why not come closer with well-targeted imagination?

You Got Nothing, You Are Nothing

You or I may one day be commissioned to design a new religion. In my case it would be self-service and all, with formulas for calculating penalty time in the contrition fields. Take luggage for example: the more suitcases and the more weight you carry, the more time you would spend in the contrition fields, all according to the formula. If you could not lift and walk with all of your luggage, if you had to drag your luggage, more time in the contrition fields. No need to speculate about your unbearable lightness of being—we would take that right from your luggage. The religion would be eagerly proactive, which meant that because of lack of access to any celestial space, the time in the contrition fields would have had to be served on Earth before passing away, and someone would have to think of renting space, say, in a desert, a volcanic caldera, or a swamp. I think the Everglades would be very convenient to Floridians, with plenty of space for all of them, and a reptile fauna to boot. All they would have to do prior is to watch *Naked and Afraid* on TV (for jungle survival), and bring their binoculars. Since I do not like to be called "sir," this would be my opportunity to request, as payment for my design, a title of religious nobility, such as prophet or vicar. Unfortunately, until a project of this caliber gets underway, I will still be called "sir."

It is clear to me now that I will remain anonymous among the masses. But maybe, even without my participation in the creative process of a new religion, I could still be considered a deity of some kind by some merciful souls. It does not have to be that grandiose—I would take anything really. Maybe a guardian angel with a spear and shield. And given that I have extended the courtesy of anointing others as deities, maybe I can also be looked upon with kindness and have my case up for favorable review. I come across somewhat dispersed through the different facets of my life. One thing I can say is that when I have had to dive into an emotional underwater cave without an oxygen tank, I seemed to have had the ability to find that hidden crack in between the rocks at the bottom, and with two seconds of oxygen to spare in my lungs, manage to squeeze through the slit into a brand new reality. I guess that's why I like people who are always looking for themselves, finding themselves over and over. I love people who are late in life, in their eighties perhaps, and still trying to find themselves. I just think it is so beautiful to see people never assuming that what they have is it.

But back to my review. Unfortunately, my life is that of a survivalist, always searching the murky waters for a little ray of light to squeeze through. It is hardly the venerable, parsimonious quality of emanating wisdom that is proper of a deity. And so, you wonder, can this person lead the life of contemplative peace of a deity? Not a chance. And so, by decision time, if we want to gather my gains from each of these many life facets and add them up like collected alms for the poor at the end of mass, I am afraid we may look inside the alms bag and find it almost empty. As I wait outside, the person in charge of locking up the sanctuary will come to the door and bring me the news: *"You got nothing, nothing. You are nothing."*

You Never Left

For my last birthday with my mom, while I was back home with her during those months, she kept asking my sister, who lives in another country, to come for the occasion. She insisted it would be the last time that we would be together, but my sister did not take the statement literally and never made the trip. Even though we hadn't celebrated birthdays in years, my mother was adamant about hosting a dinner party for mine, growing increasingly stressed at the thought it might not happen. During the party, I remember her sitting in a corner of the crowded table, squeezed by the younger generation sitting next to her. To fit in, she had to keep her elbows very close to her body, clearly showing that life was now compressing her. She looked pensive and silent, focusing on her food while the rest of us were having animated conversations. I watched. The tenderness of that moment will continue to live inside of me for as long as I walk this Earth—blessed for life. I have not known tenderness like what I felt for my mom in that instant. After dinner she began speaking at length, almost as if delivering a speech. Gradually the room grew quiet as everyone listened. Her words were about me—what she thought of me, how wonderful she thought I was, her reflections on my progression through life, and her perception of my accomplishments and successes as a person. She spoke about my ability to stay grounded enduring adversity, and emphasized that I had already become what I was meant to be. I did not realize that she was setting the table for her departure. Now I realize that her sense of urgency was to give that speech and pass the baton to me.

That night I had a dream that our doctor, all dressed in his white gown, emerged from a long corridor through big white double doors. When he appeared, he nodded to us with a somber, negative gesture. The following evening, I was in my room preparing my running gear for a 26 km run next morning. It was an uphill route through a rainforest to a mountain divide along a small dirt trail just wide enough for one vehicle. The run would take me to a ridge where I could run for a few kilometers along the mountain's divide—a route that I had just devised and was excited to experience for the first time. I heard my mom make a quick sound like "ussht," as she used to when she pinched her finger. Normally, I wouldn't think much of it, but this time something compelled me to rush immediately to her room. When I got there, she looked at me, quite surprised by the inexplicable pain in her chest. I ran to her side and held her as she began to fall, and we both fell to the floor. But by then, she was already dead from a heart attack. We called our doctor and rushed to the hospital. After a while our doctor came through those double doors that I had only ever seen in my dream the previous night, and he nodded the news. I do not know who brought me the news the night before in that dream, or why. Was it an announcement, a warning, or just a tear in the physical-spiritual fabric? I just don't know. But I know it was not a random coincidence.

As we all began to cry so intensely, I noticed her presence inside me quite vividly. I was used to deep emotions whenever I left my family of origin—feeling so close to them, sensing their presence—but this was different. It felt as though she was with me, living inside of me keeping me company. It was different. I felt as if everything we spoke, we were speaking as a duet—as if we both were saying it at the same time. And she was with me at all times, every second. On the ninth day, as we came back home in the evening from the last mass of her novenario, and we sat with family on the front porch of our house, I noticed that suddenly she was not there. I was all by myself again. I thought that I would have that feeling back, that this was just a lapse, but that feeling never came back again.

Two important issues come to mind: one is for us to just consider if something like this can happen. Can this happen? The other is how much more reassuring, exuberant, sheltering, embracing and perdurable our emotions are if we let ourselves believe our intuition without the constraints of presumed reality. Even with all our exuberance, our emotions will inevitably fall short from the actual magnificence of the emotions merited by that departure. With faith safely out of the way, we can allow ourselves to believe what we want to believe, while we wait for a definitive assertion of truth—whenever the Universe, in its own time, chooses to reveal it.

I cried for five years straight after the passing of my mom. Whenever it hurt, the private, personal pride I felt for us having been together would just swell out of my chest and protect and sweeten my wound, so I was safe. My wound was very sweet.

One month later, we did that mountain divide running route. I ran while Sister and Dad drove in the truck behind me negotiating the narrow dirt trail—the family, all of us, quietly together one more time. It was an early morning run, climbing under the rain forest canopy and emerging out to the divide for the last three kilometers, where I was touched by the sun and could see forever to both sides, and forever ahead of me. Then I left the country. Sister and Dad went to the airport and I got into this tubular metallic claustrophobic apparatus sanitized from any natural life, heat, sweat, wind, forest and sun, and I left. That was by far the hardest day of my life, and I was quite unsure I could survive it. My mom had left us a month before, but now I was leaving her and my dad and my sister. I spent 6 claustrophobic hours adding mile after mile between myself and Sister and Dad until it was open air again in a land that did not know me and did not recognize me. It had no knowledge of anything I am, I was or anything that had happened. Dumbfounded, I did not speak a word for one month.

In my home country, they know me. They are never friendly enough, never friendly to that sweaty lone runner in those country road hills. They have never seen me before, but they know me enough not to like me all that much. I must be one of those that spit on the poor and take whatever meager material possessions they have, just to convince myself I am better than those who have to work and sweat under the sun. That distance they create is a tacit acknowledgement of my presence and who I might be, but never a ratification of confidence in me. Never the benefit of the doubt, but an acknowledgement nonetheless. And I will take that any day. It feels like home to me. Acknowledgement as a presumed agreement of understanding or misunderstanding is a dying human trait. Friendliness is oversold.

Truths Worth Lying for

Sometimes it is okay to let your intuition retreat in private, since your intuition is of your own personal branding anyway. If someone were to tell me that my perception during those nine days, when my mother was with me, was a blasphemous overreach about a secular person—my mom, who had not been anointed or canonized by the church—then retreating back to my privacy would have given me even more comfort.

Privacy is comfort. Take Galileo Galilei, the Italian astronomer born in Tuscany in 1564. The Roman Inquisition accused Galileo of heresy in 1633 for advocating the Copernicus theory that the earth was not stationary nor the center of the Universe and instead it moved, it rotated around the Sun. Had he not recanted this theory, he might have been punished with death. Facing such a potential horrible death, Galileo reviewed his choices:

"hmm, I can either be burned at the stake, and my very long beard would probably be the first to catch fire, or I can continue to eat Italian and say grace by lifting my hands to the heavens and say *'ave, eppur si muove'* before every meal." He probably didn't think there was much of a choice to be made. That Italian quote is his famous saying, expressed softly as he departed the proceedings, *"and yet it moves."* So, letting your intuition or your knowledge remain private makes that private space much roomier and comfortable.

5.2. *The Dance Around Fear*

There is a correlation between belief and fear, as fear is often the ingredient that makes us vulnerable, creating an opening for the imposition of a belief.

In creating belief systems from unsubstantiated claims about near death experiences and quantum physics, proponents tend to refer to fear as an obstacle in the creation of a relationship with our non-physical selves.

Segarra (2023), in his formulation of his belief system, oversimplifies and devalues physical life as his way to give credence and elevate the value of our nonlocal or spiritual selves. He observes that people who have had NDE experiences lose their fear of death and instead very much look forward to it as a way to reunite with their nonlocal selves. Segarra and his academic friends in psychiatry go on to make the oversimplified assertion and foregone conclusion that the fear of death is the ultimate fear.

Yet, this claim is unfounded because they have not descended through the nightmare of all their own fears to find resolution, so as to know their claim to be the case.

Their conclusion can be contradicted very easily by two explanations. First, NDE survivors have been to a better place. That place is a state of being far superior in quality that reminds them that the fears of their physical life are temporary and will eventually cease to exist without any further confrontation. Therefore, these fears lose their hold on the individual and can be ignored. But this applies to all fears, not just the fear of death. There is no reason to assume that the fear of death is the biggest of them all. Second, every fear holds a prejudice—a misperception about the individual. And while that misperception is allowed to continue to be accepted, the fear will continue to thrive. When an individual has a near death experience, he or she will be exposed to a very intense form of love that conveys the message that there can't possibly be anything wrong with the person. This validation contradicts the otherwise insurmountable belief of those prejudices attached to the current fears, rendering them unfounded. The newly found happiness might dissolve those fears through the overwhelming power of the newly experienced love, shattering the misperceptions, but this does not imply that all fears are all subordinate to the fear of death. It is worth mentioning that such powerful love is not available to us mere mortals without granted access to our non-physical selves. We are mere heathens grinding our fears one by one with the modest love that is available to us.

From an existential viewpoint, the assumption that the fear of death is the root cause of all fears applied to humanity deprives individuals of their unique context in life. It separates them from the personal context they alone possess, reducing physical existence to a caricature serving a higher being—ironically, their own non-physical spiritual selves. This perspective diminishes and denigrates those who have aspirations bigger than their own lives, and those who have staked their existence on legacies intended for posterity. It dishonors the countless individuals who have preferred to give up their lives, sometimes burned at the stake or decapitated, over compromising their religious faith, beliefs, allegiances, dignity and freedom for themselves and others. Segarra does present a contradictory dual perception of us as individuals. On one hand, he exalts the happiness and joy of this wonderful physical life, but when addressing life's purpose, he presents a very unflattering, demeaned characterization of human beings as merely waiting to die, valued only through their connection—or lack thereof—to their non-physical selves.

At any rate, an intermediate fear—one that sits on top of a deeper fear—cannot be discarded because of the existence of that deeper fear. All fears are valuable because they hold misconceptions of reality that must be dismantled one by one to find the truths they hide. They are valuable because it is impossible for us to selectively bypass all these layered fears and just deal with a deeper fear totally out of context—the onion has to be peeled one skin at a time. Each fear is the solidification of a falsehood about us which we have been made to accept. The option to discover those truths is what life gives to us time and time again. Otherwise, if we translate everything as fear of death, we are once again over simplifying and leaving this life void of its layered discoveries.

Like Segarra (2023), Luján Comas and Anji Carmelo (Carmelo 2020), also describe the fear of death as the deepest fear in humans. But they attribute this to cultural and religious beliefs, thus ignoring the far more dominating influence of individuals' emotional repression—a force that in fact governs these other cultural and religious beliefs. They refer to a quote by Nelson Mandela about fear: *"I learned that courage is not the absence of fear, but the triumph over it. The brave man is not he who does not feel afraid, but he who conquers that fear."* Obviously, Nelson Mandela is an example to humanity for his ability to confront and navigate the most difficult of individual and social situations without losing his vision and his integrity.

I have a different understanding of fear, of the emotional composition of fear, seeing it as the expression of our insecurities and the internalized fallacies about ourselves. Conquering our fear is an oxymoron. Fear is not something that can be conquered because it is only the reflection of our alienation. By dominating our alienation we are imposing our will, leaving our alienation intact under submission inside. Conquering our fears is like going in circles chasing our own tail. Besides, we humans are conquerors of nothing, for there is nothing out there to be conquered. Conquest was a word invented when we began to articulate language as a way to create very clever social associations, and it is a word that will be deemed obsolete in another one thousand years. Fear is there in you, because it is perceived by you to be bigger than you. It would be very difficult and unnatural to conquer your fear when you perceive it to be bigger than you.

We can understand why fear has been installed deep in our psyches in the first place. The approach then is to surrender to the fear, allowing it to reveal the mirage or misconception of its power, allowing us to see it and be with it. Once it has passed through you, if you survive it, you can gain a better understanding and see it demystified.

Mandela himself offers a counterpoint to the fear of death being the greatest fear: *"Our deepest fear is not that we are inadequate, our deepest fear is that we are powerful beyond measure. It is our light, not our darkness, that most frightens us."* I will buy that. I would add that our fear of our own limitless power is intrinsically intertwined with the fear of our own individuality and autonomy. To experience power beyond measure, it must emanate from our clear revelation that we are not anybody else, and if we are ever lucky enough to receive that reality at its full extent, it will lead to an ensuing fear of isolation such as we never knew existed.

5.3. *All Roads Lead to Rome*

The addiction to beliefs has been a mundane infestation of our human civilization since day one, giving rise to two ailments: the viral promulgation of narratives that give rise to myths, and the deliberate enforcement of the mythical narrative as cults in multiple domains—religion, morality, politics and oppression. This makes it impossible to speak of a secular self-born approach without confronting the opposing force of the adherence to mythology, which I consider to be the primary issue affecting our civilization throughout its entire existence. Similarly, while we can evaluate the idea of living a secular, self-driven life in terms of our transition out of physical existence, it is equally primordial to assess it within the context of preserving the human race and our presumably evolving quality of life. Mythological beliefs significantly affect our ability to think and act for ourselves, and this issue cannot be addressed as a philosophical quest for truth. Truth does not emanate from the seeds of rational philosophical discourse but from our emotional complexion, where truths are formed and which precedes and ultimately replaces philosophical reasoning.

As we review the effects of our acceptance of beliefs, we could take any number of roads, each focusing on a different type of belief or mythology, and from there, we can walk through to understand its individual and societal damage. Regardless of the path we take—whether reviewing religious and mythological beliefs, spiritual enlightenment practices, social cults, the influence of philosophical conclusions, or the speculative theories spawned by hyperextended science—we will inevitably arrive at the same conclusion: the ultimate damage lies in the destruction of our own self-awareness. We can also consider quick-fix social inspirational recipes for personal improvement that make us believe that we are something we are not, or that we deeply doubt we are. Whichever of these roads we take up for review, as all roads lead to Rome, we will find ourselves sinking deeper into the swamp of misleading rationales to which these notions bring us. We will come to realize that the central issue is not the circumstantial review or correction of any particular belief system, but the harm caused by catering, accepting and surrendering to beliefs, regardless of their source or origin.

But how will we know that we have reached the bottom of the swamp, in other words, the place where revindication begins? There is no deeper bottom to reach when we realize that the paths that brought us here, though significant, are comparatively inconsequential and only serve to disguise the real issue: our surrender to beliefs. We reach the bottom of the swamp when we recognize that by far the most important issue facing our time is not any of the circumstantial beliefs that might have brought us here, but our inability to access our inner-selves cleanly without any form of mediation—without the emotional blockage of taboos and superstitions. The bigger issue is not an existential or cultural one, but a personal one of gaining clean access to our inner selves. While it is clear that some of these belief impositions—whether social or personal—may require immediate attention, such as the removal of tyranny or liberation from repression, the only enduring long-term solution will come by addressing the root cause: how mediation and internalization deprive us from access to our own inner selves.

But how do we know that this impaired relationship with ourselves is also the most important issue of our time, more important than pondering about the existence or non-existence of God? We know that because this relationship with ourselves is the starting point of any journey. There cannot be a goal, an end, or a destiny if there is no beginning. Without that foundation, any movement toward presumed greater truths or realities becomes meaningless and delirious, clouded by the anesthetic influence of mediated mythical and superstitious views.

All roads lead to Rome, but in our case, they are two-way roads. If we were to start at the other end, first introspectively realizing that it is a essential in our society to establish these inner connection to ourselves—without distractions, fears, myths, or obstructions, we would quickly realize that this cannot be accomplished without reassessing all collective and social beliefs that make up the fabric of our civilization. These beliefs obstruct our passage to our inner selves. Thus, we would realize that our goal is in direct juxtaposition and unattainable while these belief systems are generally entertained and given tribute in our society. And so, we would reach the same conclusion by going in the opposite direction as well.

This brings us to the conclusion that the most monumental issue afflicting our civilization is the impediment to recognizing our sense of selves.

5.4. *Nothing to Learn*

We understand now that all roads lead to Rome, because if we were to recognize and address the destructive power of beliefs, we would sooner or later see that the damage cannot be undone without the reconstruction of the inner emotional self. Conversely, Rome also leads to all roads because if we were to first recognize the existing damage to our inner emotional selves, we would have to trace the cause back to our addictive behavior to beliefs. Given the collective social component inherent in the adoption of beliefs, let's briefly look at its historical trajectory for any positive progression towards the reclamation of our emotional inner selves.

All we see is that the herd-oriented collective suicidal damage of adopted beliefs happens repeatedly for thousands of years by way of the massification of political and religious cults. After thousands of history books that analyze and dissect our past failures and exalt heroic successes against all odds, commending us for learning the lessons of the past so that we never repeat the same mistakes, we naively wonder why we do not learn these lessons. But we utterly fool ourselves, because there is nothing to learn. We just sleep numbed through the blood spilling hangover and are ready to recycle the experience again. We are what we are—a primitive denigrated herd society endlessly condemned to repeat failures as we have done for thousands of years, with no change in sight. This is because we refuse to acknowledge that our addiction to beliefs is merely a disguise for our inner self alienation. If we think that in 5000 years we have made progress in our collective organizational autonomy, we are mistaken.

Most of the irrational genocides throughout our civilization's history, spanning thousands of years, have been driven by a clear message of domination over others, based on the imposition of religious or political beliefs. The Roman Empire's charter was clear: conquer and kill your neighbors, turn them into slaves, and the state can become wealthier and more powerful. Exercise maximum brutality as a lesson to other neighbors. The two recent World Wars had similar origins—impossible to comprehend but easy to understand.

5. DECONSTRUCTING BELIEFS

Just recently, in the 1940's in Germany, we proved that we as a herd society could be manipulated towards unspeakable holocaust in route to the consequential collective suicide of the entire country. This did not happen 3000 years ago in some archaic, primitive society. It seems like it happened yesterday in a very modern society with a parliamentary democracy and a sophisticated industrial organization, and it could be repeated in our lifetime

And once again, in 2024, thousands of years after the Roman Empire demanded blind obedience from its subjects to support its hostile incursions for the aggrandizement of the Empire, the herd society of the country that self-proclaims itself the beacon of democracy—the shining city upon a hill—has been sedated and brought to its knees in submission under a blend of religious and political manipulation, and the promise of unrequired servitude to lesser foreign enemies and invading tyrants with genocidal blood on their hands. Servitude is the sticky smelly goo that oozes from every reasonable attempt to characterize the political climate—servitude vomited everywhere. It is a herd domesticated by an idiot seeking to kneel in servitude to tyrants, putting a nation on the brink of destruction, only to gain world ridicule, seeking the admiration of tyrants like a puppy begging for attention. Welcome to 2025, but don't be a stranger in 3010.

It is clear that this particular experiment in democracy backfires because it is not built on any individual foundation. A democracy that gives power to the individual rests on the strength and integrity of the individual. But in a democracy where reality is manipulated as fantasy, and individual liberty is defined as the inalienable right to fantasize, invent, distort, manipulate, and ignore reality, democracy becomes sheer volatility primed for explosion.

The reason we go through this exercise in passing is simply to demonstrate that in 5000 years we have made no gains in our management of beliefs and cults. If anything, it can be argued that we have gone awry, proving that we have no knowledge of the disease, no understanding of the price paid by our addiction to beliefs and no awareness of the path toward our own emancipation.

Saying that we are learning these lessons is like saying that applying reason, history, and socio-political understanding to these failures will keep history from repeating its past—it is laughable. Democracies are built on the madness of misunderstood individual liberty, which becomes the prime instrument for herd manipulation. Until society is made up of individuals who have taken the inner road to emotional self-awareness and autonomy, there is nothing to learn.

We depart in quest of a more profound secular immersion into the self as the new path for the next one thousand years.

5.5. *Enormity by Invisibility*

Wisdom is our ability to correctly interpret and reason about emotional reality. When what we perceive as reality is internalized fiction, what we regard as wisdom devolves into gullibility, deceit, and submission to myth.

If we can at least see that most issues afflicting humankind are a byproduct of our own alienation, all by way of ingestion and indigestion of external beliefs, and if we can see the pervasive damage to our collective sense of self—accepted as normal over thousands of years—then we have truly reached the bottom of the swamp. We may remain in the swamp, but we can finally lay on our backs and begin to look up. However flimsy our imagination, we are now in position to begin to speculate what an individual with a clean, direct, superior access to the self may look like in terms of individual stability, knowledge of cause, weight of opinion, profound credible sense of self, and allowance for the independent existence of others. We can now imagine how societal norms and interactions might evolve, becoming more self-reliant and founded on individuals of higher emotional and rational caliber. Even if we stay in the swamp but at least catch a glimpse of the possibility of a new self-reliant reality as it might exist in the future, this would be quite an accomplishment. For now, that vision is all we can hope for.

How can we begin to comprehend the enormity of this next leap towards self-reliance, both individually and for civilization as a whole? By understanding that it is invisible to our present cultural perspectives. The earth, for example, seems flat because it is so big relative to our individual height and naked eyes. It takes a different perspective to see that the earth is round. Similarly, the notion of a superior human being—one with greater emotional and rational stature—is not even on the table in our societies. In our societies, we frame aspirations for the future in terms of behavioral and inspirational changes, foolishly imagining that these shifts will somehow emerge after thousands of years of recycling myths. We fail to recognize that such changes must come from individuals with greater emotional presence, individuals we do not yet understand because we are obstructed by the repressing taboos that stifle our freedom of imagination in the emotional realm. These changes of behavior are meaningless as they are goals without the starting point that begins with having access to ourselves.

An example of the first ever-so-slight microscopic step away from mediated religious or moral beliefs in favor of the more powerful individual, secular context is an issue of reproductive rights. This is a clear case of difficult decisions being made individually by the person who is in direct relationship with her inner self—decisions not dictated a priori, summarily and in perpetuity by surrendering to collective political, moral, or religious beliefs imposed by servile patriarchs with overgrown jowls and over-salivated speech. This example demonstrates that secularity awards more stature to society in the form of autonomy and respect for the weight carried by a relationship of a person with herself. The movement towards reproductive rights is significant in that it marks our culture's official departure from blanket mediation in favor of individual relationships with the inner self. It represents the first rupture in the tightly woven fabric of collective beliefs that has dominated for thousands of years and signals the beginnings of a breach towards the new self-centered emancipation of the future. The significance of this cannot be overstated. By granting credibility to the individual's access to the self, we set the stage for efforts focused on enhancing that connection. With better-tuned access to the inner self, decisions are authentic, grounded, and reflective of individual autonomy. So it marks the slow movement towards gaining our access to the inner self.

Another insight underscoring the enormity of this leap towards self-reliance—and its current invisibility—is that we still continue to debate beliefs based on their presumed merits. This shows that the injection of beliefs into our society is still being administered by reasoning about the belief itself rather than questioning whether it emanates authentically from our inner selves. This means that the very process of injection or imposition of beliefs is still perceived as benign, rendering it invisible in our societal consciousness. This invisibility shows clearly how primitive and mythologically driven our society remains. Despite our cosmetic distinctions and condescending comparisons to societies of antiquity, the fact is that we have not fundamentally changed. We still perform human sacrifices, we still rely on taboos, and we are still addicted to a constantly growing number of myths.

A third example illustrating the *"enormity by invisibility"* paradigm applies to a segment of the population that does not adhere to religious beliefs or pay homage to political cults. Even within this group—where external social beliefs are absent or do not require demystification—there are often individually created precepts of life designed to paralyze access to the inner emotionally-fluent and rationally-thinking self. These privately constructed beliefs act as internalized myths, and the result is the same: a denial of direct interaction with the inner self. This again shows the enormity of this issue which has been, and is, completely pervasive in our society. It is the most alarming of all cases. This really shows that we have been, until now, an essentially mythological species. Even the slightest obstruction to our path to ourselves becomes enough of an excuse to craft intellectualized distractions that evolve into our own personal myths. As we look around, where do we see individuals with an integral unperturbed connection to themselves? Nowhere. That disconnect is pervasive as it is normal, taken for granted and damaging to anything and everything.

A new perspective reveals that the essential value of a new self-reliant morality lies not in its apparently reasonable collective justification, but in the fact that it is borne out of an individual's intimate relationship with themselves, free from internalization or persuasion. This represents a seismic paradigm shift in the outlook of our civilization. How long will society need to adopt this paradigm shift and embrace a more elevated respect for individuals who trust themselves with their own understandings of truths? This change will happen gradually, as this perspective becomes the new frontier—the natural emotional horizon marking the emancipation of humanity away from mythology. As we move towards this understanding, we will be able to unravel and begin to identify the vast, pervasive and unmeasurable damage inflicted on our society by these mythological beliefs still taken for granted as normal in every aspect of society, politics, culture, and religion. This damage remains unseen because we defend these myths on their collective reasonable value, allowing them entry into our psyches, rather than evaluating them on whether they authentically emanate from within us. This failure to recognize the root cause for our internalization of beliefs becomes the irrefutable proof of our blindness to the influence of myth in our lives.

We have not entered the era of homo sapiens as beings of wisdom because wisdom presupposes the self-reliant identification of realities. Up to now, we have only demonstrated that ability in relation to laws of nature. Lucubrations and fancy regurgitations of myths may show off high brain activity, but it is by no means wisdom that we would want to showcase before other interplanetary species. On the contrary, it is a grand embarrassment to display before the universe how an entire civilization can be manipulated like a herd at the snap of a finger. It showcases our emotional paralysis and our stubbornness to remain in the swamp of our own volition, twisting in mud. It highlights the suicidal nature of a society dressed in silk and lace for parades under the pretense that it has become self-reliant to guarantee its future. Recycling and perpetuating alienation away from reality is a form of viral irreversible contamination, and that is not wisdom. If it were not a disrespect to the monumental damages to our civilization caused by our addiction to mythical beliefs, we could say that it is utterly shameful to see adult men and women, thinkers, leaders, surrendering to these mythical beliefs in full submission without question. In light of this observation, how can we think of ourselves as homo sapiens? We cannot in all honesty accept that qualification. We remain *homo mythologicus*, and the era of homo sapiens is not yet near. It may still be another thousand years away from us, because these conceptions are baked by impenetrable emotional obstructions distracted with myths and fears that serve to rule over our species.

The impulse forward is not one of revolution or evolution driven by willpower, because willpower merely represents the forceful domination of conflicting forces, and if they are in conflict, it is because they are not real. The descent to the self, however, will be allowed by the self, not enforced over it. A willful effort would only trivialize the daunting and seismic movement, invisible in its enormity, that lies ahead—one that will unfold slowly and gradually, across a thousand years, toward a new dawn. The impulse forward is a tap of the palm on a boulder on the face of the earth, enough to impart an unnoticeable orbital shift, and off we go.

6. Reality and Duplicity

Putrid Disregard

Perhaps nothing shows the two-faced nature and contorted petty self-interest of human beings more than our relationship with reality. There is an inescapable duality in the way we choose to perceive reality. Take, for example, the classical natural laws of the universe, the Newtonian laws of physics, as they apply on earth. Empirically, every human being on this earth knows these laws intimately. They apply them instinctively, with uncanny accuracy, without needing to use formulas. Everyone knows, based on their weight, from what height they can jump to the ground and feel the burn in their feet as they land, or what height will only result in a rough roll on the ground with scratches on the knees, or from how high they could fall to be sure of a fractured bone. We all know how to throw a baseball, using our legs to produce torque and our arms for leverage and pivot. We know, for a given speed and distance of an oncoming car, whether or not we have enough time to cross the street. We know that golf ball sized hail will crack our heads. We know all this, and each of us, to the last person, respects the reality captured in these laws.

And why is there so much respect for the natural laws? Because we understand the consequences of disobeying these laws. We know cause and consequence. But a funny thing... When it comes to abstract social principles that are played out without any apparent consequence, we turn into the most slippery, opportunistic humans in order to manipulate these abstractions to our advantage, because we know we can get away with it. We twist and contort the facts in jaw dropping ways that defy imagination, and all to feed our petty, devious self-interest, or to manipulate those of others. It is striking to see the stark contrast between the perfect respect with which we accept the reality of the natural laws and the putrid disregard with which we lie about abstract realities that lack an immediate physical impact on us. This disparity reveals an alarming acceptance of a normality that includes the constant, repeated transgression of the reality that makes us a society. This is so extreme that sometimes we hold in high regard individuals who reflect truthfully the facts around us—something that should be taken for granted as the norm.

But why is this? If we take the present state of human behavior at face value, with societies largely driven by self-interest, the conclusion is that we see no adverse consequences for ourselves in lying about the world around us, even if it causes irreparable harm to others. But why even ask why? For us, reality holds zero value, and this is not about to change. It will not change for altruist reasons concerning the betterment of humanity, and it will not change because we are unwilling to admit there is something essential and significant in that change for each of us.

Masters of Reality

Arguably, the most important issue for most of us, in order to preserve our self-respect with others, is to demonstrate that our personal sense of reality is well aligned with the universal reality of all. Conversely, the worst insult that we may have to endure is that we have no sense of reality. It is peculiar that for a culture that places no value in reality, we could view it as our highest prized possession. Despite our utter disregard for reality, we still hold it as the bartering currency of the world.

Cultural manipulation of reality is not the result of random intellectual deviance. It comes as a deliberate consequence of asserting our individual make-believe realities, there to deny how forcefully we have been manipulated in the past, all constructed to ignore anything of emotional significance to us. Duplicity in society is only the tip of the iceberg; and for us to culturally dismantle the pattern, we would have to first shatter our own make-believe reality—in essence, destroying our own sense of selves as we know it. It is not that easy.

The Colossal Juxtaposition

One mildly persuasive argument that we can make in favor of change toward the recognition of reality, is that civilization has recycled itself under a proliferation of beliefs for thousands of years. If now we aim to live under the foundation of a deeper, secular, transcendental bridge to a presumed non-physical existence, that bridge must be anchored in an accurate perception of reality. If truth is what separates belief from reality, shouldn't our respect for reality be unequivocal? So back to square one:

Could there be a remote possibility that after thousands of years of total disregard for it, reality could be essential to each of us individually? And why would it be essential? Could there be another, less persuasive but more significant argument? Less persuasive because it would require a quest for dignity. More significant because the depth of pleasure, realization and testimonial of our presence in this life—the identification of purpose and destiny, as well as our present connection and eventual access to our non-physical selves upon our departure—depends on it.

Moorjani (2012) expresses the value of reality this way: *"I understood that I owed it to myself, to everyone I met, and to life itself to always be an expression of my own unique essence. Trying to be anything or anyone else didn't make me better – it just deprived me of my true self! It kept others from experiencing me for who I am, and it deprived me of interacting authentically with them. Being inauthentic also deprives the universe of who I came here to be and what I came here to express."*

After many thousands of years of being tied to mythical cults and beliefs—at least those not forcibly extracted from our cultures by blunt force, torture, beheadings, burnings at the stake, or just plain death—along with the rapid proliferation of new myths in politics, science, and religion, all we have achieved is a culture of floating, un-anchored slogans. Such duplicity in our manipulation of reality becomes institutionalized. In the United States, for instance, democracy has redefined liberty as the self-indulgent individual's inalienable right to fantasize, invent, distort, manipulate and ignore reality in any way they please. Under such conditions, even the concept of democracy itself becomes yet another misperception of the reality in which that country exists. If and when the value of reality is fully accredited, the socio-political impact of such accreditation will also be profound. The engagement in deep threaded dialogs will give us the opportunity to reach substantive conclusions of agreement or disagreement.

Let's assume for a moment that we bring our beliefs with us when we pass. What then? And what if those thought aberrations we took the time to carve into our very being are taken with us when we transition? If these beliefs are not in sync with the more powerful, general, secular and absolute laws of the universe, could we be recycling ourselves into a non-physical blocked state of being? Here in the physical realm, we can manipulate reality to satisfy our petty egos, because we assign it no value. But facts remain facts no matter how we twist them for our narcissistic convenience. Facts are what they are and not what we say they are. In the spiritual realm we may be surprised to find that reality translates to a differentiated state of being. Intuitively, it makes sense to commit to a very clean and powerful sense of reality in life that we can project well spiritually when we pass.

There are those who say that the perceptions or misperceptions of reality we harbor in our physical life are carried through afterwards. There is a recount of a very Catholic Latin American woman who had an NDE in the 1980's and who became a social phenomenon in religious spheres. She described the phenomenon of a bright light towards which individuals gravitate when passing. She made an offhand comment that people with religious beliefs had less access to that light. That statement was quickly forgotten and went unnoticed by her very religious audiences. But it was the only comment that I remembered as a child.

One possible explanation, as articulated by Moorjani (2012), is that religion represents a narrowing of reality. That narrowing stems from the submission of the self to rigid, artificially imposed precepts, potentially limiting access to broader avenues of non-physical reality. On the other hand, Moorjani (2012) offers a more expansive perspective, suggesting that all earthly beliefs are ultimately meaningless and inconsequential in the vast universal reality. Regardless of how our physical perceptions transition, we are inclined to speculate, for the same reason that we are born different, that there is continuity in the transitions between physical and spiritual. Having a perdurable perception of reality would have to mean better synchrony with our non-physical consciousness. Perhaps it is time to suspect that we did not come to this earth to tarnish that perdurable reality.

A new understanding is emerging about a secular spiritual reality. It comes from a vast collection of documented near-death and other non-physical experiences. These glimpses into a broader dimension offer profound perspectives, but they remain distant for those of us who have never experienced firsthand these non-physical overtures. What is reality for the full-time mere mortal—the grinder, the cool, the agnostic, the heathen? For those firmly grounded in the tangible, that celestial non-physical reality experienced by others does not translate. As full-time mortals we lack the ability to stand tall, look at the skies, and pierce that break in the clouds to see what lies beyond. The glimpses of that celestial reality come to us from ephemeral angels and back-again mortals who have made their life quest to bring us messages of redemption. But for many of us, those messages only give us a lift for an afternoon or a day before we are back to the grind of earthly existence. We still have to make do with the physical realities we can see and understand for ourselves. What we really want is the reality we discover independently on earth, one that endures and guides us.

It is not the abstract value of our deeds that will provide weight and meaning to our existence, but their relationship to our reality—the "why" behind them. The deeper reasons that drive actions matter far more than the actions themselves. When we are passionately committed to doing good for the world, it can be humbling—even deflating—to realize that our intentions may not be as altruistic as we believe. They are often rooted in self-compensatory motives, aimed at filling voids within ourselves. Conversely, when we confront our damaging actions, we can see that they too stem from our inner emptiness and unresolved needs.

After thousands of years in a mythological society, it is crucial that we understand the inescapable power and control that obedience to belief and myth wield over the individuals and societies today. Against this backdrop, we must rise to a new understanding: our most essential purpose as human beings, for the sake of our civilization, is to establish a genuine relationship with reality. This relationship is foundational not only for our own fulfillment in this life but also for our continuity into a non-physical existence. Our first step toward reality must be the understanding that reality is not an intellectual process. It is not something you rationalize or internalize; it is something you live in. And this awakening to the difference between belief and reality launches the most colossal juxtaposition for self-awareness our civilization has ever conceived.

PART III, Baby Steps

7. *Truth*

Lope de Vega, a Spaniard born in Madrid in 1562, was a playwright, poet, and novelist of the Spanish Golden Age of Baroque literature. Miguel de Cervantes, author of Don Quixote, said that Lope de Vega was the *"Phoenix of Wits."* In 1628, Lope de Vega wrote a poem with 28 quartets called *To my solitudes I go* (Lope de Vega 1632), one of which I share below. In 1974, the Spanish group Mocedades (1974), brought back the poem in a song.

> *They say that in antiquity*
> *Truth went to heaven,*
> *Men put it up there,*
> *And it hasn't come back since.*

Let's bring Truth home.

If we do have a timeless existence, then our physical life emerges as a manifestation of that timeless truth. Life is the expression of truth, and there would not be life without truth.

What is truth? Truth is an underground mesh of veins and rivers of volcanic emotional magma, molten and incandescent in its primordial essence, flowing beneath the earth's crust. As you walk the surface—narcissistic and naïve, unsuspecting and unaware—you will know when you have hit one of those veins because you will be engulfed in the explosion, profound and pure, as truth reveals itself to you.

Why an explosion? Because truth is always about you. Truth is the discovery of yourself; it is a puzzle piece of your being finally falling into place. It is a homecoming to a part of you that you never knew was you. And with this discovery comes reality. Discovery is the augmentation of reality. Truth brings realities into a fusion—a more encompassing, deeper, and wider reality. Such a fusion, such an augmentation of reality, is pivotal in shaping our perspective. Thus, truth is fusion. For me, I know I am sitting on an open vein of magma when the act of correlating ideas brings me to tears—tears that flow for days until the new reality, the new truth, the new discovery has woven itself into me and settled in.

And so, truth reveals itself as an internal explosion of emotions. Anything else—any other thoughts meandering in our minds or floating in the collective psyche—are not truths; they are merely thought exercises, *socially calibrated perceptions, collective sensorial alignments* that our brains confer to us so that we can participate in the social experiment of the day. They are distractions during our short time on this planet. Whether they manifest as political discourses to defend the world from deranged megalomania or as two-hour exchanges over beers with friends to ward off loneliness and boredom, they are all part of the same play.

These alignments are intertwined with some form of reasoning that gives us a social standing and provides continuity for more beers.

At best, these thought exercises, these socially calibrated perceptions, serve their purpose and buy us time—a fleeting grace period in hope of catching a flying butterfly with our bare hands—to catch this unknown concept of truth just in the nick of time before we succeed in extinguishing all life from this planet. At worst, these thought exercises can serve as over-stimulations, delusions, deceptions, so that we can pretend we are not alone in this world. They are platitudes that will deceive us until we leave this life, not accepting how sucky and lonely it really was, and what a cataclysmic waste of a life it was. The only thing is, these delusions and deceptions have no intrinsic value. We don't get to take them with us. They stay on earth, broken down into recyclable scraps for others to pick up, perpetuating the same cataclysmic rumble of self-deceit. If at the very least, a glimmer of truth could let us admit how alone we are, that we can take to the bank.

Truth is emotional volcanic magma. Everything else? Accommodations. Uncomfortable compromises wrapped in the guise of evolutionary thought, disguised as progress over past generations that did not know any better, and whom we can easily criticize because their failures are already written in stone in their epitaphs. We are natural heathens because we don't seek abstract verbiage that we can grind into succinctly enumerated articles of faith. We seek mundane truths so close to us that they have to be rubbed and scrubbed harshly against our faces like a thick mud and sand mask at a spa before we can recognize and own them.

7.1. *Truth Formation*

Because truth is emotional, it is not automatically self-evident as in the intellectual world, simply because it does not exist until it is revealed or discovered in an emotional episode. In addition to that, different emotional situations may discover the seemingly same truth from a different perspective or dimension and with a different emotional signature.

Let's illustrate with an example. Pietro makes a statement, "*I love my mother.*" That becomes an uncontested truth in the intellectual world, which can be used to establish additional assertions about Pietro. Emotionally, although accurate, it may not not even be an emotional truth; it may just be a statement of accuracy based on memorization from his past. On a later day, Pietro is in a certain emotional state and makes this same statement. Because of the emotions of the moment, the statement this time does have an emotional meaning. Perhaps it's referring to a certain enduring quality about his mother. An emotional truth, non-existent before, is beginning to form. Other emotional situations may take place that continue to form a truth about Pietro's love for his mother. There may be yet another deeply transcendental emotional situation that reveals to Pietro additional emotional facets about his love, such as his great pride in having been side-by-side throughout their lives, and how that love will endure past their deaths. Pietro's truth continues to form as it gains an extraordinary emotional composition. Pietro always knew he loved his mother, but it is only through these experiences that the emotional profound composition of his love, highly personal and non-existent in his emotional consciousness, comes into existence. In the meantime, the intellectual statement of his love was established from the first time—nothing else needed to be added compared to his subsequent repetitions of it. The intellectual memory statement is paper-thin and unidimensional, and although it applied to Pietro specifically, it is entirely impersonal. Tomorrow, depending on the transcendence of emotional events, the same statement will give Pietro an additional formation to his personal truth completely unknown today. This is what I mean about personal truths in formation. Personal truths do not exist until they come alive and bloom. An intellectual truth is never alive,

Let's review Pietro's experience again. Notice that these are all literal repetitions of the same statement, *"I love my mother."* His first statement had no living emotional value; it was merely a memorization went to the epitaph section of the brain, which Freud, in his infinite wisdom, opted to leave out from his road map of the mind, as "the emotional side of human beings" had no bearing, since the emotion, apparently, was not the engine for the mind. With this, and other statements by his younger brother Federico about his admiration for Pietro, philosophers can be cut loose as frustrated logic mathematicians and use predicate logic and ontologies in order to make inferences about the life of this family. For us, it is still a memorization exercise—an epitaph left on the curb of a street corner. As we move to Pietro's subsequent statements, we see truths coming alive gradually by the emotions creating them. These are what we call truths in bloom—live truths because they are coming out of live emotions. In one subsequent extraordinary emotional magma explosion, which we assume permeated Pietro's entire being, bringing a new, extraordinary awareness to the notion *"I love my mother"*—these assertions bloom, proliferating into bouquets, where truths are no longer solitary but form clusters illustrating the proliferation of the associative emotional experience. Now Pietro's statement has brought to life of all those times at the park when mother and son were young, owning the sun, the wind, and the morning, living for the fun of the day, not allowing anybody to interfere with their beautiful privacy, or the times when they stood together to assert their right to help someone in need. We can see how these budding truths grow with life proliferating from what a moment ago was vaguely memorized epitaphs. Now they are truths in formation. But for the intellectual world, the first *"I love my mother"* was enough to provide the paper-thin unidimensional statement to run away into their world of predicate assertions. For us, the same statement has created a formation of truths in bloom, personal to Pietro, proliferating in bouquets that have culminated in a transcendental emotional experience.

This example illustrates the emotionality emanating from a relationship; but truth formation will tend to gravitate toward the revelations about the transcendence of being ourselves and understanding the significance of our existence.

7.2. *Crying, the Perpetuation of Conviction*

When I was five years old, my mother played the Irish song *Danny Boy* for me. These are the lyrics:

Danny Boy

Oh Danny boy, the pipes, the pipes are calling
From glen to glen, and down the mountain side
The summer's gone, and all the flowers are dying
'Tis you, 'tis you must go and I must bide.

But come ye back when summer's in the meadow
Or when the valley's hushed and white with snow
'Tis I'll be here in sunshine or in shadow
Oh Danny boy, oh Danny boy, I love you so.

And if you come, when all the flowers are dying
And I am dead, as dead I well may be
You'll come and find the place where I am lying
And kneel and say an "Ave" there for me.

And I shall hear, tho' soft you tread above me
And all my dreams will warm and sweeter be
If you'll not fail to tell me that you love me
I'll simply sleep in peace until you come to me.

I'll simply sleep in peace until you come to me.

Oh Danny Boy, if you come back when summer has expired, and a bit too late, when I have passed away, I will still be waiting for you just the same, and I will recognize your soft tread above me, and you will feel my love come to you as you have come back to me. At five years old, I had never had the thought that someone could attest to the perseverance and perennial existence of their love after they had left this life. I was struck by the thought that someone could speak today for their enduring love tomorrow, when they are gone. Oh, the beautiful weight of our words today. It is that present time that lingers forever. It is when today becomes forever. As a five-year-old, I was so struck and mesmerized that I exploded into tears and understood for the first time in my short life that we could be here today and yet speak for the truths that will outlive us and perdure long after we are gone. Quite a revelation. I understood then, at five, that I had just initiated my long and gradual farewell to my mother as one day she and I would not be walking the face of this earth together. That day marked the beginning of our farewell.

As humans, we become experts in disguise and melodrama, and crying is almost always misused as an instrument for manipulation or retreat from other emotions—that is what we do. But in its true form, crying is a response to stepping into one of those underground magma veins of truth and triggering an explosion. This was evident in the case of *Danny Boy*, where the natural and innate power of conviction about the perdurability of a connection beyond life stirred such a profound emotional reaction. Crying may also inherently carry with it the emergence of a wound—if nothing else, the wound of having been unaware for far too long about a reality that has suddenly become so explicitly obvious in the present moment.

Crying is the embrace of conviction, and conviction is the reaffirmation of truth, perpetuated.

7.3. *Truth, Self-Centric*

We like to think of ourselves as light travelers, carrying no baggage, just ourselves and the well kept secret of our reality in a knapsack. But even that reality had to have been born with a sparkle of truth.

But is truth important? We must admit, the convenience of lying makes us addicted to it. Truth is important only if reality is important, because we know that truth is the instrument for mining reality. As a civilization with thousands of years of mindful intellectual exchanges, it has not yet dawned on us that living with a sense of reality might actually be important and consequential. But that would be contrary to our disdain for reality and to the pervasive notion that reality exists for us to neglect, disregard, manipulate and contort as we see fit, to satisfy our ulterior motives seemingly without any consequences. But reality is what reality is and not what we say it is. Reality does not bend to contortions. Reality is not defined by our clever intellectual explanations but by our reflective emotional understanding, recognizing that if we are wrong, we alone suffer the consequences. Reality is the anchor that connects us to the world and gives meaning, depth and realization to our lives and beyond. Our highest and most consequential purpose in this life is to be in the most gratifying state of reality that necessarily matches the bigger and more universal realities of our timeless consciousness. If we are in it, that is what we will take with us in our knapsack when we leave.

Because truth is personal, it is self-centric. The beauty of truth is that it places us at the center of our own universe, but only if we can look into ourselves deep enough to reach our center. Then and only then can we look outwards and realize that we are sheltered because everything around us is bigger and grander than we are, like a big cozy blanket keeping us warm inside on a cold day. Truth is being the center of our universe, the source of satisfaction and realization.

7.4. *Truth and Credit*

Because truth finds and creates reality, it is the means by which reality is given its due credit. The resting place of our perdurable reality is where credit is fully awarded. Truth is born in us, making it intrinsically self-centered yet centrifugal in nature because it is impossible to keep contained; it irradiates outward without interference or hesitation. But because truth lives in us, it is alive, breathing and transient.

If truth is about giving credit, this is my favorite song written by John Denver. The song is called *Matthew* (Denver 1990), and these are the lyrics.

Matthew

Had an uncle named Matthew
He was his father's only boy
Born just south of Colby, Kansas
He was his mother's pride and joy

Yes, and joy was just the thing that he was raised on
Love is just the way to live and die
Gold is just a windy Kansas wheat field
And blue is just a Kansas summer sky

And all the stories that he told me
Back when I was just a lad
All the memories that he gave me
All the good times that he had

Growin' up a Kansas farm boy
Life was mostly havin' fun
Ridin' on his Daddy's shoulders
Behind the mule, beneath the sun

Yes, and joy was just the thing that he was raised on
Love is just the way to live and die
Gold is just a windy Kansas wheat field
And blue is just a Kansas summer sky

Well, I guess there were some hard times
And I'm told some years were lean

They had a storm in forty-seven
A twister came and stripped them clean

He lost the farm and lost his family
He lost the wheat and lost his home
But he found a family Bible
Faith as solid as a stone

Yes, and joy was just the thing that he was raised on
Love is just the way to live and die
Gold is just a windy Kansas wheat field
And blue is just a Kansas summer sky

So he came to live at our house
And he came to work the land
He came to ease my Daddy's burden
And he came to be my friend

So, I wrote this down for Matthew
And it's for him the song is sung
Ridin' on his Daddy's shoulders
Behind the mule, beneath the sun

Yes, and joy was just the thing that he was raised on
Love is just the way to live and die
Gold is just a windy Kansas wheat field
And blue is just a Kansas summer sky

> *Yes, and joy was just the thing that he was raised on*
> *Love is just the way to live and die*
> *Gold is just a windy Kansas wheat field*
> *Blue is just a Kansas summer sky.*
>
> © *Warner Chappell Music, Inc*

To be clear, compared to what so many others have done for others throughout the course of humanity, the song is a microscopic gesture of giving credit back to one life lived in anonymity. Yet, despite its smallness, it beautifully showcases the self-centered centrifugal gush of pure, gratifying pleasure that comes from putting one's stake in the ground to acknowledge, appreciate, recognize, and credit someone meant to remain anonymous and unnoticed. It leaves nothing on the table, and does so in a way that only John Denver, through a perfect confluence of words, music, and a full stadium as a pulpit, had the stroke of luck to deliver, letting the story take flight. John Denver was so very lucky at that one space and time—it was his moment. I have yet to listen to that song without being moved to tears. With that song sung and delivered, I think he accomplished everything one person needs to in a lifetime to continue a never-ending celebration for many lives to come.

Jorge Drexler, Uruguayan song writer who won the 2005 Oscar for Best Original Song for *Al Otro Lado del Río* from the film *The Motorcycle Diaries*, remains mostly unknown to many, but he wrote this pop song, *Todo se Transforma*, in 2004 (Drexler 2004). This playful love song suggests that in this universe, like energy, nothing is wasted—credit circulates and always returns to where it's due. Credit is never left orphaned. Below is a translation of the lyrics in Spanish, which I modified from https://lyricstranslate.com.

Everything is Transformed

Your kiss became heat,
then heat movement,
then a drop of sweat
which became steam, then wind

that in a corner of La Rioja
turned the sail of a windmill
while bare feet pressed the wine
which your red mouth would drink.
Your red mouth in mine,
the cup that turns in my hand,
and as the wine fell
I knew that from a distant corner
of another galaxy
the love that you would give me
transformed would come back
one day to give you thanks

*Each one gives what is received
and later receives what is given
Nothing's more simple
there's no other norm
nothing is lost
everything is transformed.*

*The wine that I paid for
with that Italian euro
which had been in a wagon
before being in my hand
And before that in Turin
and before Turin in Prato
where they made my shoe
upon which the wine would fall.*

*Shoe that within a few hours
I will look for under your bed
with the morning lights
next to your flat sandals
which you bought that one time
in Salvador da Bahia
where to another you gave
the love that today
I would give back to you.*

> *Each one gives what is received*
> *and later receives what is given*
> *Nothing's more simple*
> *there's no other norm*
> *nothing is lost*
> *everything is transformed.*

The thread of the fabric of reality is credit. As pop music goes, in 1970, Justin Hayward of The Moody Blues (1970) gave us the same reminder in the song *Question*, without Drexler's scenic tour through Italy, Brazil and the Universe.

> *And when you stop and think about it*
> *You won't believe it's true*
> *That all the love you've been giving*
> *Has all been meant for you*

7.5. *Truth Ephemeral*

Truth, like us, is breathing, ephemeral and transient. Just recently, I was driving when I heard the song *Mi Viejo / My Old Man* by Piero de Benedictis, a song I consider inconsequential. It had never struck me deeply before, perhaps because I never saw my dad as an older person, never as that distant, aged old man in the song. To me, my dad was always young, with a spark in his eyes ready for incisive laughter. I never saw my dad or myself attached to an age. Maybe this is because to grow old you have to go through stages and rites of passage and I don't recall ever doing that. I never identified as an adult, nor was I ever forced into behaving like one. Perhaps it's also because I have always been drawn to the transparent manifestation of intuition—mine and others. Together, my dad and I were not old and young, just whatever, just nobody's business.

I think of age as a form of distance that gets established in the form of false respect or false deference, but a distance nonetheless. The attribution of age is one connotation of the overall concept of respect, and I think that any form of respect in the context used by our society carries that distance. So I see the association of age in a relationship as a negotiation requested by one and awarded by the other in order to make that distance more comfortable. Then any traits of distance in the relationship can very comfortably be adjudicated to age.

My Old Man

He's a good guy, my old man
Who's lonely and waiting
He has a longing sadness
From coming and going so much

I look at him from afar
But we are so different
It's that he grew up with the century
With streetcars and red wine
Old man, my dear old man

...

Now he's walking slow
As if forgiving the wind
I am your blood, my old man
I am your silence and your time

...

I have the new years
And the man the old years

...

And he has stories without time
Old man, my dear old man

My old man? not my young forever dad. That time when I heard the song, I must have been returning from an emotional face-off that left the signs of some wear and tear, a reclusion within myself, because if any thoughts were to arise, they should have been about my dad, and about how that song did not fit him. Instead, I felt greeted by my own self as a child, a child that recognized me now and was proud of the paths I have chosen, the doors that I have opened, and, with all of my decisions, what has become of him. A magma vein erupted, and truth snuck up on me. I was moved to tears receiving that gratification. But truth is transient, and it does not always stay around. The next time I heard the song, it was once again inconsequential to me. That truth had already gone and only an emotionless memorized recollection was left with the thought that someday, here or there, I will be with that boy again.

Truth is truth only while it is evident to you. If no longer in you, it ceases to be truth and becomes instead an act of faith or an intellectual recollection. An act of faith is not the manifestation of truth.

As we give credit where credit is due, at the moment and timing when credit is due, truth is alive, breathing and giving life—like a flower that reaches the peak of its bloom and opens. That is the moment when truth is expressed. Once the flower withers, there is no longer anything to be said; it becomes a remnant for recycling rationalizations, an epitaph on a tombstone, as the opportunity has passed. Truths in bloom with their myriads of colors and tinges, are what we take with us when we leave.

So, if truth is ephemeral, truth is sometimes like that prodigal son. It may find a roundabout way to come back to you.

7.6. *Truth Exposed*

Because truth is alive, it comes to inhabit us. It is not intellectual passivity we can take for granted that becomes dusty decor for our memory. When we are lucky to be in the position to have our own explosion of truth announced to us, we have to open and expand beyond anything known to us, to open our inner space and receive it. Truth does not live in isolation—it comes to life when we own it. If there is no ownership, truth does not exist.

The Cocoon that Broke the Other Way

This story of two little girls, best friends since kindergarten, highlights how truth manifests in our lives. It was a nuanced, well-developed friendship in terms of knowing each other well and being able to develop a supporting bond as they faced all dynamics related to school. At some point, while in early primary school, one of them began having trouble sleeping because of her fear that one day she might lose that friendship. As we can see, this eruption of a new truth about her emotions announced itself loud and clear, and like all truths, it presented itself with a pressing lifespan. And as we can suspect, because this eruption came with such a force, its lifespan would be short lived if left unattended, and that truth would die orphaned very quickly.

The revision of these emotions required the girl to first feel the intensity of the fear and despair for the potential loss of her best friend. Once she was able to sit side by side with her fear and understand the devastating effects it had on her sense of self, she could revise and repair the myths in her own mind. Then, she would need to understand that she would not be alone and would be fully sheltered by her family, and finally, she would need to feel free to recognize and truly cherish the value of her friendship.

The result would have been a more fulfilling reality for her to own, with renewed happiness and spontaneity toward her best friend and others. As with any truth, it came with an ask that required for this little girl to grow into a place she had never been before in order to receive this truth with the proper perspective.

These actions needed to happen while that truth was alive and knocking on the door. This required an emergency life-changing response, with all hands-on deck. This did not happen, and very quickly the girl began to simply move away from the friendship—in a short few weeks she was already ignoring her otherwise best friend as if this friend had never existed. She barely noticed her in the school hallways.

The little girl's life had changed forever and would never be the same. Truth can leave scars as it dies without recognition, but it can also die leaving no footprints of the magnificence it came to offer. For this little girl, truth died buried deep and left no visible scars and no memory. Because of the way truth was denied entry, she may for example, produce a personality that may be very assertive and with little tolerance to being toyed with, at the costly expense of avoiding situations of vulnerability, and of course, leaving her without a home to go to.

Fear of Freedom

I remember a friend from my university days, a foreigner in the U.S, like me. He was very likable and socially adept, clearly from a well-refined social background where people pay attention to others. He had a girlfriend, but it was obvious their chemistry didn't merit a relationship, and he was about to break up with her.

One night at a bar, a young woman approached him, bought him drinks, and took him home. She loved him all night, kissed him goodbye in the morning, and later sent him a big bouquet of flowers. This woman was beautiful, charming, tender, engaging, independent, and liberal. She made decisions autonomously, seemingly without any compulsion for promiscuity, insecurity, or defiance to her upbringing.

Her independence presented him with a personal challenge that was hard to dismiss. By stripping away his protective lack of freedom, her presence exposed him to an isolation he never realized had taken hold of him. Suddenly, his life without that level of engaging independence felt unbearable. If it had been obvious that she was acting out of an impersonal compulsion, he could have easily dismissed her and protected himself from exposure.

Two weeks later, he announced that he was getting married to his girlfriend after all. Truth struck like a lightning bolt and it was unmanageable, and marriage would put the cork on that isolation trying to come out of the bottle. He was able to at least recognize that truth came to check on him. Being exposed to isolation through a living emotional example can be extremely difficult to bear.

The Unbearable Weight of a Late Invitation

Sometimes truth comes as a surprise to exact justice by revealing an ignored reality. I remember watching an interview of a famous U.S. country singer after he lost his wife in the early 2000's. To an outsider like me, it seemed that, in addition to having lost his wife, he had just been assaulted with an eruption of truth—a revelation against a lifestyle where an addiction to entertainment had defined him and sealed off access to his interiority.

This was a lifestyle that suddenly felt meaningless, one that he no longer understood. It seemed as if he had never experienced a single moment of introspection, and life had come all at once to require passage through his occluded introspection. This forced him brutally open with an assault greater than he could bear, making room for him to absorb the pain of his loss. Sometimes when senile individuals are nearing the surrender of their lives, they are confronted with assaults and challenges to their lifelong perceptions of reality, leaving them defeated, exposed to all their contradictions, and ready to give up.

If instead you could give them another eighty years of life, such defeat in their perception of reality might mark the ideal beginning of a new life—one free from the fabric of pretension and servitude to the outside world, and grounded in the sobering realization that they are truly alone, the perfect start to a great life. But otherwise, this type of assault is truly an eruption of that volcanic emotional magma that leaves you awestruck and leaves you speechless.

The Suspensive Stupefaction of the Naïve

These brutal assaults are often necessary to force open our hermetically sealed sense or our self, suddenly necessary to bring our emotions out in full force. It highlights the naïveté in which we like to float, indulging in a life without introspection we don't mind wasting. As a university student, I wrote this piece below in my *Silabario* notebook, which serves as my reminder.

The Suspensive Stupefaction of the Naïve

And to remain bewildered will be my only form of aperture to a wound that deforms my face, dislocates my spine and breaks my self. And thus I will walk, in a state of animated suspension, until my own systematic naïveté, fueled by my perennial spontaneity, guides me over and over again to explode against a new reality crushing my indulgent curiosity, and that now I begin to recognize through the traces of the open wound on my face.

And there dwells the only dormant hope of the naïve, in that stupefied walk, blessed by that lack of rational fluidity, of pensive separation, open-mouthed and dumb from incredulity.

With this imprecise walk I will trip again, and from the fall on my face in the mud, I will gather one day the clear and precise form of my being. As it is my

> custom, it will not be from the instantaneous and universalized perspective of separate and panoramic reflection, but from the sense of touch that the mud on my face gives to my hands. And this will be the reward of the naïve, to have opened up unknowingly, to the sober reality at the other side of the wound, unreachable without the proximity and the spontaneity of having felt it lost forever. And the trembling, transparent bubble of the naïve will burst.
>
> And from the spontaneity for life, suspended in perpetual naïvete and carved in flesh, with blood against the rock day after day, the pure and beautiful rose of understanding is born. And this understanding in turn gives birth to the gratitude that fertilizes the eternal spontaneity for life. And the cycle of life has given fruit.

The essence of that piece is that when we are narcissistic and naive, we are bound to get hit on the face by life as a result of our repetitive, impulsive, naive actions. Yet that wound brings with it a jolt of truth that we have ignored and now we are forced to accept and receive. By staying close to the wound, we come to discover who we are, and that becomes our reward. This piece seems to mislead us to believe, with a seemingly inspirational encouragement, that such blows, such harsh life lessons framed against our gullible naïveté, can readily produce these renewable cycles of finding ourselves. While this might not always be the case, we can at least take comfort in the consideration that, with a longer-term emotional horizon in mind, this cycle would eventually bring us with the long-sought reward of a broadened perspective.

7.7. *Truth Recognized*

But how do we know that we have moved away from the world of delusions and found truth? If truth manifests itself as the corroboration of reality, then a new truth will identify itself as an expansion of our awareness of reality. As truth expands our consciousness, we may feel its effects: buried memories resurface, sometimes through factual recollection of events but more significantly by emotional flashbacks—feelings, a sense of self as it once was, vivid images, smells, or a past sensation of wind and weather. These recollections may occur in rapid succession, spanning multiple moments and periods from our past. Our life becomes an immediate testament to multiplexed instants of lived experience. Where once we stood on a single point of equilibrium, we now stand on a myriad of points of stable perspectives.

We will also know we have found truth once we have fully absorbed our newly expanded perspective. In retrospect, we may realize that this truth not only applies to us now, in the present, but also to who we were as children. Truth, then, becomes the recognition of a unification through time—a paradoxical understanding of the timeless experience. It also becomes our own fountain of youth, earned in the most old-fashioned way of all: by seeking and embracing it. After all, we will always be who we were; there is no point in trying to forget that. Instead, we can allow who we were to return to us. Truth cannot have an instamatic range; it has to encompass more and more of our past—reaching back to who we were before we decided we were not. If we came to this life with a specific purpose, that purpose needs to resonate across the entirety of our lifetime.

We recognize these truths by the introspective individual comfort they bring to us—a private comfort that eliminates the need for appeasement and renders irrelevant any urgency to impose our own reality onto others. Our truths do not demand appeasement through our external actions imposed on others; they are not a compulsion for acting upon others in order to find temporary appeasement and relief.

As a formality out of the scope of this book, it is fitting to remind ourselves that claims to truths are often used to justify misperception of reality or destructive distortions of it. To establish distinctions, we can make a couple of observations. Misperceptions of reality are typically wrapped in a form of righteous morality that require appeasement, often through damaging actions imposed on others. These delusions rely on the propagation and enforcement of misconceived realities. In contrast, the truths we seek are not injected by external imposition or manipulation. Their personal value is evident in the introspective, expansive comfort they bring to us, which contradicts the need for appeasement by projecting a misconstrued reality onto others. These are diametrically opposing experiences. Truth is what makes our present time last forever.

We will also know that we have found truth because we will see a change in our emotional stature and our empathy for others. After all, empathy is just the amoral measurement of our emotional stature and its angle of view. Just as we measure our physical stature in inches or centimeters, we measure our emotional stature by the degree of empathy we exhibit. We should not strive to have empathy as a goal or as a way to become better individuals by some inconsequential moral standard. Striving for empathy or chasing hollow platitudes that do not naturally emanate as a consequence of being ourselves, rots our entrails. It is just that when we move closer to ourselves and to the ownership of our gravitational center, we gain two things: one is the ease and flexibility to be able to look outwards, and two is an experienced understanding of how difficult it is to untangle our way toward our sense of self. We happen to call that perspective empathy. *Emotional stature is our ability to be closer to ourselves and the truth within, and empathy is just our reflection of that self of ours in others.* It is that simple.

As we accept truths and expand our reality, that expansion becomes more generalized and universal, creating a place within ourselves where our reality can no longer exist in isolation—a place that harbors credits for the context of others as well. This is the "liquid" beauty of credit—that it cannot be compartmentalized. We cannot nickel and dime credit. Credit goes where credit is due and where credit expands freely. As we have said before, truth gives credit to a reality that dwells in our sense of self—our ownership—but without a sense of self, there is no credit that can be given. So how can an individual without a sense of self have the ownership to give credit to anything? It is not possible.

Loneliness is our inability to be in touch with our own individuality. Some physicians and scientists (Segarra, 2023) assert that individuality is lost or immaterial to our timeless consciousness because of a claimed unity with a universal consciousness. But we still have to wonder, why would mediums and others speak of different energies and auras in different spiritual beings? Wouldn't we all be equal if we all had full access to that universal unity? There seems to be an individuality that is continued through our different physical lives, and if that individuality reflects varying limiting levels of awareness in quest for growth, it must also reflect an equivalent inability for that individual state to have greater access to that unity. So it does seem to make sense to say that truth and reality provide a path to our individuality, and that is our starting point.

7.8. *Truth and the Homeless Civilization*

Truth announces itself to the self. The self is the space inside us that we own and inhabit. If the space is comfortable enough, we call it home—a place truly ours where we are untouchable by misconception or mediation, untouchable because it is a magnificent space inhabited only by our own unquestionable truths, the only home that exists. It is a place where we can hear undisturbed silence. This is the place that our little girl in the *"Inside the Cocoon"* story will never be able to find. Truth is the route to our home. But because home is our place of most familiarity with ourselves, it is the place where we can find real growth. We can say that growth begins in a place of intimacy with our own selves. Growth needs privacy and the creativity of conviction reflected all around us. The self is the place where everything grows, and we know we are home when we see that immense growth happen exponentially. It is the place for a proliferation of free associations rooted in authenticity and clarity of knowledge. If we are not home, false growth will reveal itself in the adoption of new personalities more and more alien to us.

We already know very well that our civilization is a homeless place, because there is no recognition of meaningful individuality emanating from self-ownership. There is no recognition nor recollection of what our inner self was, could have been, or where it got lost. Our society is not a place where we can seek the return of our lost inner selves. But that ignorance is a fitting kind of bliss because recognizing home as the ownership of the individual self would destroy all of society's collective premises and the structures that sustain them. Life, therefore, remains an empty place—simpler because of our ignorance, but at the same time more confusing and alien because of the contradictions we construct to hide the realities we do not own.

Given that home is that centerpiece of the self where we can do no wrong because it is protected from misconception, we can see from innumerable individual stories like the one of the little girl recounted earlier in *"Inside the Cocoon,"* that our societies have always enforced the perpetuation of a homeless civilization. We can segment societies by any criteria we want—by family and friendship, educational systems, or political or religious orientation—but underneath any such segment lies the pretense of supporting a false sense of individuality, serving as a convenient facade to sustain social cohesion. The function of every one of these segments is to perpetuate homelessness. Words fail to describe the enormity and invisibility of the chasm of individual identity that engulfs our entire civilization.

7.9. The Language of Truth Formation

In my review of the book *The Closing of the American Mind*, in the chapter *"Philosophical Joe,"* I noted that philosophical discourse has not changed in two thousand years, remaining an intellectual exercise. This stagnation creates a deceiving objectivity and an insurmountable distance from the exploration of truth.

A language for emotional expression is non-existent in our society, because in an intellectual world, emotions have never been accredited. Emotions are expressed only as individual, idiosyncratic outbursts of fragility, which gain assertive value solely through the corroboration of the "objective" facts surrounding them. In essence, individual emotional expression holds no weight in our societal framework.

Parallel to our civilization's long quest to finally recognize the existence of the individual home, a credible universal emotional language will begin to emerge—a language that heralds the formation of truth. Rich in expression, it will be a language of the eyes, of silence and voice, of shock and stupor, of grace and communion. This emotional language will shift the paradigm, allowing truths to be validated through emotional expression, rather than relying on objective facts to justify them.

Emotional language will become nuanced. For example, a sense of anxiety might signal an implied, disguised attack on an individual's values, while a sense of isolation could point to someone intending to retreat with a misconception about that person. When collectively we have reached a certain emotional stature, we will be able to hold these emotions as true, even if the specific events that trigger them remain unclear. Our conversational questions will then become: *"Why is that true?"* The answer: *"Because I feel it, I know it to be true."* Then the emotional vocabulary will begin to take hold.

Poetry

If we were to consider poetry as the *word of the unstated emotion*, then we could agree that if and when emotional language begins to open a space of truth formation for us, poetry will be there drawing the contours of our exploratory paths. One beautiful thing about poetry is that in one pure form, it is not seeking truth. If it were, it would be departing towards the intellectual and becoming one with philosophy—all would be lost. We can further generalize this non-relationship to truth and say that art, like poetry, is anything that is not seeking truth but leaving an open space where truth may lie. I think Picasso would object to my definition of art, as his drawings were meant to simplify his subjects down to their essential truths. If I wanted to be militant about my definition of art, I would have to exclude Picasso by referring to him as *"the bureaucratic perpetrator of systematic communist profiling"* because of his simplified drawings, but he would likely not appreciate that characterization. I'll refrain from making my definition of art an all-encompassing generalization and just call Picasso a genius.

In terms of its non-relationship to the intellectual, we can also refer to poetry as *the wormhole of the intellectual universe*—the phenomenon that toys with and bypasses pompous intellectual laws and can move from one intellectual reality to another. On the other hand, when poetry becomes an intellectual projection, it ceases to exist for us as the emotional sustenance we seek.

7.10. *The Emotional Horizon*

A horizon represents a condition of final or eventual stability. In astronomy, an event horizon refers to the boundary of a black hole, where the gravitational pull becomes so strong that nothing, not even light, can escape it. It thus defines the black hole's "surface"—the black area where no light comes out. In mathematical infinitesimal calculus, we use geometric approximations to produce certain results. If we want to calculate the area of a circle, we can superimpose a number of rectangles to cover the area of the circle, leaving a jagged edge. We add the areas of these rectangles (height X width) to produce an approximate value for the area of the circle. If we make these rectangles narrower by decreasing the width, we will need more rectangles and the jagged edges of the circle's perimeter will become smoother. If these widths could tend towards a limit of almost zero, then our calculation of the circle's area by using rectangles would be accurate. This theory of limits consists of establishing an ideal measurement horizon that gives us a stable measurement.

Just like the event horizon, and the numerical horizon in infinitesimal calculus, there is an emotional horizon. In this repetitive, iterative process of re-encountering truths, we could assume that *we are progressing to situations of more and more stability towards the convergence of truth and reality where credit is fully awarded*—the emotional horizon. The emotional horizon is the moment where conflict becomes stable because it finally resolves. It does not mean that we will reach that state, but until we do, the conflict remains unstable and in search of resolution.

The concept of an emotional horizon is useful for understanding that even though many iterative situations may seem to depart from bringing us to a smoother, more progressively stable state (like the jagged edges of rectangles covering a circle in mathematical calculus), there is an eventual emotional horizon. We may not get there, but it is there. Whether or not we ever reach it, this horizon represents a point at which all these realities unify in peaceful resolution, when credit is finally fully awarded. We know that some truths may bring us to the jagged edges of less stability, such as when we discover that we have been oblivious to unspeakable damage being perpetuated purposefully and blatantly against us. That awakened truth will bring a great deal of despair and emotional upheaval as we try to come to terms and remember in this book *"The Suspensive Stupefaction of the Naïve"* with the malignancy we now face. We can exert patience as we continue through those iterations towards the eventual credit of more and more unifying realities. The notion of an emotional horizon is the recognition and warning that this iterative process, where truths may come to us with such force, can be as an assault strong enough to tear at the very foundations of our personality. This iterative process is a gradual one, but in general

7.11. *Truth and Lope de Vega*

As we remain uncertain, blindfolded, crawling our way to find our first steps to understand truth, we remember where we started, with one lone recognition in 1672 that truth was nowhere to be found. Then as we come back, we find it fitting to leave through the same door we came. Good cheese goes with good wine, and 300 years later, this poem now has the song to soothe the word (Mocedades 1974).

Solitudes
(Soledades)
(Lope de Vega, 1672)

To my solitudes I go
From my solitudes I come
Because to be with myself
My thoughts are enough for me

I don't know what the village has
Where I live and where I die
That by coming from myself
I could not come from any further

I am not content or discontent with myself
but my understanding tells me
That a man who is all soul
Is captive in his body

And I understand what is sufficient
And I only do not understand
How an arrogant ignorant
Can bring suffering on himself

They say that in antiquity
Truth went to heaven,
Men put it up there,
And it hasn't come back since.

To my solitudes I go
From my solitudes I come
Because to be with myself
My thoughts are enough for me

8. Life, the Personification of Truth

Our lives provide a context, a lived experience where our truths can be found and unveiled, it is the worn tapestry that we leave behind. From our physical point of view, if we could live multiple physical lives at the same time, we would multiply the opportunities where our truths could be realized in different contexts and in different variations and intensities. But we presume we have only one life to live at a time, so that leaves us with only one context—one set of experiences from which our truths can be played out, justified, explored and expressed. Then, our own life is the single physical conduit for the expression of our truths.

And what is life, in the context of truths? Life is the expression of truths. In a mundane sense, *life is saying things and tying knots.*

In life, the only things we can say or express are our own truths. Expressing a non-truth is not a manifestation of our own life. As I've said before, truths are alive and breathing. Like flowers they come into the peak of their bloom and open. That is the timely moment in our life to speak, to express those truths in bloom, and to give credit to a reality. Once the flower withers, there is no longer anything to be said. It becomes a remnant for recycling rationalizations, an epitaph in a tombstone, as the opportunity for life has passed. *Life is saying things—truths in bloom.* Truths with their myriads of colors and tinges. As those truths become our convictions, we take them with us when we leave. What matters the most is not who we are, how we come across, or what we are to others, but what we have to say and when. We know we are in close pursuit of the truth in blossom when what we have to say is more important than what we are to others. The more timely the statement, the more alive it is and the more important it is to deliver. Saying things is giving life to life.

Truths resonate in realities that bring us an understanding that does not grow in isolation, because realities reaffirm one another as they fuse into bigger realities. Each subsequent truth contributes to the peeling of the reality onion because it brings new realities that are layered deeper, wider, more general and encompassing. And as these realities touch each other at the ends, we get to tie the knots and fuse these realities together. *Life is about tying knots—realities in fusion.* We draw conclusions from these connected realities as they become one—simpler, wider, and deeper. We see how realities draw from each other, giving and receiving, serving as credit for one another. In this way, they create a fabric of understanding where credit grows and credit is given. Realities prove that credit is never orphan; it is reflective and always returns in circles to tie the knots. Tying the knots between those realities is how we corroborate our understanding, reward our curiosity and give birth to our wisdom.

8. LIFE, THE PERSONIFICATION OF TRUTH

8.1. *Descent and Surrender*

We love recipes, especially those ironclad, statistically proven ones brewed and preached by professional psychologists from renowned universities, whose names and reputations are erected behind these psycho breweries for mass consumption. These recipes bring us, free of emotional expenditure, to shed gracefully our emotional ballasts and exalt us into the immunity of a psychologically aware stratosphere.

And because of our extensive experience with daily recipes, allowing us to remain intoxicated and oversaturated, do we think that this time we found the one golden recipe we always wanted in order to access a deeper truth embedded in that fancy network of emotional magma veins that lies dormant underground? Not by a long shot.

Do we now just go shooting into the ground with a single-shot rifle like in that 1960's TV comedy, *The Beverly Hillbillies*—not to strike oil gushing out and become instant millionaires, as character Jed Clampett did at the beginning of the show, but to unearth rivers of volcanic emotional magma that will engulf us in a landscape of awareness, making us instant truth vessels capable of walking on water? No, it is not that easy. It is actually less easy than extremely difficult. Truth is not that easily accessible. Most of us will spend our entire lives and leave without ever knowing that the truth about ourselves was here all along, sitting quietly and unknowingly side by side with us.

State of Decoy

Without truth we live in an *emotional state of decoy*— enacting defense mechanisms that provide clever disguises to hide our lack of emotional understanding and obstruct our essential human nature, where we harbor the truths about ourselves.

A state of decoy is emotional obstruction by disguise.

This state of decoy exists to hide and disguise our emotional surrender—accepting emotional platitudes and a superficial, false understanding of our emotional nature. It reinforces our defense mechanisms and blocks entry to our inner selves. On the other hand, *emotional autonomy is the living awareness of our true and deepest emotional constitution*—one that exists beyond these defenses, untouched by superficial decoys and self-denials. It reflects our emotional credibility to represent our connection to a true sense of reality. It remains steadfast as we confront challenging external misconceptions. Emotional autonomy is what lies at the other side of our defense mechanisms.

An Inadvertent Winding Descent

Let's look at life styles as they relate to our access to truth. In life, comfort will only breed comfort, while desperation breeds anxiety. Resolve becomes a delusion if we believe we can "confront" our fears or explore our inner selves solely through proactive volition and willpower. These testosterone-driven impulses are precisely the inhibitors that prevent us from surrendering to the thick opaque cloud of emotions that might harbor our truths. Oh my! How quickly we have run out of options.

Sometimes, it is only when your quirky, winding route finds you unexpectedly close to your mythical fears—and you still have a tiny bit of emotional balance left, not yet spent on addictions—and maybe there is a hand to hold, that you might, on a whim, by surprise, and before you can make a decision, surrender to the whirl of your fear. You realize that there is no way you would have voluntarily chosen this path, not for all the oil in the world gushing out from the ground after a single bullet hole fired from a rifle. But now, you are inside the fear, already surrendered, against your best judgement. Then, voilà—if you stay long enough to see the fear, stay with it and look again. You may come out with a new truth about yourself, a whole lot more purpose, vindication, realization, and hopefully, a lot less reliance on will-power. The forceful imposition of willpower to overcome fears you refused to surrender to is no longer needed nor desired. You will be my hero for what you have achieved, reaffirming for me how beautiful this beautiful life is. For you, it will be the time for harvest—harvesting what you planted. The fruit will be truth, reality, understanding, and a host of other things, in bouquets and in bulk, so abundant you won't even try to count them. And to your surprise, even though you liked yourself before, but maybe not all that much, you will find that now you are actually in love with yourself.

Surrendering to our fears is then our ability to freely feel the emotions voiced by that fear with all their intensity. Like Medusa, our fears will have multiple emotional representations of those fears, meant to maximize our horror. We will somehow feel afraid in a number of different ways, but that is just a superficial dramatization of the fear that remains blocked by our defenses. Surrendering, on the other hand, is a concession to fear, allowing all its power to be felt by our emotions. It is incredibly difficult for us to reach a point where we can truly let go of our defenses, to make that concession and experience all its power. Most of us will not get a chance to live such an experience.

This piece below from my *Silabario* notebook I wrote during my university days, reminds me of that surprising, almost involuntary surrender to our mythical fears.

Inadvertent

I find myself
tasting
the sweet enticing secrets
of the lost forbidden jungle,
just retreating
at the thundering presage
of a storm that approaches.

The rain will find me
inadvertent and forsaken,
and will give way
to the cold of the night.

Tired, I will fall asleep
to wake up
to the new invitation
to go back
to the lost forbidden jungle.

8. LIFE, THE PERSONIFICATION OF TRUTH

Bewildered, one day
I'll wake up to another invitation
look around
and understand that I never left.

Wonderstruck, I will realize
that my dream
has become
the shelter of my sleep.

Inadvertent is a metaphor for the descent into the rabbit hole, our place of insanity where the rules and laws of our social behavioral norms and superficial emotions no longer apply. It's a space where we encounter conflicting, contrarian emotions that reveal a deeper, obstructed, but more sobering reality. It is insanity because our deeper state reveals that our superficial status quo has no grounding; it is a make-believe fantasy standing in quicksand. It is insanity because it is a place where our superficial delusions are proven not to exist and cannot prevent us from falling into the vacuum. It is insanity because, when we enter this space, we have no choice but to recognize and accept that our sobering inner self, grounded in truth, carries more weight and undermines everything we have lived by. For a lifetime, we resisted these truths, but now we have no choice but to accept them. This place is where our inner self lives, sitting forever next to that dichotomy—the tension between the superficial delusions and the emerging truths.

At a more intermediate level, *Inadvertent* is more specifically a metaphor for our descent—our hesitant route back to reach an emotional wound.

The Open Wound

But what is a wound? A wound is a place that holds our deepest appreciations and reflections of what we already know about ourselves. It is the place where our lived experiences have stored all the beautiful things and all the aspirations and exaltations we have for ourselves—beautiful things, not esoteric and distant but already known, lived in, tasted and experienced. It is a place where we have already found and experienced great beauty and value about ourselves, beauty and value that we were born with, and thus it is a place with immediate access to our inner self. But it is also a place where all these beautiful reflections and values were damaged, alienated, broken, and taken away against our will.

If we are hurt by a wound, it is only because we recognize the beauty and value that was damaged, because if there were no beauty or value, there would be no damage, or as lawyers would say, *"no material damage."* If we trust our emotions, our gut, we will find that more pain in the wound indicates a higher value to us of what was damaged—we understand the scale of pain from our tax returns. This is a crucial validation, as we tend to minimize our values in order to minimize our perception of damages, avoid actions, and swallow the excess of pain.

8. LIFE, THE PERSONIFICATION OF TRUTH

What is an open wound? It is a wound that bleeds to signal there is a path that grants us entry to who we are. Let an open gushing wound bleed for as much and as long as possible to keep that entry open. Never underestimate the value of an open wound, and never close it. Instead, let it bleed profusely, never interrupt its bleeding. When we have a bleeding open wound, gushing blood without control, it is impossible to know all the new wisdom and growth that it will bring, because if we knew, that wound would not exist. Truths will come in clusters. There will be revelations about ourselves and our misconceptions—disclosures about the veiled personalities of others—so we can see them disrobed in ways they themselves cannot. We will know more about others than they know about themselves. The truth in a wound is a grand prize, an immense source of wisdom to see what others cannot. Our wound is where we want to be and where we want to stay. It is a shortcut to our inner selves, a wormhole to our inner universe. In time, our new knowledge and perspective will come to embrace our wound. All of this we shall have, only if we do not buy into our cultural commands to bring closure, because we cannot grow from a wound by moving away from it and leaving ourselves forgotten behind.

An *open wound is also a trajectory in the process of landing.* If it continues to bleed, the wound will follow its own natural course, with all its surprises, and reach its landing place where it must. Then we get to grow with its trajectory, and perhaps realize that the wound was triggered, but not caused, by the given external events. Instead, it may have been stirred by something deeper inside of ourselves—a way in which, perhaps, we had betrayed ourselves a long time ago. By staying with the wound we are recognizing that the causes inflicting the wound might not have already completed their trajectory. A bleeding open wound represents the closest proximity to the self. This is the state where the most learning and growth will take place while remaining as close as possible to the wound. Think of a bleeding open wound as the place where we can decode our emotional DNA. A time will come when we may find ourselves very close to our wound, but the wound may no longer hurt. This is because we have brought a greater perspective of ourselves, where the wound is no longer a cause of damage, but is instead embraced by our expanded understanding. Most essential, we will remain even closer to our wound, our memories, our past, and our trajectory in a way that brings us to this grander reality. There is no other place like it. If you falter and tremble at the thought of walking forever with an open bleeding gushing wound, remember all of us. We the people, we the World, we the Universe, will be in receipt of the curiosity that guided you to walk the long road with that open wound, and in turn we will become witnesses to every step you take. Remember also the pride of walking with a bleeding open wound deforming your face.

If we tell ourselves that we do not want to revisit the wound, and go to that place of previously recognized beauty, that is unlikely to be entirely true. This is, after all, a place deeply tied to our most familiar and beloved experiences of self-worth and inner beauty. However, if we tell ourselves we are too afraid to go back, that rings far more true. There is too much fear in evoking the experience and navigating the damage, which involves issues of justice, accountability of others, and the examination of misperceptions that may have led us to the event.

Let's examine the cultural perspective on open emotional wounds. Society, through its surrogate disciplines, often insist that emotional wounds need to be healed towards closure. However, closure only creates separation from the wound. This response, especially prevalent in disciplines like psychology, aligns with their goal of restoring individuals to normalcy. Yet this approach overlooks the deeper path toward self-invention and communion with one's inner self, which fosters the formation of previously-nonexistent personal truths. I define closure as *an action-oriented, externally-guided approach aimed at hastening the individual's separation from the wound to expedite their return to normalcy*. But closure often alienates the wounded further from their connection to the self. It is a form of lobotomy in which you will lose a portion of your emotional memory. Closure is a very claustrophobic approach where you place your wounded self inside a coffin, with those beautiful, raw, tender, transparent emotions and values still trapped in the wound. Only undamaged slivers of the self can escape through the slits and hinges of the coffin, leaving them to rebuild themselves away from the wound. Closure focuses on gaining an understanding of the event and the individual's behavioral patterns that might have contributed to it, so that the individual learns by memory not to repeat these mistakes.

This achieves closure without healing the wound. And who is left behind in that coffin? The wounded emotions of the individual self. We know what these emotions felt before they were shattered. We have already tasted being there, and for us to put closure to it, for us to put a coffin on the beauty and values we already know we have, is a devastating loss. You cannot grow from a wound by moving away from it. That is why we should return to the wound, because we want to live in the wound and be with those things we already know exist and we have tasted. A wound is an enticing place we want to return to again and again, until it becomes a shelter for those emotions and values that made us who we were. Is there more pleasure in this life than to walk with the pride of your wounds exposed for all to see, embracing the vulnerability of public scrutiny and their uncontested condescension? An open wound represents the present moment striving for perpetuity.

Our personalities are like little vessels floating above the waters that stir all our contradictions, inadequacies and self-inflicting judgements but which do not require our immediate attention, so they stay outside the vessel. With an opening in our hull, all these waters, initially unrelated to the wound, will flow in and we will have to resolve them first on our path to the wound, prolonging our descent.

A wound brings with it a gift, presenting at our doorstep so much of ourselves trapped in the wound, waiting without requiring further discovery. While we may prefer our gifts wrapped in the season's motif paper with a big bow, Mick Jagger reminds us that we can't always get what we want. This gift is wrapped in thorns, and we will bleed as we open it. But amidst the bleeding, the gift remains alive—breathing and palpitating, as everything we touch should be. We just need to be very patient while we bleed, because we just lost our orbital center, which waits at the center of the gift. Our first step through this bleeding is simply to remember to relearn how to breathe.

8. LIFE, THE PERSONIFICATION OF TRUTH

Dungeons of Insanity

We all have practical realities that need to be addressed with actions and consequences. For example, *"should I get a loan and go to college, or should I start working right away without a college degree?"* We also have existential realities and the inner truths we seek which may or may not impact our practical lives. Sometimes practical and existential realities do not intersect. The decision of whether or not to go to college will have a life-changing impact in our lives but quite possibly a zero impact on the development and pursuit of our existential self and the recognition of our inner selves.

Our societies will say that our actions reflect who we are. And while our actions have undeniable beneficial or adverse effects socially and individually, it is our reasons for our actions that have a more substantive effect on the inner self at a much higher scale. Highly beneficial social actions may be insignificant and even detrimental to the self. The only value our actions will have to the self is in our understanding of the reasons why. We humans can articulate and justify anything, but the value of an action is measured by its connection to the owned truth and its embodiment of that truth. For example, the altruist value of donating to charitable causes is undeniable; but if such actions are motivated by the desire to impress, show off our financial capacity, show false humility, or gain religious indulgences, these actions have no value to the self. They do not produce the satisfaction or happiness so essential to the self. On the contrary, they have a destructive value because they alienate and separate us further from our own human condition. If we ever reach an understanding of those reasons, it is the well-grounded ones that will propel the self with conviction and inner satisfaction. Without them, our hollow, aimless actions become a pre-recorded reprise of a lost sense of purpose. Often, the more vigorous the argument justifying a false reason, the more it serves to conceal what truly lies beneath. Reasons why are often layered and we must descend through them one by one until we feel we hit the truly satisfying answers. We know about this layering from children because they can ask why, and then why, and then why, for every answer we provide, until we accept defeat and it becomes clear we did not know the answer in the first place.

For the thousands of years that humans have walked the earth, the pursuit of enlightenment and connection to the spiritual and divine has been almost exclusively one of sublimation, exaltation or elevation of ourselves to rarified spheres where virtue awaits. The elevation of ourselves has often been carried out with pretensions of virtue and false humility, exemplary emulations, platitudes, and fantasy—through shortcuts of self-denial or long cuts of contrite self-flagellation. We recycle this exercise, striving to go higher and higher until there is no air left, nothing else in us to deny. Maybe it is time to consider a new path—a descent into the raw, uncured realities of the emotional labyrinth within the lower chambers and dungeons of our being, where abandoned truths lie dormant and where unexploded emotional mines, covered in dusty burlap, and buried in layers of lies, pretensions, selfishness, and unforgiveness, await. Maybe it is time to check if those imprisoned emotions are still alive, capable of articulating the atrocities they have suffered at our own hands for far too long, and that they still understand freedom. Maybe it is time to undress these layers as a last resort to uncover the hidden truths, our only truths, that may still be alive within.

8. LIFE, THE PERSONIFICATION OF TRUTH

For thousands of years, we have preached goals of virtue and social love above all, through blanket beliefs which are then adopted, claimed, inducted, and canonized by societies, at the expense of too many beheadings and burnings at the stake. After all, nothing is better for the purification of the soul than the smell of burning flesh—our brethren's that is—as there had to be a price to pay for the enlightenment upon which our sanctified bare feet now stand. But it does seem that we have reached the end of the preaching by missing the beginning—that starting place from within our individual selves. So maybe it is time to initiate our descent, to our raw selves, and symbolically to our gut, and to what our gut has been waiting to tell us.

Descent is gradual—it is the peeling of the reality onion layer by layer, because true growth is gradual. It is never radical like the transformation seemingly produced by a crisis, such as when an alcoholic turns sober and becomes a religious believer overnight. This kind of change, while significant in that it may save one from physical destruction, merely replaces one compulsion with another. It reflects only microscopic growth—big enough to preserve life, yet still leaving the individual alienated and oblivious to their inner self. Segarra (2023) notes that a sure way to grow is to endure a crisis, because all your emotional scaffolding collapses, and presto—a brand new shiny one will be edified in its place. Instead, I contend that while your new look may be impressive, underneath there may be only a marginal improvement, as described in our example above.

Beliefs impede (gradual) descent. Some religions may precipitate our path to "fast-track contrition" by morally disapproving of our innate lack of repentance—our recognition of pleasure and deliberate intention to pursue questionable actions, manipulating us to accept a false contrition. But we cannot be in denial of our pleasures, even if misguided, that is, if we intend to continue our descent to emotional sobriety. As we descend, we might dismantle the superstitions about ourselves that created our motivation for those actions. Only then we may feel regret, as we own a better reality.

We may argue that we are travelers in motion—not necessarily toward the exaltation of the divine, nor toward the indulgent enrichment of the abundant experiences we believe are reserved for us because we deserve them—but rather travelers moving toward the descent. We can argue that the peace of a newly-found, deeper reality comes with a price: temporality. With the new reality comes a deeper awareness of ourselves, accompanied by more profound trade-offs that we will be hard-pressed to ignore. After a period of indulgence and reflection to celebrate our accomplishment, new challenges emerge—challenges that did not exist before and which we are likely to accept as we move on to the next layer of the reality onion.

But the path of descent to our inner selves is very difficult to find. If we think we humans are most skillful in controlling others just because we can easily manipulate relationships and situations to gain an unfair dominance without confronting uncomfortable realities, then we have not seen anything yet. The control we exercise to keep our defense mechanisms in place makes all other forms of control pale by comparison. This is where we demonstrate our most formidable, nuanced, canny, and subtle manipulation mastery—so microscopic, elaborate, and tightly woven that we do not even recognize it in action or know it is there. This is the most imposing and sophisticated trait that we all possess. Unlike other human traits—such as analytical, musical, artistic, or athletic abilities, where there are vast individual differences—we all possess similar, proficient mastery of this one trait. We use it every day to maintain the status quo of our defense mechanisms. These mechanisms were built as fortresses to protect us from our fears, and they are constructed with controls that make them inaccessible through reasoning.

Fears are shielded under the absolute control of defense mechanisms, which make an armored medieval fortress look like a hippie commune having an open house for breakfast. Fear is always protected by control, and the only way to reach fear is by surrendering or relinquishing control. Defense mechanisms are so heavily intertwined that they are virtually impenetrable. Sometimes a crisis may be deceiving, appearing to radically break through our defenses, when in reality it only produces a cosmetic gain for temporary delusion. Sometimes, the opposite of a crisis—a new emotional balance—can provide movement. And most likely, the advancement through defenses is a social process, too difficult to accomplish in isolation. Think about attempting to push a stalled car up a hill by sitting at the wheel. It is not going to happen because leverage from outside the car is necessary to impart movement.

We will need courage, but courage is not the will-powered, emotional grinder of going to war; it is not the forceful imposition against your fears. We do not conquer our fears; we are conquerors of nothing, and there is nothing in this universe begging to be conquered. Being a conqueror aligns with similar prevailing societal recipes, like giving one hundred and ten percent or never giving up. But we do give up, and in doing so, we become the best counterpart to what we give up—not a bad trade-off. Besides, better than living inside the medieval steel armor of never giving up is to give up often and give yourself the option to change your mind—again and again. If you were to conquer a fear, it would mean that the fear still resides caged inside you, and your mythical perceptions of it remain unchanged, with no wisdom gained. Conquering fear would require the hostility of a takeover, which would only make us harder, more impenetrable, and less accessible to ourselves—until one day, we implode, while holding high the social banner of pride for never having given up. The courage we need is not one of forceful triumph, but one dismissed by curiosity that catches us inadvertently and by surprise. Courage is then curiosity tucked inside our gut, fed by trust and itching to get out. Curiosity leads us to surrender, and after spending enough time inside the fear, it helps us demystify it. We will become softer, more malleable, and a lot wiser, gaining fresh insights we would never find anywhere else except within, beyond our inner myths.

So courage is more the execution of our curiosity to discover who we will become in the next moment, rather than the rehearsed, premeditated control over our fears.

If we never surrender to our fears, but at least give credit to those fears for being so much bigger than us, and we do so by coming close enough to them to size them up, I would say that is a life well lived—I hope that is in my case for me.

Loose Emotional Intensity

This descent will leave behind a new emotional foundation, unrelated to our previous ability to experience intense emotions. We understand that intense emotions have always existed in ourselves and our cultures. But those emotions were never cradled within a solid emotional foundation to give any accreditation to those emotions. Such a foundation has never existed, does not exist, is not recognized as something missing in our societies or in ourselves individually, and is not planned to exist. This clarifies the difference between an emotional foundation rooted in self-awareness and an intense, orphaned, unattached emotional experience.

8.2. *The Strength of Our Individuality*

Truths create our realities by bringing them together. As realities fuse, they become broader, more expansive, more encompassing, unquestionable, perdurable, and far reaching. It is in this fusion that we find peace. *Peace is the arrival into the expansion of our fused, perdurable realities.* Because realities were never meant to be disjointed, peace is not passive perpetual benevolence, but awareness in motion.

Our realities are the reflection of our truths, and our individuality is the signature of our realities. The strength of our individuality comes from the conviction of our truths. Through individuality, we gain a place from which to relate to the world.

Love is an outward expression of peace, awarded by our individuality. Therefore, love arises from the strength of our individuality. If we do not own our truths, our individuality does not exist, and whatever we are selling "ain't love." Without individuality, who does that love come from? So the next time you are being bathed in love, don't forget to ask, *"and what was your name again?"*

8.3. Love is Everything and Nothing

It is no wonder that survivors of NDEs have trouble describing to us the universal state of bliss they experience during their death state. They hesitate and come around in circles to call it love for lack of a better word, and that hesitation seems justified because they may find such a bliss to be so dissimilar and in sharp contrast with earthly love, which is an emotion we have made to stand upon many artifices, accommodations and conveniences, but not so much on the pillars of our own perdurable grounded reality—because we have never had one.

So love is a big word—it can be amorphous, diffused, opaque, monolithic, or it can be a sharp flash of transparency. It encompasses both the grand and the small, everything and nothing. It can mean long-term emotional alliances, a cushion at the bottom of your fall, or a flicker of innocence. It makes you warm and fuzzy, or it makes you vomit. The word does not travel well beyond our earthly confines, as it becomes meaningless in the spiritual realm. NDE survivors find that the word doesn't do justice to their experience. And yet it sits in the middle of everything—

truth, reality, individuality, and peace. To apply it, we need to open it up and see if inside we can find the roadmaps to our destinations.

One way to simplify the word and do away with all its accommodations, is to say that *love is full recognition*—the acknowledgement of our own reality. Truth, in this context, is the sheer, immaculate beauty that illuminates the reality of our presence and ignites love. Owning our truths gives us the bridge to true communication. Without full recognition, who is there to love? This connotation travels well outside earthly confines because it implies that when there is full recognition, love will shine spontaneously—and actually we don't have to see it as too much of an oversimplification. It might help us understand why full recognition in the celestial realm feels so expansive, which is why those who experience near-death encounters often describe it as such an unexplainable feeling. At the same time, that connotation shows how imperfect and misunderstood love can be in our physical realm on earth, as it is rare for individuals to be fully recognized by themselves first, then by others.

If we seek recognition without owning the truths that illuminate it, we risk falling into a cycle of futile attempts for validation that will never come. In this, we create an earthly style of dependency on false hope and reattempts. We could perhaps conclude that the deeper the recognition is, the more independent love becomes.

In our physical world, as we all know, sometimes professed love may instead be a disguised convenience, a way to avoid facing unspeakable isolation or a place to harbor resentments. On the other hand, there may be much love in the air, yet none of it given or received. Love then becomes very compartmentalized by our refusal to fully embrace our expansive sense of self—who we really are and want to be—or our refusal to undertake the initial steps in our descent into the expansive sense of ourselves.

8.4. Love in the Days of the Jaguar

I remember a close relative of my dad's. He was dry towards everybody, including his family and ours. There was nothing emanating from him that could be construed as a sign of affection—be that a hand movement, a raise of the eye brows, a wink in the eyes, a motion of the lips up or down, or the uttering of a word. His only sign of life was anger, not in his lips but in the pores of his skin—well-stitched at the seams, so you knew it would never come undone. And what was there not to love about his family or ours, about my sister and me or my parents? But getting through even the most superficial blockages on your path of descent to the expansion of love is not straight forward.

My dad was the opposite—very affectionate and playful, with us and everybody. He would come to my sister and me with his five o'clock shadow and rub his sandpaper cheeks against our faces and body until we would beg for mercy—and mercy we begged for. He would take sense of humor to places most people would not dare and have a room explode in laughter—just irreverent. You could see an entire room nodding with disapproval, thinking, *"I do not approve of this line of humor,"* but making it impossible

8. LIFE, THE PERSONIFICATION OF TRUTH 283

to stop the explosion of laughter—and very creative humor to boot.

My dad served as the engineer representing our country in a multi-national commission to re-delineate our border with Honduras, at the time when our country lost one third of its territory. That new border closely followed the contours of the Coco River, our largest, which back then was a virgin jungle. You could only move through the rain forest by opening trails with machetes. He would come home after several weeks in the jungle, covered in mud, and tell us so many stories. One time, he was walking alone at sunset, heading back to his camp up a hill, when he came face to face with a jaguar at the top. They both stopped, astonished, and simply stared at each other. My father went left and the jaguar went right. Jaguars are not like leopards, which are thin and nimble, able to climb trees with their prey. Jaguars are stocky, built for strength—they can take anybody or anything. Another time, my dad and the group went back to sleep at their camp in their hammocks hung between trees. My dad always slept with his pistol by his chest, just in case anything were to happen. In the morning when they woke up, my dad saw right underneath his hammock, the big paw prints of a jaguar that had walked right through camp during the night. No need to wake up for that one.

I thought my dad would never die. I used to take him with me every once in a while, on runs around the city in the middle of a tropical hot afternoon, and sometimes people would stare at him with surprise, and I used to think to myself, *"right—little you know that my dad has the clean arteries of a twenty-year-old guy."* He always trailed behind me in his car during my runs up to a mountain range away from the city, to bring me water and to protect me in case of any eventuality during my run, like he used to when I was little—though in reality I was more likely to protect him. He was there with me every single day to give me water. My dad always made a water stop by a huge ceiba tree about four meters in diameter. Since we had nicknames for every span and every hill in the running route, that was *Dad's Ceiba Tree*. I always see this daily run as the reenactment of my time on earth. I start zig-zagging through bumper-to-bumper traffic going in the opposite direction of those who are rushing to work, trying to make something of themselves. Gradually, as I begin my ascent, I leave that chaos behind and end up in a desolate rain forest, with birds singing and monkeys howling. At the top of the penultimate hill—which we nicknamed *The Snail* because it gets steeper as it curves—I find my passage uphill to the full tropical sun next to a huge tree we nicknamed *The Tree of Good and Evil*. I think to myself that when I die, I won't see the light of God at the end of a tunnel, since I am a heathen, so this is the only light I want to see—earned lush tropical morning sunlight that I get a preview of every day. Then I pass that and reach my life review, brought on by the final hill that opens up to a wide panoramic view of everything I left behind. Below, I can make out the city by the lake where I started, with bumper-to-bumper traffic, symbolic of starting your life in full competition. But after my life review, my life is still all mine because it is still early morning and the promise of a full day is still ahead. When my dad passed, my sister and I carved this in stone: *"Hey Papi, he who sleeps with the jaguars, the protector of our steps now sleeps. Light as a feather in the wind, you found a new shortcut in the jungle and slipped away out of sight. We stayed behind to look for that shortcut until we can find you again."*

8.5. The Purpose of Being

There is beauty in love that is given not out of eagerness to please or by mutual agreement, but through the reluctant acceptance of that bigger reality that surrounds us. So the lesson here is that when somebody holds a greater reality that resonates with ours, we cannot push them away, no matter how hard we try, as they carry too much weight. The nature of the relationship may not exist in the traditional sense, or may be one of mutual indifference, at best. It does not matter. What matters is that the perspective and realities they bring have an undeniable weight, and they become part of us. Should we expand the meaning of the term love or affection to give it some objective existential sobriety? We do not have to call it love or affection. Perhaps this vocabulary issue is a sign that we are becoming celestial beings before our time and, like our NDE ephemeral angels, we can no longer find earthly words to describe our experience. What I want to be true is that these relationships, joined by an undeniable understanding of being, will perdure after we are gone.

At the risk of sounding like Aristotle, with his sequential recipes, I will offer one of my own—though in this case, I am referring to states that deeply emanate from the emotional realm: emotional formation of truth crystallizes conviction, and conviction formulates intention, intention renders actionable purpose, and purpose is bound to individuality. *Purpose is the lifetime translation of our individuality*. Purpose can be the accomplishment of great feats, or just being.

Being can mean different things to different people. On one hand, being may refer to the act of being present in this world just to enjoy its grandeur, its majestic beauty, and the miracle of having waited billions of years to witness life this advanced. How can it not be jaw dropping every day to see life so routinely and so pervasively happening on the planet? It is still almost impossible to believe. And when it comes to ourselves as the human species, everything we have accomplished scientifically is awe-inspiring. I am still in awe of those metallic birds that fly. In this contemplative life, we must also be aware of the significance of our presence and the privilege it is to witness.

On the other hand, being may mean something entirely different to others: a state of being so self-absorbed, so oblivious to the miracle before us, that we become narcissistic parasites—where the earth exists only for our consumption, heading toward its own obliteration. Obviously, this cannot in any way be elevated to a purposeful state of being.

8.6. *A Tale of Three Purposes*

Peace comes first, then love, and the hippie movement of the 1960's got that right: it is peace and love, not love and peace. For the hippie movement, peace and love symbolized that last moment of lucidity for those unknowingly on the brink of generational extinction—a soul sacrifice behind the hypnotic notes of the new music of Hamelin, a new make-believe reality, blurry and psychedelic, promulgating a disparate disarray of intersecting thoughts of cool. Like in a play of football scrimmage where everybody runs in a different direction, they left an open path for the vibrant and consequential civil rights movement to march through the center of the field with full determination and historical purpose, resonating through each subsequent generation. The 1960's generation did not survive two asymmetrical assaults. One was the opening of the pressurized can of pretension of the early forties and fifties, the poison of farce, pretension, and cultural repression that you could no longer pretend to ignore with a change in look, hair do, or dress code. After all, you cannot remove putrefaction when you cannot smell it, but if you open the can, can you smell it then? The second assault was napalm bombs and rosaries of deaths in a hot jungle with a name never seen in our primary school history books. How to ignore that? Music says it will stay around to remind new generations of the one who was obliterated and pulverized. But these new generations are busy shaping their own footprint, born alien to the conditions at stake but retro-receptive to the music they were made from. But hey, peace and love—thanks for saying that, man.

Ave Caesar! Morituri te salutant! Two thousand years ago there were those gladiators who knew they came to this life only to die at the circus; their purpose was all too clear. Bypassing the luxuries of due process and argumentative lucubrations, their purpose was imposed, weighted in iron armor, a life already forfeited but still awaiting formal surrender in the arena. Truth arrived for them as a crushing assault, stipulating their worthlessness to others with no ambiguity. Truth arrived on Sunday afternoons of *panem et circus*, but it came only to those who were about to die in horror—yet still afforded the grim dignity of knowing their purpose. It is a badge of honor to live with the clarity of knowing one's purpose. Hippies were street philosophers, but purpose is not in the words you exhale in order to let smoke escape from your lungs. But purpose is still that conviction for which you will give your life, and even when involuntarily, it is still a life given, and gladiators knew that well. So as we in modern life try to fill the void of those Sunday family matinees at the circus—where your children would laugh and tell anecdotes of that time when their faces got splashed in blood—and with all the philosophical respite afforded to a hippie generation in recess, granted the right to lack purpose, it is unclear whether we can claim moral superiority over the gladiators, whose sole possession was the certainty that their only purpose was to die for others' entertainment.

Moral superiority does not lie in the eloquence of street corner philosophical verbiage that grants the right to dismiss purpose as a convenient excuse for consuming air, nor in the intellectual posturing we radiate from a moral or intellectual pulpit. It lies in the magnitude of the choices or impositions we explicitly accept and confront. Ultimately, life tells a tale of three purposes to die for: the imposed, the hazy, and the vibrant.

9. Present Time

9.1. The Echo of the Past

Now is the time for us to speak the living, breathing truths that may perdure forever or just linger for a little while. Truth is what has the power to make the present eternal—when today becomes forever. If present time is meant to live with us perpetually, it must also embody the recollection and presence of our past. And recollection, in turn, is the art of being present. This suggests that truth lives in the present time because it shapes and sustains it by integrating our past. Thus, present time becomes the art of being in our own presence.

Truth, as the expansion of our awareness, suggests that in a fully engaged state of being, the echo of our past would remain alive and breathing within us, keeping us in perfect company. This companionship would be similar, though to a lesser extent, to the timeless existence we often imagine. After all, why should the past not live with us? If there were wounds in our past, would we not want to embrace them? And live under the exposure of those raw wounds until, one day, they become our shelter?

When these wounds become public, visible by anyone perceptive enough to see them, their exposure becomes our pride. Who would not want to go back and live with their wounds?

As part of the new belief systems proliferating from discoveries in quantum physics and near-death experiences NDEs, scientists such as Luján Comas (Carmelo 2020) and Segarra (2023), among others, tend to trivialize our physical life as serving only as a transition to our spiritual or timeless existence. They argue that living life at its fullest equates to "living the moment," which is valid but often presented in an unidimensional way—focusing only on being absorbed in the present moment while disregarding the so-called "distractions" or issues deemed irrelevant to that one moment.

We don't view present time as merely being absorbed by the circumstances of a moment, such as a relative's graduation. The experience of present time is complemented by the resonating echoes of our past, which bring perspective and add richness to the present moment.

Presumably, according to Moorjani (2012), our timeless consciousness does not exist in a physical linear sequential progression of time but in a state where all time is always present. It is an elevated form of consciousness where all time exists always. We can assume that if the live echo of our physical past is also present in our sequential life, our life will be richer, more evocative and seamless with our timeless consciousness. This creates a multi-dimensional resonance in our presence—more than a symbolic validation of our past, it reveals that we have arrived at the present with all of our might, carrying everything ours into the now.

Regaining our ability to exist in the present—truly in the presence of ourselves—is not straightforward. Achieving this fresh recognition of our inner selves requires shedding baggage and recanting the shortcuts and compromises we made along the way. Those repeated decisions to diminish ourselves, discount our presence, and shortchange our stature, day in and day out, create a false reality not easy to overcome.

It is sometimes easier to experience fleeting flashes of recognition of your child self within you, as I have done and recounted in the section *"Truth Ephemeral."* However, this stands in stark juxtaposition with the more serious process of bringing all of your past with you. This challenge is difficult, as recollection is an emotional process that requires opening those avenues where many truths lie hidden. These pathways are often blocked by the burden of lesser decisions that must be recanted and the weight of consequences that demand mourning before those paths can be reopened. Do we know how extremely difficult it is to bring back our absent child in order to give meaning to our presence today? Extremely difficult. And if we cannot even accomplish bringing about that past presence into our physical selves, what business is it of ours (and what a farce) to be marching forward with inflated pride thinking about our spiritual transcendental selves? We have to first plant our feet on the ground. In 1964, Pablo Neruda (1964) published an autobiographical collection of poems titled *Memorial de Isla Negra*, which included the poem *"El Niño Perdido,"* translated below.

The Lost Child

*A slow childhood out of which,
as out of long grass,
grows the durable pistil,
the wood of the man.*

Who was I? What was I? What were we?

*There is no answer. We happened.
We were not. We kept on being. Other feet,
other hands, other eyes.
Everything kept changing leaf by leaf
on the tree. And you? Your skin changed,
your hair, your memory. You were not that other one.
That other one was a child who passed, running
after a river, after a bicycle,
and with movement
your life was gone with that moment.
A false identity walked in your footsteps.
Day after day the hours gathered,
but you were not there now, the other one came,
the other you, the other until you became,
until from the train, from the wagons of your life,
from substitution, from your traveling self,
you brought a new self into being.
The child's mask began to change,
his pain diminished,
his self stopped shifting.*

*The skeleton held still, v the bone structure stayed firm,
the smile, the walk, the odd gesture,
the echo of that naked child
who started from a lightning flash,
but growing up was like a new suit
which the other one, the man, borrowed and wore.*

That's what happened with me.

*From the woods
I arrived in the city, gas, cruel faces
taking stock of my being and my size,
I arrived among women who sought themselves in me
as if I had lost them,
and so he went on happening,
the impure man,
child of the pure child,
until nothing was as it had been,
and suddenly there appeared in my face
the face of a stranger
and it was also I:
it was a growing I,
it was a growing you,
it was everything,
but we change.*

> We no longer knew who we were,
> and at times we remember
> the one who lived in us
> and we ask him something, perhaps to remember us,
> to know at least we were he, that we speak
> with his voice,
> but across the used-up years
> he looks at us and doesn't recognize us.
>
> *Translation:*
> *https://unmasking.tripod.com/poemless/pn9.htm*

Who was I? What was I? What were we? There are no answers—we just happened, Neruda says. But there are answers, because we were, and who we were did not disappear—it still lives locked within us. In this evocation by Neruda, it lives locked among plenty of male stereotype imagery. But with those answers would come recognition from the child.

When I think about Neruda, much like Gabriel Garcia Marquez, I see them as such a gold mine for translation. Rubén Darío, on the other hand, I don't look to him so much for introspective content, only for resonance, exuberance and syncopation—qualities in which I have never seen an equal. I grew up reciting his poems with bombastic splendor, walking to school with the resounding beat of poetry in my eardrums, in a country where everyone was a writer and a poet, or so it seemed. In his poem *Triumphal March*, I only see him marching alone as a one-man marching band with 100 instruments. But he is untranslatable.

In the walk to truth, we would like to think that somewhere, sometime, nothing would be more enticing than to go back inside our time and be that child, be with that child that we have so conveniently ignored and disdained, so that we can hear and realize that their truth is likely simpler, bigger and more encompassing than the little collections of pseudo-truths we fabricate as adults. We just cannot not bring our whole selves forward until we can go back for what we left behind.

9.2. Elusive Togetherness

Part of being in the present is being together with the people we like and love. We all experienced those moments of being together, with emotions that linger, wrapping us in the feeling of that moment. Despite such experiences, I think that the feeling of existential togetherness is quite elusive. This is because it is not just related to affection or love but to a more transcendental conclusion—the recognition that we are being with each other in this precise existential confluence of time and place. It is the significance of having been together on Earth at the same time, of being together in each other's present time. But an inability to live in present time will make us numb to the importance of this transcendental togetherness.

There is a clear difference between the longing for and the privilege of being with loved ones—such as your parents—and recognizing the existential value of it. I can connect this to an example of my own. My adult relationship with my mother became quite rich and my understanding of her amazingly clear. I think her transparency came from how uniquely vulnerable my mom was in giving her love to us. When we were hurt by disappointment, you could see how her vulnerability was pierced—how a big long needle had trespassed all through her heart. I could literally see it, and I was zoomed into that vulnerability. People are not in the business of making themselves vulnerable. Love is contextual, and like a planetary system, it takes place in different concentric and contextual orbits. The more concentric, the more contextual and the more tightly connected the relationship is. It is its gravitational force. For example, with my mom, we were in a contextual orbit inside and unscathed by an outer orbit of morality—where morality judgements impair and mediate relationships. This means we had our own private sense of morality. It wasn't amoral, just uniquely ours—not imposed by external currents, but designed to account for us being together above all else. Obviously, this makes the relationship much more private and comforting—like it was home, like we were it. And because to us, everyone else existed in outer concentric orbits, they were not it.

I wonder how that relates to the more generic notion of comfort and home. NDE survivors describe it when they say, "I felt I was home." What was present as "home" in that afterlife experience that was absent in their physical life? There has to be a context associated with it—something that makes that existence more theirs than their physical life and that could include a more encompassing recognition of themselves.

There never seemed to be enough time to spend with my mom, and when I had to leave, the break in that unity was very palpable and hurtful. Even with all those explicit emotions in life, when my mom passed away, the wound of that departure was overwhelmed by a new sense of immense existential private pride of having had the privilege of walking side by side on this earth with my mom. Then I cried continually for the next five years about how meaningful and private that pride was. But it would have been impossible for me to experience that existential pride in present time when she was alive. I think this is because for a relationship to be existential you have to see it gone before you can make it yours beyond a lifetime. Otherwise, it is existential only in theory and the comfort of the still existing physical relationship overpowers your imagination to the raw feeling of the existential. That is why present time is so elusive.

9.3. *Intuition and the Blink of an Eye*

Intuition is the forward ability to see the inner self of another individual in a flash of transparency and pure emotion, turning time into beauty.

Being in the present time means that the eyes of our intuition and curiosity are immersed into everything that surrounds us.

There are countless dimensions that contribute to the attractiveness and likeability of us humans. Personality-wise, we present ourselves naked, with all our layers on display—our personal history tattooed on our bones and served on a silver platter for all to see. For example, some of us reveal how we have been victimized and either continue to allow that victimization or, conversely, show what we have sacrificed to prevent any further harm. Others demonstrate how they live in pretense, maintaining friendships without requiring any disclosures from them. Some of us show how we overcompensate for our inner isolation by being overly solicitous to others, striving to avoid falling into an emotional abyss. And on that silver platter, we may encounter the humbling beauty of one who does not have two dimes to rub together, just one shirt between sun, skin, a daily sweat of eight hours and a cup of beans—but whose private life is so profoundly private and thus preserved to remain forever unseen.

Our ability to read others from their silver platters becomes part of what makes us attractive, as it stems from our ability to read and know ourselves. I remember one time, shortly after arriving in the U.S. as a graduate student, I attended a noisy party, talking to whoever, when a female student came up to me and said *"you know, you can walk with anybody along their path, but nobody can walk with you in your own path, you have to do it alone,"* and then disappeared. It is so humbling and so beautiful to know that we are on our own pilgrimage walking barefoot, limping with our scars and imperfections, so visible to the naked eye for all to see. And when our curious intuition that sees others finds a landing and comes out in a flash of transparency, and pure emotion is given for just that moment, it turns time into beauty that lingers flamboyant and uncontained. Intuition sparks curiosity—the spontaneous curiosity of a child, the only curiosity that there is.

Adult curiosity does not exist—it is a fabrication to endure the low-grade rumblings of our daily capitulations. Intuition is love without a safety net. What we see in others laid on a silver platter only comes to us by the sheer strength of our intuition, until fear of owning it and holding it high on a banner brings doubt and we deny ourselves and take back everything we saw. There is a price to pay for intuition: it is an insight that opens up a private channel to an external reality. The more our spontaneous intuition goes out on a limb, the more vulnerable it becomes to the flicker of fear that rushes back into that opening, flooding it to deny and vilify our intuition for daring, in the blink of an eye, to trust nothing else but ourselves.

We know we live in our intuition when we become the personification of beauty. *Self-trust is the engine of our intuition, and curiosity is the flight of our intuition, looking for a place to land.* The world would be a permanent celebration of life and suddenly unrecognizable if we never took back what we see with the eyes of our intuition.

We can also look at intuition more specifically by contrasting it with the fear of intimacy. Let us oversimplify and define fear of intimacy as a fear of entrapment, and love as a process of emotional exploration. Intuition is the grand entry to our Inner Sanctum, and individuality and autonomy create the conditions for intuition to emerge as the guiding compass.

Given that our trust in our intuition is still fragile and underdeveloped, the bolder the intuition, the quicker the backlash that crashes against the fear of insecurity, doubt and exposure. This leads to the subsequent vilification of our own intuition to protect against the perceived threat of entrapment. There is no other way to escape the perceived threat but by the vilification of our intuition. The fear of entrapment is conveniently justified by the individual's religious and moral beliefs. The cultural symptom of our current generations is the failure to fully realize intuition and exploration. This fragile sequence goes from intuition to fear of entrapment, leading to the perception of threat and the vilification of intuition—all while preventing genuine exploration. Leaving exploration unexplored is a key condition to perpetuate this cycle of fear; otherwise, exploration would confirm our initial intuition and further complicate our hurried exit. This suggests that our best individuals in these generations are those most likely to see their intuition and sense of exploration crushed. This generational loss is unsustainable and underscores the need for future generations to establish a cultural framework that fosters individual autonomy and gender emancipation, allowing emotional explorations to flourish.

This direct emotional exposure to the effects of intuition is a beautiful trait in the prevalent U.S. culture which is nowhere to be found in many other cultures, mainly because cultural roles quickly permeate and diffuse direct interactions. It is beautiful partly because it reveals, in full transparency, the reverse vilification effect of our fears, which perpetuate our isolation and confine us to our own self-entrapments. That retreat by vilification shown in full transparency is a form of cultural generosity exposing the retreat. In a perverse twist devoid of all sadness, it resembles a glass wall laboratory where behavior can be anticipated with mathematical predictability.

Still within our simplified view of the fear of intimacy, we see that initial opening of intuition as a shortcut—a shortcut through layers of social norms, conditioning, and stereotypes. A spontaneous flash of intuition may be second guessed, reinterpreted as an attempt at domination or a threat of entrapment, triggering the vilification of intuition as the only perceived way to preserve our misunderstood sense of freedom. Vilification, in this context, is the refusal to give credit to our intuition and turning against our original perceptions. It is the betrayal of our intuition. Such self-betrayal never sits well within us, because it is so extremely difficult to justify or hide. The unconcealable transparency of the reversal and self-betrayal of our intuition is what brings me to the clearest signal of hope for the future of the U.S.

If we had enough emotional margin to spare, we could consider another option that takes us beyond the entrapment paradigm. We could understand our intuition as not merely speaking for someone entering our space but instead revealing an undiscovered reality about ourselves that this person is bringing to light. It is a reality that will resonate with us for the first time. If we trust that our intuition operates in our best interest, then it suggests that this new, enticing undiscovered reality holds the power to shatter the concept of entrapment in favor of an expansive view of ourselves.

9.4. *Arrival to Present Time*

I don't know if there is anything more beautiful and magnetic in this life than a human being who has made a descent and has a clear path to their inner self, devoid of any naïveté, crutches or addictions, devoid of any chronic emotional white noise which, like a vehicle running idle, poses a permanent distraction from a transparent coexistence with the surroundings. It means that a person with that depth can read the rest of us like a book and smile at our pretense but not buy it or cater to it. That transparency is infectious, awe inspiring and truly exemplary, and it signals the person's arrival to present time. But being blessed with such an experience is not that common. I have encountered it once or twice, and the experience will stay with me until I die, because to me they are my proof of who we are.

I can describe two of those experiences. I remember one time, watching a friend of mine as he was walking on his way back from lunch and going into his office for the afternoon. There was nothing commemorative or eventful about the moment, except that I noticed how grounded he was. He had no emotional idle stress engine driving him. Those engines running in automatic keep us absent or distracted and prevent us from just being in the moment. I could see, as he casually looked at the trees and the wind and the clouds, that he was aware of his surroundings without an overt interest in them. I could see he was ready for a hopefully not-so-boring afternoon at work. He did not have to be one moment ahead or behind where he was. I looked at him from inside my car and thought: *"that is present time, that is exactly the emotional place where I want to be."* But I also knew it was not likely to happen. It is not so easy to get there. It's not as if I haven't been to wonderful places inside myself.

I remember situations in which I had to understand heavily encrypted emotional dynamics that were stagnant and harmful to me. I had to dissect them carefully to uncover the specific underlying issue, understand the reasons behind it, and ensure that the issue was fully encapsulated, leaving no room for it to escape through false reasoning. Then I had to present it in a way that made the argumentation compelling and precise, like an ultrasharp scalpel cutting deeply without causing bleeding, leaving no room for confrontation.

Those moments for me have raised the presence of my emotional self to an art form, and they brought that beautiful sense of present time. But they were the result of riding the crest of an accomplishment, and over time they faded. I think my friend's experience revealed a higher state of being, because it represented his natural routine. That is a great place to be, but it is not that easy to get there.

In another situation, I had to meet with a woman many years ago to review a social topic we had to address. Though we never spoke about ourselves or any individual emotional accomplishments during our time, I found her emotional presence to be jaw-dropping. Out of all the individuals, whether from public or private life, leading major or minor political or social causes for gender, racial, or political equality, I have never encountered anyone who lives outside of the emotional cage imposed by society. But she did. She was a woman outside of any emotional cage—a woman who had obviously surrendered to her fears to move past them and reach the beautiful inner self awaiting her. Her presence had no sign of fear or hesitation, just love as sweet as honey and gratitude from being surrounded by beauty.

Recognizing this beauty everywhere was now her reward, and it had become clear for her to see. Recognizing surrounding beauty is easier said than done—everyone will say they recognize it, but the devil is on the level at which they recognize it. I felt she saw me as a man, a boy, and everything in between, as well as what I was before a boy—the more pure, genderless being that I am quite fond of. Everything that I still doubted about myself, was not in doubt to her. With her love and awareness, everything about me was accounted for. I experienced this with her without ever speaking a word of it. Why would we speak of what was already obvious to us both? When I left, I said *"I love you,"* and she said *"I love you too,"* and that was the end of the afternoon. Later I cried like a baby, for the love of course, and for having been seen that way, but more for the ratification of who we really are inside, so essential for the survival of our human race. I had the proof of who we were—a proof that I will take with me to my grave. I have not seen another person outside the cage, either before or after this experience.

This brings gender issues to a social context. For a social oppression situation to take place, both sides have to be severely repressed to accept their respective roles. It seems that women are more likely to move their inner selves forward into noticeable progress, because they seem to show enough malleability of emotion to accomplish just that. I have a blind spot in that I don't believe in us men. We are just too stiff, mechanical and subservient to our gender roles. Emotions do not really flow for us because they become a smelly, stagnant manifestation of self pity. The best you can get out of us is "understanding," which is another word for convenient passivity and reluctance to find our own entrails. Understanding is a transitive verb—a way of passing the buck. We don't want or need understanding; what we need is to become what others do not understand—socially for others but foremost for ourselves.

It is well known that individual emotional progress has to spill into social gender issues to become the propulsion for advancement. We men find ourselves in a very compromising situation, difficult to escape. In his article, *Caverns of Rage*, Dougherty (1993) refers to the bind we men find ourselves in, which requires a male-centric approach. After all, as we argue that any emotional movement must be self-centered, this approach should at some point consider the male personification in men and address gender preferences in those born male. Before we men can look at feminist issues, we have to own our male personification. As I have said before, changes will not be sustainable if we do not start at the beginning—the center.

Among those of us who will never reach our transparent self, I do love those with an insatiable curiosity for who they might be, always looking for themselves. I love people who are late in life, and still trying to find themselves, never assuming that what they have is it, though sometimes what they already have is a lot more than what most of us could hope to find. Even for a moment, they just want to see who they are and who they were all those years past—the self they humbly missed—just so they can say *"I found me and I was with me. I saw myself."*

There was a soapy movie called Cleopatra (Aleandro, 2004) about a retired school teacher in Buenos Aires, Argentina, who lived all her life as a housewife. She would go about her day—going to the market for groceries, remembering to bring her umbrella, purse, bag and enough change for the metro, preparing food for her husband—and would wonder if there was a world outside all those house chores and duties. One day she collects all her cash to make enough change for the buses, puts on her mid-heel shoes, handkerchief around her head, brings her purse and small luggage, waits at the bus stop and takes off out of the city. While on the road, Cleo befriends a young woman who has just ended her TV acting career, tired of the gender roles imposed on her as a beautiful woman. Later, they befriend a young man in an old rusty truck in the middle of nowhere. Eventually, the three of them set off together, traversing the great American open spaces of the place we call La Argentina. Flamenco composer Paco Ortega wrote the song that plays in this movie clip—*La Rumba de Cleo* (Ortega, 2004). The song is the musical inner voice of Cleo, sung by Ortega, a man, using the feminine Spanish pronouns: "*me espera otra mujer, que soy yo misma, y tan contenta,*" "*another woman awaits, which is me, my own woman self, and I am so girl happy,*" which is so beautiful and gives such a sense of togetherness, of echo, to Cleo's voice. Following is a translation of a portion of the lyrics:

La Rumba de Cleo

Like a trail in the forest
That little by little
Is disappearing
That is how life is escaping from me, searching...
Searching in the thicket
Searching blindfolded
Searching for an exit
For an entire life
Without realizing.

Searching for an exit
Searching for my destiny
Searching blindfolded
Dreaming of an open forest
And an immense sky
To surprise me.

From the inside out
Another woman awaits
Who is myself
A heart awaits
Which is my own heart

And I am so happy
And I am so happy
What a moment
What a moment
When my thoughts explode
Inside me
What a moment
What a moment
When my feelings explode
Inside me

Searching for an exit
Inside my soul
Searching for strength
To throw high up
All of my life trembling

Searching in the thicket...

9.5. Blossoms that Cling to the Vine

If I run into a situation where someone is vociferating and spewing anger against me, with foam dripping out of their mouth, ready to pulverize me with verbal attacks, I will select my defiant walk from my repertoire, channeling the James Caan walk in the movie *The Godfather*, and walk up to that person and say, *"If you have something to say to me, say it with a song!"* This applies today to the thoughts we now entertain. If we have something to say, let's say it with a song. Below are the lyrics to a song called *Today*.

Today

Today, while the blossoms still cling to the vine
I'll taste your strawberries, I'll drink your sweet wine
A million tomorrows shall all pass away
'Ere I forget all the joy that is mine, Today

9. PRESENT TIME

I'll be a dandy, and I'll be a rover
You'll know who I am by the songs that I sing
I'll feast at your table, I'll sleep in your clover
Who cares what the morrow shall bring

Today, while the blossoms still cling to the vine
I'll taste your strawberries, I'll drink your sweet wine
A million tomorrows shall all pass away
'Ere I forget all the joy that is mine, Today

I can't be contented with yesterday's glory
I can't live on promises winter to spring
Today is my moment, now is my story
I'll laugh and I'll cry and I'll sing

Today, while the blossoms still cling to the vine
I'll taste your strawberries, I'll drink your sweet wine
A million tomorrows shall all pass away
'Ere I forget all the joy that is mine, Today

Today, while the blossoms still cling to the vine
I'll taste your strawberries, I'll drink your sweet wine
A million tomorrows shall all pass away
'Ere I forget all the joy that is mine, Today

This song says all I can say. It makes the thoughts in this chapter redundant or at least unnecessary to explain. It goes to show that reading is overrated.

The song speaks of truths as living, breathing, ephemeral emotions, as they can be spoken only when they are alive, while the blossoms still cling to the vine. And the truth that I bring will stay alive for a long time. A million tomorrows shall all pass away, 'ere I forget all the joy that is mine, today. The truth that I bring is all in me, and you will know who I am by the songs that I sing. I live in the present time, and today is my moment.

Well, maybe the song does not say everything I want to say, but you get the idea.

I think soloists like John Denver and others who sing this song, do a disservice by singing it solo. The song evokes the voices of all of us—a murmur of our shared humanity—and it should be sung as such, by a group, so no single voice stands isolated. In this way, the song becomes a collective echo, resonating with all of us together.

10. *While Today is Still Forever*

My life changed over these last few months, from me being somewhat spacey—watching my thoughts drift with the wind, leaving me disowned of what once upon a time, one minute earlier that is, was my thought—to becoming the reporter of my own self. During the summer of 2024, I turned my river running into a pilgrimage of sorts, with frequent sudden stops to claim temporary ownership over my brain and scribble on my phone a thought in fleeting suspension, before letting my brain continue to roam free with my run. My brain is a big hollow space where the wind enters to swirl and gain speed as it blows out to the other side, and once blown, everything in between is gone forever. The moral of this story is, never run without scribbling your testament as you go, for I say you, torture is trying to retain the wind with your hands to hold on to a thought when it has already blown by you.

I seek forgiveness from poems unwritten, which remain forever patient, dormant and unattended underneath the pressing rush of contrasting sobriety that gives body to this book, which shall remain incomplete, because every place it touches creates ripples that extend out of reach. Who would I be if I were to say that a journey is ever completed? I would be negating the premise of truth formation that gave birth to the book to begin with.

Whether or not this book has any value for reader, for me it has been a road to myself. The road ahead that now comes to me frontally, wider, open, plain and free of hurdles, and with a new visual further into the horizon. It's as if this road had been waiting for me all along. It is the road that impels me to put my stake in the ground for those individuals I saw day in and day out walking the face of the earth, as if the earth belonged to them. On the one hand, they were living in anonymity and ignored by society, walking their imperfect walk, stuttering or not, making do in life with whatever they thought might be good enough in their pockets to barter their autonomy and stay afloat outside society and in clandestine appropriation of their own lives. On the other hand, they were living in anonymity and ignored by society because society could never give them credit for what it could not understand. Understanding them would have meant recognizing the farce of wasting a life of *pleasing and placing*—pleasing society submissively, in order to place into society's ranking, buying the delusion that such ranking had any value, any comfort, any shelter.

These individuals brought with them the eyes for a reality that with their sarcastic laughter dismantled a world of elaborate pretensions and disrobed it into a world of make-believe. And for that, inconspicuously, anonymously, they owned the day, and they owned reality—all of it. They owned their own reality and they owned everyone else's. I thought these individuals immortal because they made life their own possession. Without them, life would be replaced by a paper fantasy glued only by sleepless

10. WHILE TODAY IS STILL FOREVER   313

nights and the eternal anxiety of living in a make-believe alienation. It is for them that the song is sung and that my wide-open road brings me to plant my stake in the ground as my own reward for writing this book.

Antonio Machado, poet from Sevilla, Spain, and his mother, Ana Ruiz Henández, went into exile and crossed the French border on January 27th of 1939 during the Spanish Civil War and the ensuing Franco dictatorship. He died of physical exhaustion a month later on February 22nd, and three days later his mother died too. His verses still stay at the tip of our tongue. After all, *"today is still forever, and our entire life is now."* He wrote *Cantares*, which awkwardly translates like this.

Cantares

Everything passes
and everything remains
but our fate is to pass
to pass making paths
paths over the sea.

I never chased glory
Nor to leave in the memory
Of mankind my song;

I love subtle worlds
Weightless and gentle
Like bubbles of soap.
I like to see them colored
in sunshine and scarlet, fly
below the blue sky, suddenly
Tremble and burst.

Wayfarer, the path
is your footprints and nothing else;
wayfarer, there are no paths,
You make the path as you walk
and when you look back
you see the path that you will never
step on again.

Wayfarer, there are no paths,
They are wakes on the sea.

When the goldfinch cannot sing.
When the poet is a pilgrim,
when it is useless to pray.
wayfarer, there are no paths,
You make the path as you walk
Blow by blow, verse by verse.

10. WHILE TODAY IS STILL FOREVER

Joan Manuel Serrat is a songwriter from Catalonia, Spain, and storyteller of one thousand years of Mediterranean history (1971). Serrat (1969) wrote a pop song for *Cantares*, which shaped a generation of high schoolers with that secular thought of individuality and destiny and gave us the banner for our own autonomy. But it also taught us to endure that little bitter taste of loneliness with stoicism, as we walked the solitary path that only we could carve for ourselves.

We are no longer willing to bathe in stoicism, but what we take now is Machado's pronouncement of not wanting to chase hollow glories, not leaving our names engraved in the mossy history of humankind. There will always be a present time awaiting in our lives to give every second back to us, more overpowering, fulfilling and spontaneous than any premeditated notion of living for history.

As we move in the great human procession, we await another poem, another song and another century, with a new reality for another generation of highschoolers. A poem that will delineate our very own path, carved by both predetermined destiny and free will, and sustained with the comfort of the entire humanity watching in suspense, celebrating, and staying with us, as if there were nothing more important in the universe than every step we take along our individual way.

U.S. pop singer Paul Simon wrote (1966):

> *So you see, I have come to doubt*
> *All that I once held as true*
> *I stand alone without beliefs*
> *The only truth I know is you*

And thus, while we bring our today to remain forever, we stand alone, at peace or not with our doubts, disrobed without beliefs and with even less certainties, but one step closer to everything. We want our timeless consciousness to sneak through the physical cracks and reach us while today remains eternal, to reward our infinite curiosity by revealing the reasons for our existence and past lives, and to join us in celebrating this majestic, wonderful experiment we call life.

∞

PART IV, Addendum

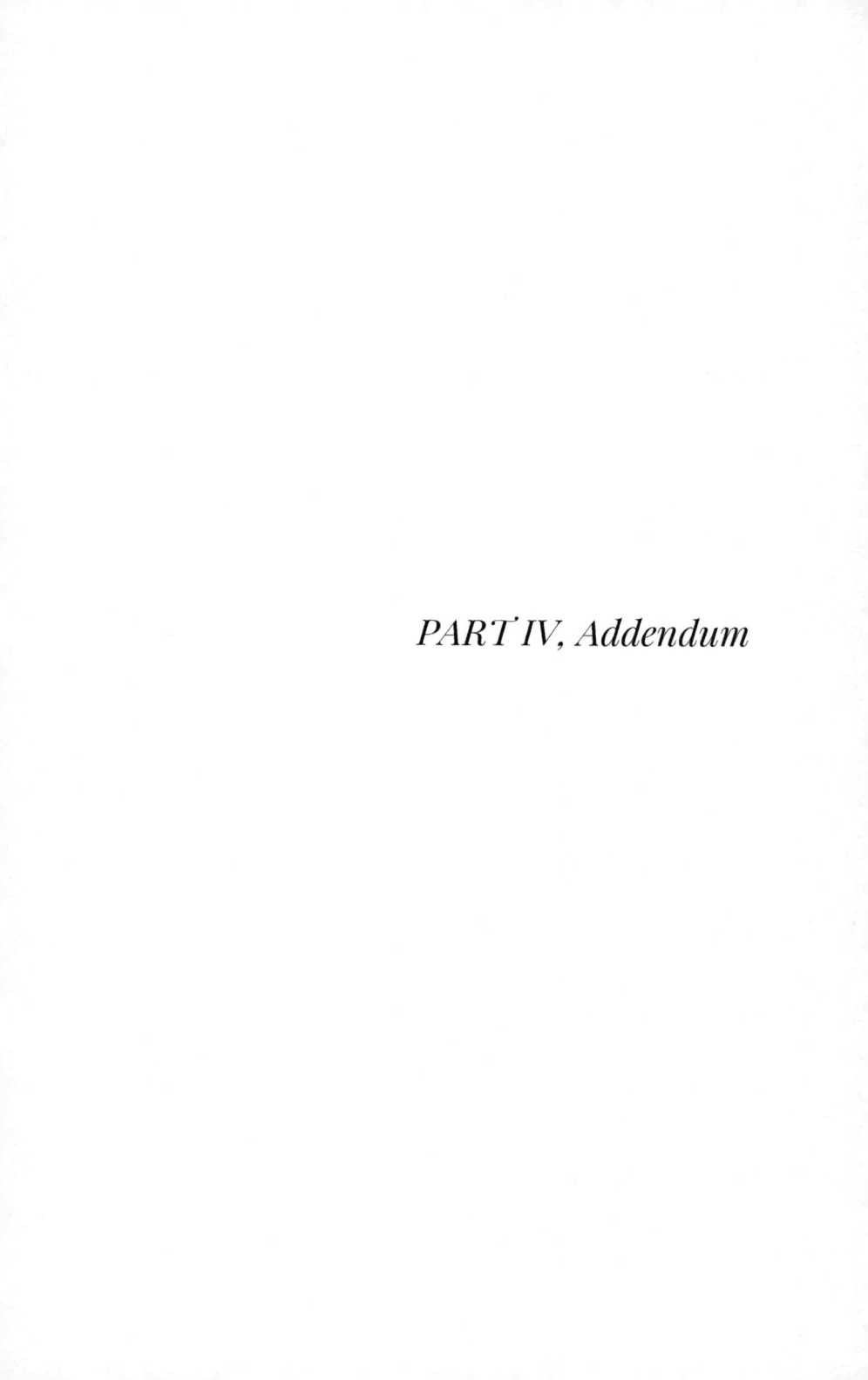

A.1. Unsubstantiated NDE Cases

In this section we briefly refer to cases that gained quite a bit of popularity, but which I would not offer as reference because of seeming contradictions or lack of verifiable evidence.

The externally verifiable credibility of each case must stand on its own. Eben Alexander, a U.S. neurosurgeon, recounts his own NDE on his best seller (Alexander, 2012). He has been featured in Time Magazine, Newsweek, and Oprah Winfrey. His book was endorsed by Raymond Moody, Jr., award-winning author of twelve books, including *Life After Life* (Moody, 1975), and he is the person who coined the term NDE, as he states that *"Dr. Eben Alexander's near-death experience is the most astounding I have heard in more than four decades of studying this phenomenon. (He) is living proof of an afterlife."* Eben Alexander states he became very ill with acute bacterial meningoencephalitis and fell into a coma, where he experienced his NDE. He describes going through a tunnel of white light and beautiful complex music as he felt as if he was being born, then flying over a beautiful lush earth-like landscape where people celebrated with great happiness. He was not flying alone and a beautiful girl, his biological sister whom he never met before her passing, was guiding his flight. Seeing and hearing were not separate in this place as he could hear visual beauty and see beautiful sounds, and that he could not hear or listen to anything without becoming part of it. His silent questions were answered with an immediate explosion of light, color, beauty and love in the form of thoughts that entered directly into him, as knowledge was stored without memorization, instantly and for good. He entered into the infinite void of an omniscient omnipresent being who explained that there were multiple universes with life, good and evil, for without evil there would not be free will. He conveys that his NDE was very peculiar because he did not have a sense of himself and therefore was deprived from access to his past or future. The following observations can be noted regarding Alexander's credibility surrounding this case:

1. (Dittrich, 2013a,b) states in his article in Esquire that back on April 13, 2001, Dr. Eben Alexander's employment as a surgeon at the Brigham was terminated for unknown reasons, and in August 2003, UMass Memorial suspended Alexander's surgical privileges *"on the basis or allegation of improper performance of surgery."* Dittrich (2013a,b) and DailyMail (2013) state that Alexander was sued for malpractice five times and provide details of the nature of these lawsuits. The last one for three million dollars was still pending at the time of his illness and was related to the allegation that Alexander had fused the wrong vertebrae in surgery and later attempted to change the medical records to cover up his mistake.

2. Contrary to Dr. Alexander's statement that he was in coma and brain dead for seven straight days caused by his illness, Dittrich (2013a,b), in an interview with Dr. Laura Potter, the

A.1. UNSUBSTANTIATED NDE CASES 321

attending ER physician, establishes that the coma was instead chemically induced by her because Dr. Alexander's extreme state of conscious agitation required that he be physically restrained for his own safety, and every time they tried to let him wake up, he was in exactly the same conscious but agitated state, so they would go back to inducing the coma again. Mays (2016) defends the veracity of the original statements made by Alexander and refutes the characterization of Alexander's coma in Dittrich's article in Esquire, by posting a subsequent written statement provided by Dr. Potter. Instead of absolving Alexander, this statement only created more damage, because surprisingly, Dr Potter did not set the medical record straight, which would have put the issue to rest. Instead, she says that her statements presented by Dittrich were "out of context" and "misrepresented." But misrepresented how? What was the context then? Was the nature of this misrepresentation only about her tone and intention not to damage Alexander's credibility? Were there any material misrepresentations or lies? She also states that, *"I believe Dr. Alexander has made every attempt to be factual in his accounting of events,"* but there is a big difference between *attempting* to be factual and being factual. Khanna et.al. (2018) states that he remained sedated for the first five days but that *"his medical records suggest that his coma was not drug-induced."*

3. In an Oprah Winfrey interview (Winfrey, 2012), Alexander states that the reason for him to return to his physical body was a compelling experience he had when his son pulled his eyelids to look at his eyes and talked to him. But if he had a recollection of that event, wouldn't that mean that he was somewhat conscious and not in a coma? Wasn't he already

present physically on Earth? And contrary to his statement of spiritual amnesia, wouldn't this assume that his spiritual self was aware of his physical presence and state? And wasn't then his physical self making that decision from a position of control over his spiritual self? This narrative only brings too many contradictions to the case.

4. Khanna et.al. (2018) states that his vivid memories of the experience suggest an NDE, but that would never be proof of one. However, they do state that Mr. Alexander recalled events that he claimed to have perceived from a visual perspective outside his physical body, such as a group of individuals praying around his ICU bed.

5. There is no point in second guessing the source of the experience, be that a true NDE (comatose or not), a hallucination, or just a creative mind. Contrary to most NDE accounts, where individuals describe a heightened nonlocal awareness of their physical world, Mr. Alexander contradicts himself by first stating that in the spiritual realm, everything is remembered forever without requiring memory. Yet in his own spiritual state, he claims to have had "spiritual amnesia," with no recollection of his present physical identity. He claims it was his semi-awaken physical self who called him back to his physical realm. For the reasons outlined above, I cannot offer this case as a reference.

A.2. James 3, a Past Life Remembered

This case was summarized in the subsection *"James 3"* of the section *"Spontaneous Recollection of Past Lives."* It is revisited again in order to provide additional details, including a review of Philosopher Sudduth's re-examination of the case.

Tucker (2016) describes the case of James Leininger, which I summarize below, and which he also includes in a later book (Tucker, 2021). This case was also presented in a Netflix documentary (Netflix, 2020b).

James Leininger was born on April 10, 1998. When he was 22 months old, his father took him to the Cavanaugh Flight Museum outside of Dallas. James showed a great deal of interest in the airplanes, but in particular in the World War II exhibit. After three hours in the exhibit, James left with some toy planes and a video called *It's a Kind of Magic* about the Blue Angels, the Navy's flight exhibition team. James often surprised his parents with his passion and knowledge of airplanes. Tucker states that the video was not the source of James's knowledge about World War II, since the Blue Angels was a group founded in 1946, once the war had ended. His father took James to the museum for a second trip that spring, on Memorial Day weekend. Once again, James was excited to be there but he grew quiet in the World War II exhibit, and stood in awe staring and pointing to the planes.

Shortly within two months of the first trip to the museum, James developed a habit of saying *"airplane crash on fire,"* and simulating an air crash by slamming his toy airplanes, nose first into the table. He repeated this behavior with great frequency, leaving the table full of scratches and dents. James' father travelled a lot and when James and his mother would see him at the airport, he would continue to stress that single theme by saying to his father, *"Daddy, airplane crash on fire."* This behavior was repeated constantly, despite his father's admonishments and reprimands.

This single theme started to appear outside James' conscious behavior, as he began experiencing nightmares. They started out as screams at first, but then evolved to include words as well: *"Airplane crash on fire! Little man can't get out."* Tucker notes that in their book, James' parents quoted him using a longer sentence, *"Airplane crash! Plane on fire! Little man can't get out."* but in a prior interview, they had referred to the shorter quote. It seems these nightmares surfaced with a great deal of emotional content, as James would be very agitated during these episodes, shouting the same sentence over and over, while kicking his legs forcefully. After several months had passed with the same behavior, James had several conversations with his parents about the nature of these dreams, and he was beginning to add more details at that time. He recalled that they were memories of events from his past. He stated his plane had crashed on fire and that he had been shot by the Japanese. He continued to provide information, and two weeks later, James said his plane was a Corsair, and he mentioned he flew a Corsair several times. The Corsair was a fighter plane developed during World War II. When James was just 28 months old, on August 27, 2000, he told his parents he flew his plane off a boat named "Natoma." James' father was able to corroborate online the existence of the USS Natoma Bay, an escort carrier stationed in the Pacific during World War II. Tucker notes that James' dad printed the information he found about the USS Natoma Bay, and that the date of the print was shown at the footer of the printout. With that information in hand, James' parents asked him repeatedly for the name of the little man in the airplane crash. He always responded by saying *"me"* or *"James."* They also asked him if he remembered the name of anybody else, to which he responded *"Jack Larsen."*

When James was two and a half years old, his father was looking through a book called *The Battle for Iwo Jima 1945*, which he was going to give to his own father for Christmas. As reported by his father, James pointed to an aerial view of the base where Mt. Suribachi is located and said, *"That's where my plane was shot down, my airplane got shot down there, Daddy."* A week later, a veteran from Natoma Bay told James' father that he remembered a pilot named Jack Larsen, but that he never returned from one of the fly missions and no one knew what had happened to him.

At that time, James' parents contacted Carol Bowman, who was the author of a book about children's past-life memories. Following her advice, James' mother began acknowledging to James the veracity of the events he described, while reassuring him that they were part of his past and that he was now safe. The nightmares then grew less violent and less frequent.

The theme of his past life experience continued to manifest itself. When James became old enough to draw, he drew hundreds of airplane battle scenes, and he signed them "*James 3.*" When his parents asked him about the reason for the number 3 in his signature, he always stated that it referred not to his age but to his being "*the third James,*" as he continued to sign his drawings that way past age 3.

In June 2002, James' parents as well as Tucker were interviewed for an ABC News segment called Strange Mysteries. The segment never aired but Tucker received copies of the supporting documentation for the segment, which outlined an initial profile of the still unidentified pilot in the crash. Correspondence between James' father and the producer of the ABC News segment at that time, serve as documentation of the father's efforts to locate Jack Larsen, which proved unsuccessful at that time. James' father later attended his first Natoma Bay reunion, where he learned that the one Jack Larsen from Natoma Bay had survived the war. He was absent at the reunion and he was alive, and soon James' father was able to visit him. At the reunion, he learned that there was only one casualty during the Battle of Iwo Jima, a 21-year-old from Pennsylvania named James M. Huston, Jr., making the boy James Leininger James III. His father then turned his attention to Huston, and such efforts were documented by a posting he made on a website.

A.2. JAMES 3, A PAST LIFE REMEMBERED

James' father found out that James Huston Jr. did not actually die in the battle for Iwo Jima per se. He was one of eight pilots from Natoma Bay who took part on a subsequent strike against transport vessels in a neighboring harbor at Chichijima, as the Japanese were preparing a troop and supplies buildup. Huston's plane crash site appears to coincide exactly at the location James had described, and there were charts of the paths each pilot took, and Jack Larsen is shown to be flying the plane next to Huston's. Given that Huston was the only Natoma Bay pilot killed during the Iwo Jima operation and his details were closely matched to James' statements, his parents reached the conclusion that Huston was the man being recalled by James.

Philosopher Sudduth (2021) provides a detailed, 94-page re-examination of the James 3 case, where his objections to the veracity of the case I classify in 4 categories: a) alternative sources of knowledge for James 3 from his own childhood, b) omissions in the construction of the case, c) redactions and revisions of the original narratives, and d) "dark data" as in statistical reasoning— what you don't know matters and may further disrupt your evidence. Sudduth exemplifies his observations to point out that an event with explanatory value does not necessarily rise to the scrutiny of an evidentiary force. In other words, an explanation is more likely to be credible, if there are no other explanations that contradict it. However, it is worth noting that a) unless an explanation of an event is shown to negate or contradict the event itself, the plausibility of the actual event still stands, and b) the negation, contradiction or alternative explanation of an event, does not necessarily propagate the same invalidation to other events in the case, regardless of how related they may seem. The latter is a common sense rule that we apply routinely in our arguments, and is equally found as a standard legal clause in every legal contract (the *salvatorious* or severability clause is a provision in a contract that allows the remainder of the contract's terms to remain effective, even if one or more of its other terms or provisions are found to be unenforceable or illegal), but Sudduth does not apply it as he uses questionable evidence to dismiss all other events. One of Philosopher Sudduth techniques to summarily discredit the case is to apply a singular isolated technicality, narrow as a needle, to dismiss an event and with that, the entire case, without accepting that other interrelated events may be validated independently and will stand alone as the verification of the case—what we might call *"the anti-salvatorious"* clause. So if the salvatorious disclaimer has been part of the vernacular human dialogue for millennia, and routinely granted by lawyers to their contractual adversaries, why is it not part of Philosopher Sudduth's formulation? These are some of the objections raised by Philosopher Sudduth in his re-examination:

1. James 3's vast knowledge of aviation might have been acquired through his visits to the museum or the Blue Angels video.
2. His nightmares might have been caused by related stimuli in his childhood such as the Blue Angels video.
3. James 3's signing of his drawing as "James 3" when he was 3 and 4 years old "probably" refers to his age.
4. Neither the parents nor Dr. Tucker were aware of the title and content of the Blue Angels video.
5. The details of the James Huston crash as documented in the historical reports is described differently than as it was

recalled by James 3. The recollection gathered in the historical record seem to imply that the airplane did not catch fire in mid air and that James Huston might have died upon impact with water.

6. There was no evaluation by an accredited psychiatrist or psychologist concluding that the nightmares were a manifestation of PTSD.
7. Notes made by the parents were lost or thrown away by the time their book on the subject was published. This begs the question, how can original notes be lost or thrown away, and for the mother not to know whether they were lost or thrown away?

These are some observations to Sudduth's objections:

1. Philosopher Sudduth fails to invalidate the plausibility of this case on the possibility that James might have acquired his avionics knowledge from sources in his childhood, but either possibility is immaterial to the case. James could have had that information a priori or else refreshed and revised during his experience in the course of his childhood. Either way, his unusual and most significant interest in avionics prevails from day one. It does not change the validity of the rest of the experience. As a researcher, Sudduth needed to establish the relevant value of all the avionics events to the essential experience of flying and dying in the airplane crash. Knowing about the Corsair, flying a Corsair, dying in a Corsair, and having nightmares about being on his Corsair on fire (nightmares which did not come from being exhilarated at a museum), have relevant value to the specific in-

dividual experience far beyond liking the colors of the airplanes at a museum. Sudduth's criticism can be dismissed simply by the fact that the source of James' avionics knowledge is inconsequential with respect to his other essential recollections.
2. James 3 seems to have been an extremely happy boy otherwise, and all of James 3's daily experiences regarding aeronautic events were positive and filled him with enthusiasm, thus unlikely to be the provocation of recurring nightmares.
3. It was clearly stated by James 3 that the number 3 in his drawings' signature alluded to the fact that he was the third James in the generational succession. A boy with a voice said that.
4. Apparently, neither the parents nor Dr. Tucker were aware of the title and content of the Blue Angels video.
5. Sudduth discounts James 3's recollection of the Huston crash because it might not seem to correlate with some unverifiable reported description of the event by others that were actively engaged in battle, presumably under gunfire themselves. We are splitting hairs here. Even if we assume the airplane was not a big ball of fire as a result of the direct frontal hit, it is hard to imagine that there was not even smoke or a small fire in the cabin, not visible to others at a distance. If James 3 reports the trauma of fire in the airplane and his desperation about trying to get out, that suggests that he was not yet engulfed in flames, but trying to avoid them, and that suggests a small fire. It would also be natural to describe a fear of drowning before reaching the water, because that would be an expected horrifying outcome while falling from the sky into the water. Cuomo (2004)

presents an interview with Ralph Clarkberg, who was a rear gunner on a TBM Avenger flying on March 3rd, 1945, next to James Huston Jr, under the most intense enemy fire he saw in the war, and he recalls suddenly seeing a flash on the nose of Huston's plane as he was hit head on, just as James 3 had described, and contradicting the report of the crash without a fire cited by Sudduth. The crucial issue is the recollection of the event itself in a manner that coincides with other related, significant, material events of the day; that specific day, that specific location, that specific battle and that specific pilot.

6. This is another example of Philosopher Sudduth's summarily discounting events on the basis of a technicality. He discounts the recurring nightmares, occurring 3 to 4 times a week, only because there was no professional certification by a psychiatrist or psychologist to conclude that they were a manifestation of PTSD. The question is, do they have to be a product of PTSD in order to have evidentiary weight? There are interrelated events that shed light into the nature of those nightmares, for example, the fact that they significantly subsided when James 3 began to consider the possibility that he lived that experience in a previous life. A nightmare by any other name is a nightmare.

7. Sudduth refers to redactions and revisions made by the parents to their original statements, including the loss or discard of the original notes when their book was published. However, before using these alleged redactions to summarily discredit the case, Sudduth needed to review the context for those redactions in two significant ways: One, there are no indications that these alleged late-stage revisions were supporting a premeditated effort to fabricate

a hoax a priori, from its inception. These redactions are moderated revisions that took place after the fact and did not change the original explanations of the events. Second, there are early-stage chronological proofs provided by the parents, of their early accounts and efforts, including a) the dated printout of the USS Natoma Bay information, b) timely correspondence with ABC News producer about the attempt to locate one Jack Larsen, and c) the dated attempts to obtain information about James Huston Jr. The summary dismissal of the case on the basis of presumed late-stage redactions would require the dismissal of the parents' documented early chronological efforts, which Philosopher Sudduth is unable to dismiss. Without the dismissal of the chronological evidence, any late redactions, or revisions that might have been allegedly carried out by the parents, have no bearing on the dismissal of the case.

Philosopher Sudduth goes to great lengths to show that his assessment can only get worse because of the presumptive existence of "dark data," which are unknown additional facts that might exist to only further discredit the case (but never to prove it outright), but remain yet undiscovered. This case does not require that all the events be verified with evidentiary force, and thus Sudduth needed to classify these events in order to arrive to sets of minimal "essential" potentially evidentiary events—events that would prove the existence of a past life relationship regardless of the veracity or lack thereof of any other peripheral events. These essential events need to be selected so that, if verifiable, they would prove not so much a reference to a past life, but more importantly, to the life of WWII pilot James Huston II. As an example, let me briefly indulge in that exercise. Consider

A.2. JAMES 3, A PAST LIFE REMEMBERED

the following events: nightmares ("nm"), James repeatedly crashing his toy planes in the coffee table ("coffeetab"), James 3's catharsis at the sea by the crash site ("cath"), and his early signature as James 3 ("j3"). Would the verification of both "j3" and "nm" events be sufficient to prove this past life relationship? Or would "nm" and "cath" be sufficient? This exercise omitted by Philosopher Sudduth is sine qua non in the impartial evaluation of this case. Without this, we cannot even begin to speak about other peripheral events surrounding the case.

It seems that in his extremely detailed 94-page case re-examination, Philosopher Sudduth was unable to provide enough amplitude in the formulation of the case, to allow us to arrive at a natural conclusion.

It does not escape our attention that in these sets of essential events with potential substantive evidence, the lone actor without hearsay or intermediaries is the boy, James 3. His nightmares are clear. It is him crying in his crib, him providing the details surrounding the events, his signature in his drawings, him crying at the crash site, and him as an adult recollecting his relief at the crash site and expressing his lingering anxiety for having lived through a horrible prior death. It is James 3 speaking to us directly, and so Philosopher Sudduth must realize that he is not answering just to Dr. Tucker or James' parents, but to the boy himself. It is Sudduth who, through his intellectual pursuits, sees daylight to appropriate James 3's experience in order to take liberties as if it were his own to manipulate. Ignoring the boy's testimony in favor of pursuing an intellectual brawl, like a pit bull chewing on a bone, can be construed as a form of adultism—"philosophical adultism" in this case.

Cuomo (2004) offers a video recount of the James 3 case, while James was a boy and therapist Carol Bowman was already involved. Professor Emeritus of Philosophy at the State University of New York at Buffalo Paul Kurtz intervenes in this segment to state that these events are the product of misinformation supplied to James 3 during his childhood and not from a past life. But in a surprisingly generous gesture, he awards the parents the freedom to believe in what he already has predetermined to be nonsense without any inspection. In order for James' parents to feed this detailed historical and aeronautical information to James, there would have to have been a prospective, premeditated effort to deceive years before James 3's birth, with advance knowledge about James Huston Jr and surrounding details, notwithstanding James 3's own accounts.

In making his assertions, Professor Kurtz, the American philosopher and father of anti-superstition and the paranormal, does not bother offering a scientific foundation to support his dismissal of the case, but instead engages in his own brand of witchcraft: casting a blanket spell of reckless, invented, incoherent, and improbable hearsay to explain how the James 3 case came about. In the process, this great American humanist calls everyone involved a liar without a thought to their humanity or human motivation. He makes no attempt to at least salvage his own unredeemable credibility, or that of his university, instead merely rehearsing his denial of the paranormal with unrelenting certainty. His certainty is so blind and unequivocal that it can only have come to him from God and delivered in a thunderbolt of paranormal enlightenment. What that thunderbolt did to the rest of his ability to reason remains a subject of speculation.

We can feast all we want on a depiction of professor Kurtz, but he is only one person. It is a sad commentary on what he has been made to represent in our society and what that says about our quest for enlightenment and the course of our civilization.

A.3. Joe and the Closing of the American Mind

I want to review the philosophical book *The Closing of the American Mind* written by Allan Bloom in 1987 for the following reasons: 1) to show that the philosophical discourse has remained stagnant for 5000 years and remains intellectual and aloof from nuanced, intertwined reality, and 2) to show the dominance of intellectual discourse over emotion, as evidenced by the great popularity and praise the book received upon publication.

The Closing of the American Mind, a #1 New York Times National Best Seller written by Allan Bloom (1987), comes from the realm of classical philosophy and received a great deal of attention and overwhelming reverence because of its criticisms of the modern culture of the second half of the twentieth century. Bloom's thesis of the book is a criticism of higher education in the United States, arguing that it has failed to teach students of the 1960's and 1970's how to think and therefore has impoverished their souls. He claims that U.S. universities have been taken over by moral relativism, the notion that morality is entirely subjective and depends on individual perspectives, rendering the concepts of right and wrong indefinable. According to him, this has led to a decline in intellectual curiosity, exacerbated by a lack of religious upbringing, which he also sees as a contributing factor to the spread of moral relativism.

As we will see later, the book fails in a fundamental way. In 5000 years and with respect to the search for truth, it has never been the role of education or philosophy to teach people how to think. No one can teach you how to think, and to believe otherwise has been the false existential premise that erases philosophy from the face of the earth as a credible pillar of society.

This book is an example of how intellectual judgment of an entire generation can be forcefully imposed by flooding the thought process with seemingly related but otherwise unfounded philosophical assertions. In other words, it is an intellectual tsunami aimed at giving an audience a reason to believe what they already believe before any argumentation, as we saw in Europe before World War II. This process is designed to alienate a generation from the deeper realities beneath their experience. This review is particularly relevant in the context of belief systems because it shows how philosophical argumentation can be used as an intellectual surrogate for religion and myth to block our access to individual emotional realities. Heavy argumentation is a way of imposing intellectual views that block a more pensive, reflective access to emotional understanding.

At the heart of the failure of this book lies the gross misunderstanding that human depth is found solely through intellectual pursuit. Bloom attributes what he perceives as the failure of the 1960's and 1970's generations to the sudden and surprising failure of the educational system. But education has nothing to do with it. Throughout 5000 years of civilization, education has never served or had an understanding of the essential emotional composition of humans. Bloom's misstep lies in his unquestioning adherence to the principles of classical philosophy, which command intellectualism over emotional understanding and are entrenched in the framework of educational pursuits. This blind allegiance to ancient philosophical ideals undermines his critique, making classical philosophy itself a key contributor to the book's colossal failure.

If we want education to provide a paradigm shift and become a protective emotional space for truth formation—a space where truths cannot be taught but discovered—it must become entirely different from what has ever been in the history of civilization, and certainly nothing like the intellectual philosophical predicament Bloom wanted it to be.

Another major failure of the book lies in Bloom's eagerness to showcase his superiority and pass a condescending judgment on an entire generation. He encapsulates the turmoil and imperfections of the generation but fails to acknowledge or explore the causes for this generation's predicament as the natural evolutionary consequence of prior generations, whose values and structures had reached their limits, were showing their cracks, and were destined to collapse. The more insightful and nuanced the reasons why, the more we would have an insight into our future, and the more we would find generational continuity, so essential for this understanding. The problem with searching for causes is that it completely undermines Bloom's stance: instead of preaching from the comfort of a pulpit, he would have had to step down, sit side by side with his students, and engage as a peer to understand their perspective. Instead of starting at the end, giving conclusive professorial summations about his findings, he would have had to start at the beginning, at the perspective from which his students view the world. He would need to immerse himself in their experiences, to the point of forgetting he once stood in the pulpit. But what is the point of writing a book if you have to abandon the pulpit altogether?

I can offer a commentary on this book from three different levels or vantage points.

Education, Know Thyself

Despite the book's all encompassing, high-level perspective, Bloom the philosopher stays confined to classical philosophical slogans, mined for their collective and presumed universal value. He sees education as the path to enlightenment and self-knowledge. As I explained before in the section *Philosophical Joe* regarding similar slogans, to intellectually "know thyself" is an impossibility—an oxymoron—because it requires relying on non-existent "self-evident" truths as a foundation for self-knowledge. This results in building upon an alien foundation, creating a contradiction. If in addition, it is through education that such a goal is to be reached, it means that such knowledge must undergo endless levels of collective mediation by way of self-evident truths, confirming its implausibility. That thesis, propagated all over his book, is false and superficial and becomes the major failure of his book. His main thesis—that deepening our sense of self, or the "knowing thyself" as he puts it, rests in the hand of education—falls apart as a fallacy, reducing the self to a caricature and leading to a complete loss of orientation in the search for human nature.

First of all, the notion that education can teach us to think for ourselves, or to be with ourselves, is a fallacy that uncovers a mediation or indoctrination process. We can reframe this by saying that education teaches us to be ourselves by first learning not to be ourselves—that is, through an external mediation process that distances us from our true selves. In addition, how can education in the social sciences and humanities offer an individual entry into self-understanding when what it offers is a goal-oriented collectivist approach? Any process of self-recognition must begin with the individual perspective, where the underlying self is, by all accounts, shielded by an impenetrable and deceiving armor—almost unreachable in the best of circumstances. Bloom sees the social sciences and the humanities as a path to human healing (pp 135), a direct philosophical derivative of the idea that rational thought drives everything. This notion is not only an indescribable platitude but also a profound misunderstanding of human nature. Yet, it forms the book's core premise—that education is the world's source of self-knowledge—a jaw-dropping misunderstanding. He insists on this topic, stating how the eros is intertwined with the higher reaches of the soul and that the most delicate part of education is maintaining harmony between the two (pp 134). Again, from what I have stated before, how could this be the role of education? Take a moment to swallow the absurd grandiosity of that statement. How can education touch the higher reaches of the soul, your transcendental self, when it has never known that you are an emotional being? And worse, this would mean that such a delicate balance must be established for individuals by way of mediated collectivism? This just does not make sense. How can individuals be left uncontested to make these statements? This thesis also represents a failure because it is based on the philosophical presumption that it preemptively owns the truth, pending a few rewarding syllogisms as merely academic formalities. Thus, he conveniently removes himself from searching for a truth in formation that does not yet exist. Bloom's is an intellectual exercise that does not guide us back to the tabula rasa of an emotional contemplation of our human state.

At the risk of turning criticism into insight, let's consider a simple example that highlights the fallacy of his fundamental premise—that education is the source of philosophical enlightenment of the self—when in fact it is the institution that feeds the philosophical stereotypes to the herd. This is where his elevated discourse devolves into a street brawl, a competition for the leftover crumbs of self-knowledge spread by education. He states that *"Rousseau, the founder of the most potent of reductionist teachings about eros, said that the Symposium is always the book of lovers. Are we lovers anymore? This is my way of putting the educational question of our times."* His commentary begs for a few observations:

1. Plato's Symposium, written in 385 BC, is an intellectual classification of stereotypes of love, is a way to rationalize and generalize personal not-yet discovered emotional immersions which cannot be rationalized, replicated or generalized. Do we need to assume that this philosophical exercise stems as a substitute for our inability to discover these emo-

tional immersions? How can we bring this form of collectivization to the most personal emotions of self-irreplicable discovery?
2. Given that the Symposium was never the book for lovers to assert their already found love, what they knew was love, we excuse both Rousseau and Bloom for immortalizing it as the book of lovers for the rest of us, haunted by a slippery notion that will never be ours.
3. Are we lovers anymore? He bases his criticism on the 1950's and 1960's generation on his implied statement that we were lovers before these times. For his statement to gain traction, we anticipated his account of when we were lovers. Was it during the love and marriage inspiring years of Henry VIII? Was it in the immediate past of the 1920's or the 1800's when prejudice straightjacketed any exploration for love? We would like to know so that we can go back.
4. Now comes the big philosophical delivery. For Bloom, this is the educational question of our times: are we lovers anymore? This is where the absurdity of his philosophical machinations come to play. Not only is he trying to collectivize platonic stereotypes that only exist in the distant hollow gaze of lost souls looking for meaning, but he unapologetically goes the extra mile to see this as a massive induction, an educational question. Are we to understand that education, the great collective, impersonal mediation mechanism, is now the prime means to rationalize, attest and grade any stereotype of love turned into a personal irreplicable discovery? How can education have anything to do with it?
5. It becomes clear that these are just unanchored statements thrown randomly into the air in the hope they will be found in a cloud of exorbitant intellectual confusion.

6. When reasoning begins to leak at the seams and through too many holes, the focus shifts back to questioning the writer's motives, inevitably leading to a backflow. Why would anyone look to love under some rational, impersonal classification? And what does it say about the emptiness of those who adhere to the dry intellectualization of the emotion?

Instamatic Philosophy

At a second, more specific argumentative level, his reasoning about the entire generation of the 1960's and 70's is controversial because it is positioned from his arbitrary instantaneous external perspective, which leaves no room for consideration of past cause and future consequence, no accountability for the generational dilemmas set in motion by previous generations.

By eliciting reasoning in this instantaneous fashion, the reasoning becomes lame and loses its natural ponderation and counterbalance, decaying into arbitrary, banal criticism—a caricatural, dislocated snapshot of time, like the cheap Instamatic cameras introduced by Kodak in 1963. It also highlights his double standard, because he is happy to trace back to ancient classical philosophy to formulate the delivery of his attacks but not any immediate history to formulate a defensible position for the generations he intended to criticize. To clarify, no generation is an island in time, and Bloom offers plenty of examples of greatness in previous generations, but he offers nothing from previous generations to explain or justify the behavior of the generation in question, leaving the generation fully exposed to receive his criticism. Bloom's book is plagued with examples of this. Let us take a look.

He claims that in this generation of question, eroticism and relationships have become lame, boring, lethargic and lack a number of endearing philosophical attributes of times past. As a thinker, he needs to bring context into his observations. While it is true and depressing to see the boring soporific state of many relationships in that generation, we have to put that in perspective with respect to their immediate past. The world had just come out of two wars, the U.S. had the unjustifiable horror of the war in Viet Nam, which only accentuated the hollow morality of the time and the no longer sustainable pretension and appearance of society in the fifties.

No thought whatsoever is given to this generational behavior as a backlash from the tightly wound pretension and preservation of appearances of the 1950's, or the generational sacrifice in Viet Nam. Maybe the way for a new generation to survive all this is to sleep for a little while, as sometimes sleep is the deflating language of the non-pretentious, a restful time to wash off the putrid smell of an entire generation being sacrificed. And if we establish a comparison, it would be between the unbearable pretentious tension of the 1950's—marked by the implosive impositions to marry a socially appropriate partner to maintain the status quo, seeking marriage without friendship, knowledge, respect, or love, merely to endure until retirement and death—and on the other hand, the unassuming, boring deflation of relationships in the subsequent generation. I will say this has been a total net gain, as we rest and prepare to look at love and relationships in the next generation. With a bit of perspective and context, we would see the generation in question as a reflection of a putrefaction brought into the open, air-exposed for sanitization. This obvious perspective, offering absolution for the generation, is not provided by the relentless criticism shown by Bloom.

Let's look at his criticism of the gay and same-sex movement in the 1960's. Everything that the gay and same-sex movement embodied in the sixties, he chose to nickel and dime, criticizing the melodramatic noise this movement produced. Every movement is entitled to some baby fat, especially after the millennia of relentless repression already endured, and now we can see from the results that all of it was justified and has paid off.

To make matters worse, Bloom himself goes out of his way to quote a passage from the 19th century French novelist Flaubert to illustrate the importance for the generation in question to see the present as a consequence of the past, while at the same time failing to follow his own advice as he has a field day criticizing that generation without providing any perspective from the past. Although it would be great for a generation to have a cultural historical perspective, it does not have to have it, as they are too busy living the present without premeditation from the past. On the other hand, it is Bloom's responsibility to bring that perspective to his commentaries, not only to provide an understanding of a generation, but also to justify the reasoning for a future prediction. But for someone so loquacious, Bloom only offers silence.

Plowing with a Rake

Let us go to a more specific, third-tier level of detail. I see Bloom take a number of unjustified, narrow comparative positions, wielding a rake like a plow, leaving much context and substance behind. He misses the counterpoints and the writing loses the force of breath, failing to sustain a case. Instead of making irrelevant comparisons intended to demean a generation, it would be far more enlightening and philosophically authoritative to just ask why. Why is this generation moving in a given direction? Why? The more insightful and nuanced the reasons, the more insight we would gain on our future.

The problem with searching for causes is that it totally debunks Bloom's use of the pulpit: instead of preaching from the comfort of his pulpit, he would have had to abandon it and come to sit side by side with his students, begin to understand their perspective. Rather than starting with conclusive professorial summations, he would have to begin at the start—where the students are— becoming one of them to the point of forgetting he ever had a pulpit. Had he done that, he would have found a clear connection between these generations, such as the abysmal fear of intimacy. In the fifties, there was no fear of intimacy because roles dictated behavior. In contrast with having the right brand-new car or belonging to the right social clubs, being asked for intimacy would have been the legal grounds for a divorce, so it was off the table, and men and women felt relieved and free to pursue their gender-based pretend roles without any outward insecurities. For the next generation, it was no longer off the table. This only deepened the fear because, while there were still no concessions to intimacy, the awareness of it was sitting a lot closer to us.

He comments on how *"The student who made fun of playing the guitar under a girl's window will never read or write poetry under her influence... It is not that he will fail to adorn or idealize the world; it is just that he will fail to see what is there"* (pp 135). This is a point well taken, but it is placed against an idealistic scenario that most often does not exist. In most cases those idealistic scenarios represent infatuations caused by emptiness and loss of self, fueled with significant anxiety—hardly the idealistic model to follow. He criticizes lame love relationships in contrast with Socrates' divine madness, the enticing awareness of incompleteness, and the quest for perpetuity (pp 132); but these manifestations have never been a signature of any of our previous generations. On the contrary, the repression of previous generations have taken reality away from it in favor of escapism, so these love exaltations have never been on the table. These precocious idealistic manifestations, though very enticing, may often disguise preemptive defense barriers of the emotional self—not always transparent reflections of the inner self, but just one more deceitful turn, a gender ambush where predator awaits prey.

Is Bloom asserting that these alternative relationship frameworks, built on great postulates, represent states closer to a truth? Without a social context, his proposed pursuits ring hollow and become mere slogans. In fact, the closer intergender relationships of recent generations have understandably taken the umph from the idealistic power of those pursuits, which bank on fuel and combustion from societal separation between genders.

Once gender separation is taken out of the equation, self-combustion gives way to a gradual form of intimacy and de-mythification, thus less conducive to dramatic exaltations of self-discovery, but still a higher level of living nonetheless. You cannot describe the generational shift as the closing of a mind that was previously more hermetically sealed; such a progression cannot be called a closing. I see in his work a precipitous quest for cherry-picking classic slogans to justify assigning blame, not as a showcase of intellectual conviction, but as a substitute for his own creative thought.

The Backflow

When we see such a systematically flawed perspective, we may begin to experience a backflow in our focus of attention. The tide begins to turn and the focus shifts to the author and his motives, and the book becomes instead a referendum over the state of the author himself. It is also useful to contrast the conclusions I am drawing with those of reviewers in the past. Take Billy Krystol of the Wall Street Journal, *"Brilliant... No other book combines such shrewd insights into our current state...,"* or The New York Times Book Review, *"An unparalleled reflection on today's intellectual and moral climate... That rarest of documents, a genuinely profound book."* All these reviewers needed to do was to take Bloom at his word and ask themselves his educational question of our times: *"Are we lovers anymore?"*, then ask Bloom *"are you a lover anymore? were you a lover before?"*—simple questions, simple answers, no need to get convoluted—rhetoric is not for lovers.

Throughout these thematic layers I've discussed, I find no way to align myself with Bloom's perspectives, which appear whimsical and self-serving—an opportunity for him to elevate himself to a high pulpit. In addition, as this was a scathing condemnation of a generation, I would have expected him to bring a prediction for this alarming state. What we see now, as society has continued to move, is that the implied warnings encapsulated in his book have not come to fruition: the amoral segment of our society, the one targeted with his criticism, has moved progressively forward beyond our expectations. Gay people and same-sex relationships have now become part of the mainstream stable family units, which is an amazing social accomplishment in such a short time. On the other hand, the moral minority that has long advocated for his principles, contained by a hermetic straightjacket sustained by these pillars of classical morality, has decayed to an extent that could never be predicted. So, it is safe to say that the opposite to his implied predictions is what has taken place, which then casts doubt on his premise of the closing of the American mind. By adding just a bit of historical perspective to his book, he would have had plenty of titles to choose from, such as *The Ripping at the Seams of the American Fabric*, or *The Underbelly of Progress in American Society*. Bloom's book cannot be endorsed because of its aimless reasoning, clever disguise of moral conviction, dislocated blame delivery, and his erratic prediction of future consequences. Requiescat in pace.

Acknowledgments

Very special thanks to my friend and editor Jessica Pierson Russo, who despite being so busy with life, took over the entire editing of the book with such quality and blinding speed. This book would not be here today if it weren't for Jessica.

Jennifer Skuza (Jenny) was by my side making sure I stayed on message—something not so easy to do with a storyteller gravitating to the most scenic and convoluted routes. She opens spaces just in time for you to discover them, as if they had always been there, as part of an ever-expanding seamless private fabric of universality.

Sofía Skuza Rivera made my dream of becoming a girl dad come true. She has taught me that the most significant roles in life are sometimes the simplest. In my case, it was just sitting back, watching, and learning how someone can enter this world and, from day one, form her own opinions without seeking approval from the world, exercise her judgement, and make everything her own. I always knew, even before she was born, that she would be a writer, because when you walk freely on the face of the earth, poetry follows you. If poetry floats in the air around her,

I figured I was entitled to take on the rudimentary grinding of writing a book.

My sister Glenda Sofía Rivera and I share the same singular historical context shaped by our life experiences. As co-witnesses, side by side, day in and day out, we have the perspective of a private world all our own—a private world that just opened up in this book, but for us to forever remain private.

Author Quotes

art: anything not seeking truth but leaving an open space to find it

blanket belief: internalized notion or ideology that cover all aspects of our entire relationship with our own self

collective sensorial alignment: a form of social engagement when emotional truth is nowhere to be found

conviction: the reaffirmation of truth

courage: curiosity tucked inside our gut, fed by trust and itching to get out

credit: an outward emanation borne from the sense of self—liquid in liquid state as it cannot be compartmentalized

crying: the embrace of conviction—perpetuated

curiosity: the flight of our intuition

democracy: an indulgent, fragile, self-destructive political experiment where the inalienable power of individual liberty combined with the certification of imaginary realities sets the table for inexorable, spontaneous self-combustion—can only be defused with individual emotional autonomy and the accreditation of reality

emotion: the place for truth formation

emotional autonomy: the living awareness of our deepest emotional constitution, untouchable by misconception and self-denial

emotional autonomy: what lies at the other side of our defenses

emotional horizon: convergence of truth and reality where credit is fully awarded

emotional stature: a unit of measure, the more of it there is, the greater our ability to be closer to ourselves

emotionality: juxtaposed to philosophy, the creative reverberating engine of thoughts not yet conceived

empathy: the amoral measurement of our emotional stature and its angle of view to the outside world

equality: a caricature under pressure burdened with the overstressed responsibility to bring inequality in peaceful reductionary collectivization

faith: the proactive, unquestioning acceptance of an entire internalized belief in advance of any proof or personal verification

fear: the reflection of our alienation

giving up: becoming the best counterpart to what we give up

home: the inner self dwelling of unquestionable truths and undisturbed silence, untouchable by misconception—the only home that there is

home: the inner self dwelling where all associations land to create exponential growth

idiot: a recalcitrant individual with no sense of reality

indoctrination: the process of persuasion or imposition to internalize a belief

inequality: differentiator unrelated to motivation for oppression, domination or exploitation

internalization: the unconscious assimilation of a belief, implies that awareness of the self has been lost, alienated, and relegated by this take over

insanity: a destination that demarks a beginning

insanity: a void state of heightened awareness, where our lifetime superficial make-believe fantasies crumble confronted by the revelation of our deeper, sobering reality never before exposed—a dichotomy yielding unbearable anguish

intuition: the forward ability to see the inner self of another individual in a flash of transparency and pure emotion, turning time into beauty

intuition: the grand entry to our Inner Sanctum

intuition: the personification of beauty

liberty (in a democracy): the inalienable unchecked right to arbitrarily invent, distort, trash, neglect, manipulate, circumvent, retract, ignore, destroy, and recreate reality

life: saying things—truths in bloom—and tying knots; realities in fusion

loneliness: inability to be in touch with our own individuality

open wound (emotional): a trajectory in the process of landing

peace: the fusion of our perdurable realities

pleasing and placing: pleasing society submissively, in order to place into society's ranking

poetry: the word of the unstated emotion

poetry: the wormhole of the intellectual universe

power: autonomy of being and becoming

purpose: the lifetime translation of our individuality

purpose: the most gratifying state of reality

quantum physics: the "seeing is believing" plausibility of our non-physical consciousness

reality: the footprint of emotional truths

resolve: the delusion of confronting fears through willpower

respect: a measurement of distance between individuals

resting place: where the credit of our perdurable reality is fully awarded

secularity: disaffection for ideological fabrications

selective beliefs: internalizing them only affect specific aspects of our lives

self-centricity: not selfishness, but the recognition that everything about us begins within us

socially available behavioral ranges: limited behaviors that do not require confronting impenetrable defense mechanisms

socially calibrated perceptions: thought engagements when truth is nowhere to be found

state of decoy: behavior enacted by defense mechanisms to obstruct by disguise, access to our essential human nature—it is obstruction by disguise aimed to mislead

superiority: off center, a weight that dwells outside ourselves—impossible to intern and own

surrender to fear: a concession to freely feel in all their intensity the emotions elicited by the fear

surrogate beliefs: selective beliefs with indoctrination power stemming from adherence to comprehensive blanket beliefs.

trust: the engine of our intuition

truth: emotional volcanic magma, engulfing you in a personal explosion, profound and pure, revealing a state of new awareness—truth is personal

truth: the means to mine reality, and by which reality is exposed

truth formation: the gradual process for non existing personal emotional truths to come into being as a result of emotional experiences

trust: the repeatable corroboration of an intuition that already lives in us without surrendering or lending out our sense of selves

willpower: the forceful domination of conflicting imaginary forces

willpower: the absence of wisdom

wisdom: the absence of willpower

wisdom: ability to correctly interpret and reason about emotional reality

Bibliography

(Aleandro 2004) Aleandro, Norma, et.al. *Cleopatra*, movie fragment. http://y2u.be/Am3j5AkqIZc, 2004

(Alexander 2012) Alexander, Eben. *Proof of Heaven*. Simon & Schuster, 2012.

(Andrade 2017) Andrade, Gabriel. *Is Past Life Regression Therapy Ethical?* NIH Library of Medicine, Journal of Medical Ethics and History of Medicine, Vol. 10, 2017.

(BBVA 2023) BBVA. *Frontiers of Knowledge Awards, 15th Edition, Steven Pinker Awardee.* https://tinyurl.com/yc5reamw March 9, 2023.

(Bloom 1987) Bloom, Allan. *The Closing of the American Mind.* First Touchstone Edition, 1987.

(Carmelo 2020) Carmelo, Anji, Luján Comas, M.D., (2020). *¿Existe la Muerte?*. Plataforma Ed. 8th Edition, 2020.

(Cuomo 2004) Cuomo, Chris. *Carol Bowman and James Leininger, the Boy Who Died in His Past Life as a WWII Pilot*. ABC PrimeTime, http://y2u.be/QRefj5Mqg6U 2004.

(DailyMail 2013) DailyMail Reporter. *'Proof of Heaven' doctor faced a $3 million malpractice lawsuit when he fell into a coma*. DailyMail.com, December 24, 2013. https://tinyurl.com/3t23m47v

(Dawkins 2001) Dawkins, Richard. *The God Delusion*. Black Swan, January 1, 2001. New York Times Bestseller, International Bestseller.

(Deccan 2023) Deccan Herald. *Oscar, a Therapy Cat Who Could Predict Deaths*. https://tinyurl.com/3tjws6vt , October 15, 2023.

(Denver 1990) Denver, John. *Matthew (Live at Farm Aid 1990)*. http://y2u.be/RPhUYD1jkbl

(Dion 2024) Dion. *The Wanderer* (Remastered). Caribe Sound. February 7, 2024. http://y2u.be/vh0L6rmcKEU

(Dittrich 2013a) Dittrich. Luke. *The Prophet. Debunking a bestselling account of the afterlife*. medium.com, July 23, 2013. https://tinyurl.com/bp7f9zyn

(Dittrich 2013b) Dittrich, Luke. *The Prophet*. Esquire. July 2, 2013. https://tinyurl.com/4y7ms4jj

(Dosa 2007) David M. Dosa, M.D., *A Day in the Life of Oscar the Cat*. https://www.nejm.org/doi/full/10.1056/NEJMp078108, The New England Journal of Medicine, July 26, 2007.

(Dosa 2011) Dosa. David M. *Making the Rounds with Oscar*, Hyperion Ed., April 5, 2011

(Dossey 1989) Dossey, Larry. *Recovering the Soul*. New York, NY: Bantam, 1989.

(Dougherty 1993) Dougherty, Patrick. *Caverns of Rage*. Networker, March/April 1993.

(Drexler 2024) Drexler, Jorge. *Todo se Transforma*, http://y2u.be/QfhEKpFiepM, 2004

(Ebah 2021) Ebah, Emmanuel. *Reincarnation was Removed from the Christian Scriptures by a Roman Emperor Named Justinian I*, Kindle April 10, 2021.

(Ehrman 2012) Ehrman, Bart D. *The Bart Ehrman Blog*, https://ehrmanblog.org . 2012-2024.

(Ehrman 2014) Ehrman, Bart D. *How Jesus Became God, the Exaltation of a Jewish Preacher from Galilee*. Harper One, First Ed. 2014

(Gibbs 2010) Gibbs, John. *Near-Death Experiences, Deathbed Visions, and Past-Life Memories: A Convergence in Support of van Lommel's Consciousness Beyond Life*. Journal of Near-Death Studies, 29(2), Winter 2010.

(Goswami 1993) Goswami, Amit. *The self-aware universe*. Los Angeles, CA: Tarcher/Putnam, 1993

(Goswami 1994) Goswami, Amit. *Science within consciousness*. Sausalito, CA: Institute of Noetic Sciences, 1994

(Grant 2023) Grant. Adam. *Think Again*. Penguin Books, December 26, 2023. #1 New York Times Bestseller

(Grant 2024) Grant, Adam. *Wharton psychologist Adam Grant: To understand yourself better, try this—'it's one of my favorite exercises'*, CNBC, August 1, 2024. https://tinyurl.com/4axve3yk

(Greyson 2013) Greyson, Bruce. *Getting Comfortable with Near-Death Experiences, An Overview of Near-Death Experiences*. University of Virginia School of Medicine. https://tinyurl.com/5brpe5bh

(Henry 2022) Tyler Henry. *Life After Death*, Netflix Series, 2022.

(Henry 2024) Tyler, Henry. *Here & Hereafter: How Wisdom from the Departed Can Transform Your Life Now*. St. Martin's Essentials Ed, January 30, 2024

(Husserl 2017) Husserl, Edmund. *Ideas: General Introduction to Pure Phenomenology*. Martino Fine Books. August 23, 2017.

(Jobim 1962) Jobim, Antônio Carlos. *Garota de Ipanema*. August 1, 1962. http://y2u.be/rOAGNjCYprY

(Khanna et.al. 2018) Surbhi Khanna, Lauren E. Moore, Bruce Greyson. *Full Neurological Recovery From Escherichia coli Meningitis Associated With Near-Death Experience.* The Journal of Nervous and Mental Disease • Volume 206, Number 9, September 2018.

(Liberman 1995) Liberman, J. *Take off your glasses and see.* New York, NY: Crown, 1995.

(Little Richard 1958) Little Richard. *Good Golly, Miss Molly.* January 1958.

(Little Richard 1995) Little Richard, *Tutti Frutti.* 1995. http://y2u.be/ZSx91WBQLpg

(Lope de Vega 1632) Lope de Vega y Carpio, Félix, Alan S. Trueblood (Editor), Edwin Honig (Editor). *La Dorotea.* Harvard University Press, 1985.

(Mays 2016) Mays, Robert George. Eben Alexander's *Near-Death Experience: How an Esquire Article Distorted the Facts.* January 2016, Journal of Near-Death Studies 35(2):65-93. https://tinyurl.com/mryu2mfh

(Mocedades 1974) Mocedades. *Soledades*, 1974.
http://y2u.be/kDgd9QAqfWA

(Moody 1975) Moody, Raymond. *Life After Life*. Mockingbird Books, 2nd Edition, January 1, 1975.

(Moody Blues 1970) Moody Blues. *Question*. 1970.
http://y2u.be/eaTiFbuuI14

(Moorjani 2012) Moorjani, Anita. *Dying to be Me*. Hay House, Inc., 2012,

(Neruda 1964) Neruda, Pablo. *Memorial de Isla Negra*. Visor Libros, S.L., January 24, 2024.

(Netflix 2020a) Netflix. *Surviving Death*, Netflix series, chapter 1, segment 1, 2022.

(Netflix 2020b) Netflix. *Surviving Death*, Netflix series, chapter 6, 2022.

(Ortega 2004) Ortega, Paco. *Rumba de Cleo.*
http://y2u.be/Am3j5AkqIZc http://y2u.be/z5h9qmeKexQ

(Pinker 2003) Pinker, Steven. *Blank Slate: The Modern Denial of Human Nature.* Penguin Books, August 26, 2003. New York Times Bestseller, Pulitzer Prize Finalist.

(Pinker 2019) Pinker, Steven. *Enlightenment Now: The Case for Reason, Science, Humanism and Progress.* Penguin Books, January 15, 2019. New York Times Bestseller.

(Pinker 2022) Pinker, Steven. *Rationality: What It Is, Why It Seems Scarce, Why It Matters.* Penguin Books. September 27, 2022.

(Ring et.al. 1997) Ring, Kenneth, Sharon Cooper. *Near-Death and Out-of-Body Experiences in the Blind: A Study of Apparent Eyeless Vision.* UNT Digital Library. Vol 16, No. 2, 1997. https://tinyurl.com/ytw7r7rn

(Sagan 1987) Sagan, Carl. *The Fine Art of Baloney Detection,* https://tinyurl.com/bdn3khtn Parade Magazine, February 1, 1987.

(Sartori et.al. 2006) Sartori, Penny, Paul Badham, Peter Fenwick. *A Prospectively Studied Near-Death Experience with Corroborated Out-of-Body Perceptions and Unexplained Healing.* Journal of Near-Death Studies, 25(2), Winter 2006.

(Segarra 2023) Sans Segarra, Manuel. *La Supraconciencia Existe.* http://y2u.be/c5ewaGJ5AuA , Regenera Health, June 16, 2023.

(Segarra 2024a) Sans Segarra, Manuel. *El Pensamiento Condiciona la Acción.* https://www.tiktok.com/@motivarte365/video/7348200653698632965?lang=en, 2024.

(Segarra 2024b) Sans Segarra, Manuel. *La supraconciencia existe. Vida después de la vida.* Editorial Planeta. 2024. ISBN 978-84-08-29128-2.

(Serrat 1969) Serrat, Joan Manuel. *Cantares.* Festival de Benidorm 1983. http://y2u.be/6ilxz7FT0y4

(Serrat 1971) Serrat, Joan Manuel. Mediterráneo. 1971. http://y2u.be/7JJByYw9pe0

(Simon 1966) Simon, Paul. *Kathy's Song*. 1966. http://y2u.be/0faGrAq5C5o

(Soggy Bottom Boys 2008) Soggy Bottom Boys. *Man of Constant Sorrow*. April 2, 2008. http://y2u.be/hr8UcGU6_ls

(Stevenson 2000) Stevenson, Ian. *Children Who Remember Previous Lives: A Question of Reincarnation*. University of Virginia Press. December 15, 2000.

(Sudduth 2021) Sudduth, Michael. *The James Leininger Case Reexamined*. Journal of Scientific Exploration, Vol. 35, No. 4, pp. 933–1026. https://tinyurl.com/5n7s9es8, December 30, 2021

(The Commitments 1991) *The Commitments*, Geffen Records, http://y2u.be/mgn5roohu-g , 1991.

(Tucker 2008) Tucker, Jim B., MD. *Ian Stevenson and Cases of the Reincarnation Type*. Journal of Scientific Exploration, Vol. 22, No. 1. 2008.

(Tucker 2016) Tucker, Jim B., MD. *The Case of James Leininger: An American Case of the Reincarnation Type*. University of Virginia School of Medicine, https://tinyurl.com/4sczhfy6 March 2, 2016

(Tucker 2021) Tucker, Jim B., MD. *Before: Children's Memories of Previous Lives*. St Martin's Essentials Ed, April 13, 2021

(Tucker 2022) Tucker, Jim B., MD. *Response to Sudduth's "James Leininger Case Re-Examined."* University of Virginia School of Medicine and Journal of Scientific Exploration, https://tinyurl.com/mr3jxxz7 May 2022

(Utah HR 2011) Utah Historical Review, *The Argument over Reincarnation in Early Christianity*. Utah Historical Review, (S.l.), v. 1, ISSN 2374-1570. December 27, 2011. https://tinyurl.com/3t93nv23

(van Lommel 2010) van Lommel, Pim. *Consciousness beyond life: The science of the near-death experience* (English edition; L. Vroomen, Trans.). New York: HarperCollins Books. (Original work published 2007)

(van Lommel 2011) van Lommel, Pim. *Near-death experiences: the experience of the self as real and not as an illusion*. Annals of the New York Academy of the Sciences. 2011;1234:19-28.

(van Lommel 2014) van Lommel, Pim. *Getting Comfortable With Near-Death Experiences: Dutch Prospective Research on Near-Death Experiences During Cardiac Arrest*. Mo Med. 2014

Mar-Apr;111(2):126-131. PMID: 30323518; PMCID: PMC6179502.

(van Manen 2023) van Manen, Max. *Phenomenology of Practice: Meaning-Giving Methods in Phenomenological Research and Writing*. Routledge; 2nd edition. June 8, 2023.

(Weiss 1988) Weiss, Brian. *Many Lives, Many Masters: The True Story of a Prominent Psychiatrist, His Young Patient, and the Past-Life Therapy That Changed Both Their Lives*. Fireside, July 15, 1988.

(Weiss 2000) Weiss, Brian. L. (2000). *Messages from the masters: Tapping into the power of love*. New York, NY: Warner.

(Weiss 2004) Weiss, Brian L. *Same soul, many bodies: Discover the healing power of future lives through progression therapy*. New York, NY: Free Press, 2004.

(Weiss et.al. 2012) Weiss, Brian L., Amy Weiss. *Miracles Happen: The Transformational Healing Power of Past-Life Memories*. Hay House, January 1, 2012.

(Winfrey 2012) Winfrey, Oprah. *Terrifying Part of Dr. Alexander's Near-Death Experience*. Oprah Winfrey Network. http://y2u.be/7ljnWH9JJBY November 29, 2012.

Index

1950's, 5, 140, 141, 142, 343, 345
Adamantius, Origen, 67
agnosticism, 36
Aleandro, Norma, 305, 361
Alexander, Eben, 48, 49, 59, 319, 320, 321, 322, 361, 366, 372
alienation, 87, 90, 107, 201, 209, 355
    all encompassing, 118
    forceful, 88
Andrade, Gabriel, 59, 60, 66, 70, 361
    past-life regression unethical?, 70
    psychotherapy unethical?, 71
    religious practice unethical?, 70
    spiritual and somatic correlations, 60, 66
appeasement, 118, 151
    inferiority of the herd, 173
    reality imposition, 103, 251
Appeasement
    through preaching, 163

Aramaic, 113, 114
Argentina, 305
Aristarchus, 128, 129
Aristotle, 132, 133, 285
art, 103, 129, 190, 220, 256, 289, 303, 353
awareness, 43
    expansion, 50, 55
    omnidirectional, 54
    self, 15, 48, 75, 125, 203, 208, 221, 279
    suprasensorial, 40, 53, 56
Aztecs
    Tenochtitlán, 92
Badham, Paul, 369
BBVA, 148, 155, 361
beauty, 268
    being, 286
    conceptualization, 103
    credit, 252
    humbling, 298
    inner, 270
    personification, 299, 356
    reality, 281, 285
    surrounded, 303
    truth, 234

turning time into, 297, 298, 356
universe, 42
values, 268, 271
wisdom, 185
belief
    blanket mediation, 210
    imposition, 86, 87, 211
    surrender, 204
beliefs, 3, 4, 5, 10, 11, 13, 14, 19, 20, 23, 81, 82, 94, 96, 102, 103, 105, 106, 119, 177, 179, 275
    blanket beliefs, 94, 97, 106
    collectivization, 4, 102
    congruent beliefs, 82
    entry criteria, 104
    exclusivity, 4, 103
    indoctrination, 78, 85, 86, 94, 96
    less access to afterlife?, 219
    moral, 140, 210, 299
    obligatory, 180
    pseudo-science, 120
    scientific, 119
    selective beliefs, 96, 97, 105, 116, 357, 358
    softer indoctrination, 97
    surrogacy, 4, 20, 105
    transfer to the afterlife?, 219
    unfounded beliefs, 81, 86
Beverly Hillbillies, 263
    Jed Clampett, 263
Bierce, Ambrose, 152
Bloom, Allan, 136, 337
Bohr, Nils, 30, 31
Bowman, Carol, 325, 334, 362
Caan, James, 308
cancer, 38, 41, 60
Cantares, 313, 315, 369

Carmelo, Anji, 98, 201, 362
catch-22, 134
Catholicism, 67, 72, 93, 95, 104, 114, 219
Cecil B. DeMille, 115
Cervantes, Miguel de, 225
Christianity, 78, 83, 95, 110, 112, 124, 180, 371
    Moses, 109, 114
circus, 160, 170, 287
    contortionists, 170
Cleopatra, 305, 361
Closing of the American Mind, 5, 7, 136, 137, 141, 142, 255, 337, 361
Coco River, 283
collective sensorial alignments, 15, 226
Comas, Luján, 59, 98, 100, 201, 290, 362
consciousness, 32, 35, 39, 42, 44, 55, 170, 364, 371
    higher, 32, 39, 42, 44, 170
    nonlocal, 55, 91
    non-physical, 25, 56, 125, 220, 357
    omnidirectional, suprasensorial awareness, 54
    omnipresence, 19, 27
    omniscient, 54, 320
    scientific proof of transfer?, 67
    secular, 79
    timeless, 26, 35, 234, 253, 290, 316
    truth expands, 250
Constantinople, Second Council, 67
contrition, 191, 276
    fast-track, 117, 275
convergence, 26, 42, 258, 354

conviction, 6, 231, 233, 262, 285, 353
Cooper, Sharon, 368
Copenhagen interpretation, 30, 32
Corsair, 63, 64, 325, 329
Cortés, Hernán, 92
courage, 158, 201, 277, 278, 353
creator, 42
credit, 238, 252
crying, 10, 64, 65, 182, 232, 333, 353
crying in baseball, 182
Cuauhtémoc, 92
   am I in a bed of roses?, 92
Cuitlahuac, 92
Cuomo, Chris, 330, 334, 362
curiosity, 26, 122, 187, 248, 278, 353
DailyMail, 320, 362
Darwin, Charles, 42
   natural selection, 42
Dawkins, Richard, 42, 107, 108, 123, 170, 362
   universe without a designer, 42
De Benedictis, Piero, 240
De Broglie, Louis, 28
De Niro, Robert, 190
Deccan, Herald, 71, 362
   therapy cat, 362
decode our emotional DNA, 270
defense mechanisms, 143, 144, 145, 148, 152, 157, 160, 264, 276, 277, 357, 358
   emotional guardians, 143, 144
   state of decoy, 145, 152, 264, 358

delusional, 87, 186, 264, 277, 312, 357
democracy, 5, 164, 165, 166, 167, 168, 170, 207, 218, 354, 356
   self-combustion, 164, 167, 349, 354
   unreality hiccup, 167
Democritus, 128, 129
Denver, John, 234, 237, 310, 362
   Matthew, 234, 235, 236, 362
designer, 42
Dion, 184, 363
   The Wanderer, 184, 363
Dittrich, Luke, 48, 49, 59, 320, 363
dogma, 41, 43, 68, 83, 84, 121
Don Quixote, 225
Dosa, David M., 71, 363
Dossey, Larry, 55, 91, 363
Dougherty, Patrick, 305, 363
   caverns of rage, 305, 363
Drexler, Jorge, 237, 240, 364
   Todo se Transforma, 237, 364
Ebah, Emmanuel, 67, 364
education
   lovers anymore?, 342, 343, 349
   mediated, 340
   mediated collectivism, 342
Ehrman, Bart D., 112, 114, 364
Einstein, Albert, 31
   a very spooky phenomenon, 31
emotion, 11, 12, 14, 20, 134, 136, 153, 155, 157, 161, 229, 256, 280, 297, 298, 304, 337, 344, 354, 356
emotional

autonomy, 9, 13, 14, 21, 26, 166, 167, 168, 172, 174, 264, 354
    credibility, 264
    emancipation, 25
    magma, 226, 230, 247, 263
    stature, 127, 169, 252, 256, 354
emotional autonomy, 14, 166, 264
    civilization far away, 172
    convergence, 26
    democracy, 164, 354
    pure expression of beauty, 42
empathy, 252, 354
equality, 149, 165, 168, 169, 170, 171, 172, 173, 174, 182, 185, 188, 303, 354
faith, 4, 26, 88, 92, 95, 236
    absolutely no faith required, 41, 43
fear, 5, 6, 21, 198, 201, 245, 277
Fenwick, Peter, 369
Flaubert, 346
founding fathers, 170
Freud, Sigmund, 101, 124, 126, 146, 161, 229
Galilei, Galileo, 25, 197
    eppur si muove, 198
Gibbs, John, 46, 364
giving up, 278, 355
god, 72, 95, 96, 107, 123, 166, 186, 188
    as Dawkins' gradual evolution, 42, 124
    as Segarra's first intelligence, 123
God, 46, 67, 111
    backed by guns, 186
    conferred equality?, 170
    delusion, 42, 107, 108, 123, 362
    God and Caesar, 109
    god-forsaken, 72
    in our image and likeness, 116
    more important than God?, 204
    passing the buck, 170, 304
    Sodom, Gomorrah and San Francisco, 115
    universal, 95
    worship as distance, 107
gods, 5, 20, 83, 94, 95, 107, 166, 167, 179, 180, 182, 185, 188, 191
    designing our gods, 108, 109
    of democracy, 166, 356
    surrender and blind obedience?, 108
    universal, 94
Goswami, Amit, 55, 364
Grant, Adam, 145, 148, 159, 364, 365
Greyson, Bruce, 37, 58, 365, 366
Harvard University, 148, 157, 160, 366
heathens, 199, 227
Heisenberg, Werner, 30
Henry, Tyler, 343, 365
    wisdom from the departed, 365
herd mentality, 86, 87, 158, 166, 167, 206
Heston, Charlton, 114
hierarchy
    domination, 44
home
    untouchable by mediation, 253
    untouchable by misconception, 253, 354, 355
homo mythologicus, 213

homo sapiens, 213
human nature, 25, 86, 145, 148, 150, 151, 152, 153, 154, 155, 156, 175, 264, 341, 358
Hume, David, 128, 129
Husserl, Edmund, 60, 158, 365
Huxley, Thomas Henry, 128, 129
idiot, 72, 167, 168, 207, 355
inequality, 169, 171, 172, 173, 354, 355
inner self
    mediation deprives, 204
insanity, 135, 161, 163, 267, 355, 356
inspirational, 4, 22, 79, 86, 97, 98, 99, 101, 115, 203, 210, 249
intellectual
    mediation, 154
internalization, 4, 85, 88, 102
intimacy, 139, 253, 299, 300, 347, 349
    grounds for divorce, 140
    requesting, 140
intuition, 7, 140, 141, 297, 298, 299
    beliefs undermine, 84, 85
    exposure highly cultural, 141, 300
    guiding compass, 140, 299
    trust, 93, 359
    vilifying, 140, 182
Iwo Jima, 63, 64, 325, 326, 327
Jagger, Mick, 272
jaguar, 7, 282, 283
Jesus, 67, 112, 113, 114, 118, 364
Jobim, Antônio Carlos, 181, 365
Jung, Carl, 124

Justinian, 67, 95, 364
Khanna, Surbi, 49, 321, 322, 366
    neurological recovery, 366
knapsack, 233, 234
Koine Greek, 114
Krystol, William, 349
Larson, Jack, 63, 64
Last of the Mohicans, The, 142
Leininger, James (James 3), 3, 7, 63, 64, 323, 326, 327, 328, 329, 330, 331, 333, 334, 362, 370, 371
    airplane crash on fire, 63, 324
    James Huston Jr., 64, 327, 328, 331, 332, 334
Liberace, 156
Liberman, J, 53, 54, 366
liberty, 36, 164, 165, 166, 167, 208, 218, 354, 356
life
    saying things, 261
liking yourself
    in love with yourself, 265
    not all that much, 265
Little Richard, 184, 366
loneliness, 226, 315, 356
Lope de Vega, 6, 225, 259, 366
    La Dorotea, 366
    Soledades, 259, 367
lovers, 342, 343, 349
magnificence, 39, 41, 196, 245
Mandela, Nelson, 201, 202
Mays, Robert George, 321, 366
Medusa, 265
Messi, Lionel, 72
Michelangelo, 191
MIT, 148, 156
Mocedades, 225, 259, 367
Moctezuma, 92

Moody Blues
    Hayward, Justin, 240
Moody, Raymond, 48, 50, 51, 240, 319, 367
Moore, Lauren, 366
Moorjani, Anita, 3, 38, 42, 43, 44, 45, 54, 57, 59, 60, 62, 75, 78, 116, 126, 218, 220, 290, 367
    not to take ourselves too seriously, 45
moral superiority, 45, 288
more important than God?, 204, 217
most gratifying state of reality, 233, 357
Mother Teresa, 43, 127
Mt. Suribachi, 63, 325
mythology, 27, 84, 107, 173, 203, 212, 221
Natoma, 63, 64, 325, 326, 327, 332
Neal, Mary, 3, 46
near death experiences, NDEs, 3, 27, 28, 31, 32, 37, 38, 39, 41, 48, 49, 50, 51, 58, 75, 79, 98, 101, 116, 122, 132, 280, 290
    brain activity, 37, 213
    cardiac arrest, 37, 46, 47, 58, 371
    clinical death, 37, 38, 39, 58
    coma, 38, 39, 48, 49, 319, 320, 321, 362
    general anesthesia, 37
    near-death studies, 364, 366, 369
    prospective studies, 37, 58, 334, 369
    retrospective studies, 37

Neruda, Pablo, 291, 294, 367
    El Niño Perdido (The Lost Child), 292
    Memorial de Isla Negra, 291, 367
Netflix, 46, 64, 323, 365, 367
    Life After Death (see also Henry, Tyler), 365
    Surviving Death, 367
neuroscience, 38
Newton, Isaac, 27, 33
    classical physics, 27
non-physical consciousness
    energy and not matter, 26, 27, 28, 30, 32, 35, 41, 56, 57, 62, 108, 120, 123, 124, 237
    omnidirectional, suprasensorial awareness, 40, 53, 54, 56
obscurantism, 128, 154
omnidirectional, 40, 53, 54, 56
open wound, a trajectory in landing, 248, 269, 272, 356
Ortega, Paco, 306, 368
    Rumba de Cleo, 306, 368
out-of-body experiences, 368, 369
Out-of-body experiences in the blind, 368
oxymoron, 134, 172, 201, 340
Paine, Tom, 128, 129
past life regression, 361
past-life therapy, 372
People Magazine, 161
phenomenology, 60, 158, 365, 372
    grand colander, 59, 61
philosophy
    rationalized beliefs, 131

self-evident truths, 131, 133, 134, 170, 171, 175
philosophy:, 131
physical realm, 19, 37, 42, 49, 57, 124, 129, 219, 281, 322
   physical life experience, 40
Picasso, Pablo, 256
Pinker, Steven, 5, 148, 149, 150, 151, 152, 153, 154, 155, 156, 157, 175, 361, 368
   blank slate, 149, 150, 153, 157
Plato, 125, 342
   Symposium, 342, 343
pleasing and placing, 312, 356
poetry, 256, 257, 294, 348, 351, 356, 357
power as autonomy, 42
Presley, Elvis, 180
psychology, 161, 162, 164, 263
   closure in psychotherapy, 158, 162, 164, 269, 271
   psychotherapy, 16, 145, 146, 147, 148, 157, 159
Psychology Today, 161
quantum physics, 19, 25, 26, 27, 28, 32, 33, 55, 120, 121, 122, 123, 124, 126, 198, 290, 357
   double-slit experiment, 29, 32
   non-locality, 30
   principle of uncertainty, 32
   quantum entanglement, 30
   subatomic particles, 25, 27, 28, 29, 30, 120
reality, 5, 21, 117, 166, 215, 217, 233, 251, 281, 312, 357
   cosmetic gain, 277
   deeper awareness, 135, 267, 276, 356
   democracy, 165, 207

   emotional, 15, 130, 209, 359
   expansion, 226, 250
   individual, 133
   misperception, 13, 81, 200, 251
   nonlocal, 84, 124, 285
   primary source, 50
   reaching, 168
   secular, 26, 78
   self-reliance, 209
reanimation, 98, 100
rebel without a cause, 181, 184
   die young, 184
recipe, 12, 117, 125, 127, 159, 161, 167, 263
reincarnation, 59, 61, 62, 65, 66, 67, 95, 364, 370, 371
   previous lives, 370, 371
religion, 4, 106, 110, 118, 164
   animal kingdom, 44, 171
   eternal damnation, 44, 82, 95
   excommunication, 68
   humanly-conceived indoctrination, 110
   image and likeness, 108, 183, 184
   inclemency, 45
   mediation, 111, 210
   narrowing, 26, 41, 42, 43, 116, 117, 154, 165, 187, 220
   original sin, 44, 82, 83, 104, 112, 126
   punishment, 44, 83, 87, 106
   salvation, 43, 44, 77, 110, 118
   unaffordable downside, 95, 112
remorse, 117
respect
   distance, 183, 241, 357
   natural laws, 216
   reality, 165, 167, 168, 172, 212

sarcasm, 190, 241
secularity, 210
subservient, 107
resuscitation, 46, 47, 58
Ring, Kenneth, 49, 50, 368
road to perdition, 180, 181
Ronaldo, Cristiano, 72
Rousseau, 342, 343
Sagan, Carl, 120, 127, 128, 129, 130, 368
Sans Segarra, Manuel, 100, 101, 120, 121, 122, 123, 124, 125, 126, 127, 132, 198, 200, 201, 253, 275, 290, 369
sarcasm, 182, 184, 187, 190
Sartori, Penny, 37, 58, 369
Schrodinger, Erwin, 31
secularity, 19, 26, 36, 43, 76, 77, 78, 90, 100, 170, 210, 357
    mediation, 78
seeing is believing, 25, 357
self-centricity, 91
Self-evident truths
    passing the buck to God, 170
Serrat, Joan Manuel, 315, 369
servitude, 15, 77, 79, 94, 102, 107, 143, 207, 247
Simon, Paul, 316
sine qua non, 162, 333
socially available behavioral ranges, 144, 145, 152, 357
socially calibrated perceptions, 15, 226, 227, 358
Socrates, 134, 139, 348
Soggy Bottom Boys, 101, 370
    Man of Constant Sorrow, 370
Sophocles, 128, 129
Spain

Christian bothers as main export, 72
spiritual hierarchy, 41, 44
    absence, 42
spiritual realm
    spiritual families, 40
Stanford University, 148, 156
Stevenson, Ian, 65, 66, 149, 370
Studi, Wes, 142
submersion, 162
Sudduth, Michael, 64, 323, 327, 329, 330, 331, 332, 333, 370, 371
superiority, 17, 83, 89, 90, 109, 138, 174, 187, 188, 189, 288, 339, 358
Taracena, Gerardo, 142
The Commitments, 189, 370
trust, 74, 93, 140, 212, 268, 278, 299, 301, 353, 358, 359
truth, 6, 225, 234, 240, 243, 250, 253, 255, 259, 291
    formation, 6, 131, 134, 138, 146, 153, 175, 228, 230, 256, 312, 339, 354, 358
Tucker, Jim, 63, 65, 323, 324, 326, 328, 330, 333, 370, 371
unexplained healing, 369
Utah Historical Review, 371
van Lommel, Pim, 37, 46, 58, 364, 371
van Manen, Max, 60, 158, 372
Vigilius, Pope, 67
Wall Street Journal, 349
Weiss, Brian, 46, 47, 68, 69, 70, 372
    sadness clouds the eyes, 69
    tsunami in Santorini, 3, 68, 338
Wharton Business School, 159, 365

willpower, 214, 264, 265, 357, 359
Winfrey, Oprah, 48, 319, 321, 372
wisdom, 42, 45, 102, 111, 116, 163, 193, 209, 213, 229, 262, 269, 278, 359

witchcraft, 161, 334
World War II, 63, 64, 323, 325, 338
Young, Thomas, 29, 142, 372

Printed in Great Britain
by Amazon